BYGONE BRITAIN

CHILDHOOD
1900–1970

LONDON: HMSO

Researched and prepared by Publishing Services, Central Office of Information

© Selection and introduction Crown copyright 1996

Applications for reproduction should be made to:

HMSO, The Copyright Unit, St Clements House, 2-16 Colegate, Norwich NR3 1BQ

ISBN 0 11 701899 6

Published by HMSO and available from:

HMSO Publications Centre
(Mail, fax and telephone orders only)
PO Box 276, London SW8 SDT
Telephone orders 0171 873 9090
General enquiries 0171 873 0011
(queuing system in operation for both numbers)
Fax orders 0171 873 8200

HMSO Bookshops
49 High Holborn, London WC1V 6HB
(counter service only)
0171 873 0011 Fax 0171 831 1326
68-69 Bull Street, Birmingham B4 6AD
0121 236 9696 Fax 0121 236 9699
33 Wine Street, Bristol BS1 2BQ
0117 9264306 Fax 0117 9294515
9-21 Princess Street, Manchester M60 8AS
0161 834 7201 Fax 0161 833 0634
16 Arthur Street, Belfast BT1 4GD
01232 238451 Fax 01232 235401
71 Lothian Road, Edinburgh EH3 9AZ
0131 228 4181 Fax 0131 229 2734
The HMSO Oriel Bookshop
The Friary, Cardiff CF1 4AA
01222 395548 Fax 01222 384347

HMSO's Accredited Agents
(see Yellow Pages)
and through good booksellers

Acknowledgments

We would like to thank the staff of the British Library Newspaper Library at Colindale for their ready and cheerful assistance and co-operation, and for their expertise in problem-solving. The staff at the British Library at Bloomsbury have also helped in turning up rare and distant journals. We are also indebted to the following, who so kindly allowed us access to their archives: the National Magazine Company (*Queen*, *Harper's Bazaar*, *Good Housekeeping* and *She* magazines) and the National Federation of Women's Institutes (*Home and Country*).

We stress that copyright in the extracts quoted belongs to the newspapers and magazines concerned, and to their successors in business. Present owners have been most kind in granting permission to quote. These include Times Newspapers Limited, Express Group Newspapers Ltd, Associated Newspapers, Mirror Group Newspapers Ltd, The *Observer*, IPC Magazines Ltd, Punch Publications Ltd and D.C. Thomson and Company Ltd, incorporating Beano Group.

In spite of all our efforts, it has not been possible to trace all present copyright owners in some of the extracts quoted. If we have in any way offended, we invite those concerned to get in touch with us.

We would like to thank our colleagues in COI Pictures Section for helping us to choose the photographs for this book.

The centre cover illustration is by courtesy of Meccano, S.A. (France). The photo on the right, showing bathtime in a Manchester kitchen, is from the *Daily Herald* (1949); that on the left shows a Girls' Indian Club class at Cromer Street LCC school (1906).

PREFACE

By Sir Harry Secombe

There's nothing quite like coming across a 50-year-old newspaper or magazine – when you're moving house, perhaps, or having a particularly vigorous spring-clean. The shape and size of their yellowing pages may look familiar, but their contents seem to come from another world.

The Bygone Britain series explores our past through the pages of these old newspapers and magazines, which were only ever meant to be bought, read for a day or so and thrown away, but often end up lining people's drawers or wrapped round their crockery.

I find them endlessly fascinating. On the one hand here are events familiar through the reasoned analysis of history – battles, political upheavals – reported with vivid immediacy. Yet news items such as Chamberlain's successful appeasement mission to Berlin can only be viewed through the lens of hindsight. There are also the news stories that took a long time to happen: the earliest of many items about the Channel Tunnel in Bygone Britain is dated 1907!

Quite unselfconsciously, the articles, letters and advertisements reveal completely different priorities from our own. It is quite shocking that a small and ostensibly sentimental item about the discovery of an abandoned baby finishes with the casual disclosure that the infant was then consigned to the workhouse. Conversely, the behaviour of these aliens from another age has the power to amuse us in a way that would make them quite indignant: the excruciating niceties of visiting cards are surely no laughing matter, and what on earth is wrong with attempting to banish grey hair with radium? Likewise, in these knowledgeable days of niche marketing and core business, we find it absurd to see an advertisement urging hairdressers to sell the odd bicycle on the side.

But there are many hints that the people who populate these pages are not such strangers to us after all. Get-rich-quick schemes and dubious books already feature prominently in the small ads, and the slimming advertisements seem as widespread as in our own press. Some of the ideas voiced in the articles are ones that we thought our own generation had come up with: domestic science as a subject for boys, the dangers of too much exposure to the sun. And, needless to say, affairs of the heart loom large across the pages, whatever the decade.

The things that we can recall ourselves exert their own particular attraction. Coverage of events we remember, pictures of celebrities, advertisements for objects we coveted excite a warm glow of recognition and affection. Other pictures may arouse quite opposite emotions: horror and self-loathing to think that we ever went around with lapels like that! Our reactions to our memories are as much a gauge of how we as individuals have changed as of how society has changed.

So what conclusions can we draw from leafing through the pages of the Bygone Britain books? The increasing pace of technological change is evident, as is the growing informality – in manners, in language, and in address to the readers. The problem page letters confirm this. Early in the century, the letters themselves do not appear; all we see are the replies, addressed to a mysterious correspondent with a fanciful name: Heart's Ease or Sapphire. Fifty years later many writers think nothing of revealing their true identities along with their troubles. (In passing, let us be thankful for the demise of the enterprising service offered by the *Hairdressers and Toilet Requisites Gazette*, whereby people sent in samples of falling hair – and worse – for trichological analysis.)

Does the very different look of the articles in the 1900s and those of the 1960s – tiny, dense text with small headlines giving way to more spacious type with *Sun*-style screamers – mean that our powers of concentration are declining? That papers and magazines have to try harder to wrest our attention from television is obvious, but modern technology, availability of newsprint, and more widespread literacy have all played their part in shaping our contemporary press.

Whether you have a serious interest in British history and society, or you're an avid consumer of trivia; whether you can remember most of the first seventy years of this century, or you weren't even born, you will find plenty to wonder at, to mourn and to laugh about in the Bygone Britain series.

INTRODUCTION

Extracts from newspapers, magazines, journals and comics give a revealing overview of the lives of children during the first seven decades of this century. Overall, a clear desire to improve the lot of our children emerges, although there are often miserable failures on the part of adults to meet their needs. Then, as now, anxious parents received often conflicting advice from a plethora of sources on the best way to mould their offspring into upright, healthy adults.

The health and nutrition of children have been a constant source of interest and concern. In 1904 a public meeting to discuss state maintenance of school children concluded that attempts to teach 'underfed and ill-clad children' were doomed to failure, and the first step towards complete state maintenance should be for the Government to provide free meals and clothing (*Carlisle Patriot*, 1904). In 1916 a report by the School Medical Service stated that one in six school children were physically and mentally incapable of benefiting from the education provided by the state and therefore much of the public money spent on education was being wasted (*Common Sense*). An article in 1934 reported that although 90 per cent of children were born healthy, bad housing conditions, poor diet and general neglect meant that 35 per cent suffered physical defects by the time they started school (*Edinburgh Evening News*, 1934). A group of undernourished children in 1923 had the dubious privilege of being the subject of an 'experiment in feeding'. Their deficiencies of weight and 'red colouring matter of the blood', and poor academic progress, improved significantly as a result of being given a pint of milk daily. The reporter confessed to finding it 'touching' to hear that a month after the experiment stopped, the children's health began to deteriorate again (*Schoolmistress*, 1923).

However, the overall success of efforts to improve the health of children can clearly be charted in the pages of this book, and is perhaps most apparent in the great reduction in infant mortality. National Baby Week was established in 1917 to raise awareness of the measures needed to improve the health of infants; at that time, according to a report in the *Edinburgh Evening News*, 1934, one in seven children died before the age of 12 months. By 1955 the infant mortality rate had fallen so dramatically that National Baby Week was devoted instead to promoting the emotional needs of children, adopting the slogan 'Happy Homes Rear Happy Children' (*Townswoman*, 1955).

Inevitably there are painful contrasts between the childhood experiences of the rich and the poor. The voices of working class parents are seldom heard, although the wellbeing or otherwise of their children is a subject of constant debate among the middle and upper classes. Workhouses and orphanages feature along with advertisements for swanky schools and expensive clothing; one particularly bleak advertisement of 1907 states that the Hackney Guardians will send 100 abandoned children to the Colonies unless they are claimed before the New Year (*Reynolds's Newspaper*). Although a strong drive to do the right thing by children emerges over the years, some attempts to help seem at best a little misguided. 'Slum parties' for poor children were popular in the early decades of the century, especially at Christmas-time; however, one account describes the sadness of those children left to stand outside the hall because there was not enough space for them to join in. One also wonders how the party-goers felt when the festivities were over and they had to return to their poverty-stricken homes.

A range of childcare philosophies and methods emerges in these pages. During the early part of the century there was concern with preserving an ideal of 'Englishness', which seemed to be equated with sound moral development. A letter in *Comic Journal*, purported to be written by a child, informs the reader that 'the only way to bring a child up into a good, honest and loving Englishman is to thrash him when he deserves it'. This view is endorsed by one Dr Cornelius, a vicar of 1933, who recommends 'a good thrashing' for 'breaches of home commandment'; he informs us that the best leaders of Church and State emerged from such an upbringing (*South London Press*).

By no means all the vicar's contemporaries were advocates of a harsh and repressive approach; a report in the *Halifax Courier and Guardian* of 1931 discusses the need for guidance rather than a strict and disciplined regime, and other writers discuss the need to set a good example by treating children with the same respect as adults, and allowing the physical and emotional freedom they need for healthy development.

Clearly all approaches to childcare had failed in the case of a 'Terror Aged Seven' described in a 1912 edition of *News of the World*; the young rascal bullied and intimidated his father to such an extent that he was able to compel him to fetch beer and cigarettes, threatening him with a good thrashing if he refused. Eventually, his father could cope no longer, and the boy was committed to an industrial school.

The question of the desirability or otherwise of children being cared for outside the home surfaces throughout the book. A journalist writing in *Good Housekeeping* in 1922 felt that if public opinion were healthy 'the woman who would let any outside work prevent her giving her personal service to her children would be regarded as the unnatural freak she is'. During the Second World War, the Government was doing its best to ensure that public opinion was strongly in favour of women arranging care for their children in order to take on 'war work', and hundreds of nurseries were set up to help make this possible. After the war opinions shifted again, and by 1963 Denise Robins, an agony aunt in *She*, was advising that women were born to be wives and mothers, and that the child whose mother goes out to work suffers psychologically. Her view is endorsed by no less a luminary than Eartha Kitt, who reveals herself as a devoted mother, caring for her child all day, while singing at night.

Predictably, when it comes to entertainment there is a gulf between the perceived interests of boys and girls. A 1937 edition of *Hobbies* introduced the budding Englishman to the art of making stink bombs, while his female counterpart was no doubt enthralled by instructions on how to make a 'sweet little feather broom' with which to spring clean her dolls' house (*Rainbow*, 1936). A cartoon in *Champion*, 1951, features Ginger's plans to cure tubby fourth-former Jumbo of being a snob, while in *Roxy*, 1959, a swooning female is 'crushed joyfully' to a manly chest, discovering 'what it meant for the very heart of you to float!' Perennial favourites like Rupert Bear and Noddy make an appearance, while the increasing popularity of television ushered in new entertainment in the form of characters like Muffin the Mule and Sooty.

Changes in children's fashions can be traced from the beginning of the century. The mother of 1913 was told how to dress her son when he was of an age to put petticoats aside: combinations, knickers, a bodice, and a blouse or tunic were what was required (*Hearth and Home*). Advertisements for tailors to make the uniforms needed at Britain's top public schools are in sharp contrast to descriptions of the children who attended a 'slum party' in West Ham, 'without stockings or boots' (*Daily News*, 1905). Wartime mothers worried about having enough clothing coupons, and advertisements appeared for 'siren suits'. The youngster of 1960 sported a tight zip-up cardigan and baggy shorts, while in 1966 a 'dreadfully unhappy' teenager was driven to write to the problem page in *She* because her parents would not allow her to wear mini skirts.

Much has been written about the attitude of the British towards their children, but what emerges from the hundreds of extracts in this book is that their wellbeing and development are a constant source of concern, fascination and pleasure.

Julie Halls
COI
March 1996

1900 ▆ 1909

No. 2679.—SAILOR SUIT, made in serge, for a boy from ten to twelve years of age The sailor collar is edged round with three rows of white braid. The vest is of white flannel, edged with braid. Quantity of 50-inch serge required, 2¼ yards.

Mother's Help and Little Dressmaker 1900

THE ORDER OF CHIVALRY.

Princess Victor of Hohenlohe yesterday opened a bazaar at 10, Cornwall-terrace, Regent's Park, for the benefit of the children of "The Order of Chivalry."

This order was founded by the late Earl of Winchilsea to bind together "young people in every sphere of life, so that by kind words and deeds passing from one to the other, especially from the rich to the poor, a spirit of sympathy and large-heartedness may be encouraged in early youth."

The stall-holders at the bazaar yesterday included Lady Bristol, Lady Strafford, and Lady Muriel Paget. at whose house the bazaar was held. Excellent concerts were given during the afternoon, among those who kindly assisted being Mme. Belle Cole, Countess Valda Gleichen, and Mr. Hayden Coffin.

The bazaar remains open to the public today, and it is hoped that the convalescent homes and country holiday funds belonging to the order may reap substantial benefit.

Daily Mail 1900

THE KIPLING POEM.

Mr. Cameron, the present lessee of the Lyceum Theatre, has hit upon a very happy idea in aid of the Kipling Poem Fund. He will devote the proceeds of the performance of "The Snow Man" at the Lyceum on Monday evening, January 15, to the cause we have at heart. "The Snow Man" is a piece pre-eminently pleasing to children, hundreds of whom daily crowd the Lyceum. Mr. Cameron's idea is that the children should fill the theatre on January 15, and in that way they will all be helping "Tommy's kiddies."

The work of children in aid of the Kipling poem fund is always gratifying. Master Stanley Evans, of Brynteg. collected £4 12s. 2d. at the Merthyr Hospital annual children's fancy-dress ball. Master Evans appeared as the A.M.B. Master Vernon Rause, of Mill Hill-park, aged five and a half, got 15s. for his recitation of the poem, and Miss Violet M. Firth, Miss Amy L. Moses, and Miss Lena F. Moses, at the Craigside Hydro, Llandudno, organised an entertainment on their own account, and collected 10s.

Daily Mail 1900

THE CHOICEST OF BABY CLOTHES AT MESSRS WOOLLAND'S.

THE proverbial fascinations of the baby clothes department at Messrs Woolland Brothers', Knightsbridge, have been strongly enhanced since the return of the buyers who have represented the firm at the Paris Exhibition. It was a good old custom, which should certainly not be allowed to fall into disuse, that of making the first christening in a family the occasion for instituting an heir-loom in the form of a choice christening robe, to be handed down for use at all succeeding functions of the same kind. A most favourable opportunity now arises for anyone who has a disposition to carry on the time-honoured practice, for much of the exquisite liliputian apparel selected by Messrs Woolland from the exhibition is well worthy of being treasured and passed on to successive generations. First may be described a christening robe, quite a dream of beauty, with its masses of soft-toned Valenciennes, and the delicate stitchery making the beholder marvel at the skill and patience that must have been expended on this regal little gown. The material is French muslin, falling in the softest folds from a tiny Empire bodice, all lace and *plis broderie*, over an underskirt of white silk; frills of lace and pin tucks innumerable form the trimming of the robe to a considerable depth, above which are inserted cone-shaped medallions of transparent lace set in with the finest hem-stitching. A cloak well worthy of being worn with this lovely robe is of ivory satin, edged with a deep flounce of rich point lace, sewn on in rounded scallops over a full ruche of white chiffon; a powdering of lace incrustations adorns the full underskirt and the detachable cape above it. The finishing touch to the suite is a filmy lace cap, worked *à merveille* with minute tucks and drawn thread borders. The well-appointed baby of to-day must include in its wardrobe one or two smart little tea jackets to be worn for the afternoon visit to the drawing-room. In these there are some charming little models, with Capucine hoods to match, some in white satin trimmed with real Cluny lace, others in fine French cambric, with frills and insertions of lace over pale coloured glacé. Then there are lace-trimmed bibs ornamented with the fine classic embroidery which now characterises nearly all the best lingerie, little guimpes or chemisettes of lace and cambric made with a high neck and long sleeves for wearing under a low-bodiced robe, diminutive lace-covered satin shoes; indeed, every possible detail which could be required to make a thoroughly luxurious outfit for a baby in long or short clothes. A corbeille must not be forgotten which would well accord with such a layette as may be ordered at Messrs Woolland's. It is of the French, tall-handled shape, lined with satin, lace, and chiffon caught with small posies of flowers, the fittings being of the finest ivory. When no longer required for nursery use, it might well continue its ornamental existence as a work-basket of the most elegant description. Contributions to the wardrobes of older children have also been levied from the Paris Exhibition, and in the same department are to be seen the smartest of coats for small boys in pastel cloth with the new Lincrusta trimming, and party frocks for little girls, dainty creations in silk or muslin, enriched with point de gaze or some other choice lace, and made beautiful with fine embroideries. The children's millinery, too, is no less worthy of attention than all the other items of the juvenile toilette which may be studied to perfection at the famous Knightsbridge house. Nor are these the only departments to which important additions have been made from the stores at Paris. Quite as much might be written upon the charms of the graceful and recherché models in tea gowns, the fascinating lingerie, and the newest makes of French corsets, at which, however, a lengthened visit to the attractions of the children's department permitted of no more than a fleeting, though admiring, glance.

Queen 1900

Physical education at a London County Council school, c. 1901.

DRILL FOR OUR BOYS.

SCOTCH EDUCATION TAKES A NEW FORM.

The lessons of the war have apparently not been lost on the Scotch Education Department.

By direction of Lord Balfour of Burleigh the attention of school boards and managers of schools in Scotland is to be called to the importance of physical exercise, "and particularly of those forms of military drill which most effectively develop the physical capacities of the pupils."

In emphasising the importance of such exercises, it is pointed out that "they bring the individual into contact with the principles which lie at the foundation of national defence, and they bring home to him his duties and responsibilities as a citizen of the Empire."

"Whatever form," it is added, "the military service of our country may hereafter assume, it is evident that the strength and security of the Empire as a whole, as well as that of every individual citizen, must depend upon the extent to which the moral elements of responsibility, duty, and readiness of judgment, along with the physical capacities, may be developed."

As a means to the desired end, Lord Balfour suggests the formation of local associations, which he says "might aid in providing the most simple and essential elements of military drill, and in the formation of cadet corps for those who have just left school. In seaboard parishes it might be judged expedient to develop specially that nautical training for which their situation gave opportunities.

Daily Mail 1900

INFANT HIGHWAYMEN.

Frederick Dutch, aged eleven, and George Dutch, who is only nine, offered to a pawnbroker a ring, value 15s., producing as their authority a letter purporting to have been written by their mother.

He got Frederick to write his name, and as the writing was similar to that of the letter, both boys were arrested.

On Frederick was discovered a note giving the amounts they had taken from other children in the streets, scriptural quotations, and a list of regiments now serving in South Africa.

At the North London court yesterday it was stated that they had a wretched home, and their guardians were of indifferent character. They were remanded.

Daily Mail 1900

A very pretty and enjoyable "boy and girl" dance was given on Monday last by Mrs. Arthur Harter for the birthday of her daughter, Miss Gladys Chester-Master, commencing with a dinner-party, at which the guests were Miss Edith Raye, Miss Ethel Lindo, Miss Victoria Wood (the youngest daughter of Sir Evelyn Wood), Miss Diane Creyke, Mr. Frank Curzon (a brother of Lord Curzon of Kedleston), Mr. Guy Chetwynd, Mr. J. Tarver, Mr. Walter Stopford, and Mr. James Lumsden. The dancing commenced quite early, and lasted till two o'clock. The young hostess looked very well in a pale blue picture dress, copied from a Romney shown in the English Pavilion at the Paris Exhibition. Miss Victoria Wood, a handsome dark girl with Irish blue eyes, wore rose-pink, with encrusted motifs of lace, and touches of black, a chou of black tulle on the bodice, and a black tulle sash. Miss Edith Raye wore a pretty French frock of striped Pékin, pale green and white, with pale green chiffon draped across the bodice, and sash of the same, with choux of green chiffon holding the graceful long pleats of the skirt; Miss Creyke wore black, with an artistic arrangement of white tulle and lilies-of-the-valley on her corsage. Miss Ethel Lindo, in oyster-white satin with lace and silver embroideries, had a twist of pale blue chiffon threaded in her dark hair. And amongst those who arrived later for the dancing were Miss Dora Labouchere, dressed in white mousseline de soie over white satin; Miss Muriel Barnby, who came with her brother; Miss Moore-Brabazon, who also was chaperoned by her young brother in the Coldstream Guards; Miss Bainbridge, Miss Vibart, in white, with roses in her hair; the Misses Gould-Adams, three pretty daughters of Mr. Henry Arthur Jones; Miss Stella Faudel-Phillips, looking pretty in white, who came with her brother, Mr. Benjamin Faudel-Phillips; Miss Sylvia Creyke, in white satin, with touches of black jet embroideries, and a black tulle sash; Miss Naomi Anstey, in a pale blue Liberty satin frock, and many others; whilst among men were Lord Rosslyn, Mr. Cyril Streatfeild, Mr. Oppenheim (Scots Guards), Mr. Labouchere, Mr. Thornton, Mr. R. Wodehouse, Mr. Victor Hodgson, Mr. F. Jonson and Mr. Percy Jonson, Mr. Hart-Davies, Mr. Gerald Wheeler, Mr. de Lissa, Captain Seymour Fortescue, General Sauterelli, and others. The young people were all chaperoned by their hostess, Mrs. Arthur Harter, and her sister, Mrs. Anstey, and only a few really grown-up people were invited as lookers-on.

The Lady **1900**

"WHAT A BOY OUGHT TO KNOW," by Rev. Sylvanus Stall, D.D. London : Vir Publishing Co., Imperial Arcade (pp. 190).—This is one of the "Self and Sex" series, which are issued uniformly and are neatly got up, though their cost is but four shillings. The volume before us ought to be placed in the hands of all boys ten years of age and upwards. No boy ought to be sent to a boarding school without taking a copy with him. Parents cannot do better than give copies to their boys, and see that they read them. The book is of absorbing interest, faithful, lucid, and comprehensive, and yet it is delicate and refined. It is the highest recommendation of our leading moral reformers, and those who know it best think most of it. It amply meets a keenly felt want, and so deserves the widest circulation.

Gentleman's Journal
1901

A department which is known and beloved of all little folks in Liverpool is that devoted to English-made toys, which includes what is locally known as "Bunney's Zoo." In the Zoo are represented animals of every known species, wild and domestic, most of them in the harmless aspect of felt, soft wool, india rubber, or padded skin. Of the superiority of English-made toys over foreign productions there can be no question. In point of strength, quality, and finish they are unequalled. With the martial spirit still rampant, it is not surprising to find that military toys are chiefly in demand. At Bunney's every detail for a mighty army is to be found, including military equipments, swords, guns, cannons, Maxims, "Long Toms," and soldiers in the uniform of every British regiment. With a laudable impartiality, Bunney's also supply the combatants on the other side, Boers, Chinese, etc.

Gentleman's Journal **1901**

"SONS OF THE BRAVE."

LORD ROBERTS PRAISES THE DUKE OF YORK'S SCHOOL.

The Commander-in-Chief was highly pleased with all he saw yesterday at the brilliant annual inspection of the 545 boys of the Duke of York's Royal Military School at Chelsea.

His lordship acknowledged the great services rendered by an institution which had no fewer than 1,673 old boys in the Army on January 1 last, many of whom had brought credit to themselves and the training they had received.

They should be proud, he said, in addressing the scholars, of the fact that one of their old boys—Corporal Shaw—had gained the V.C. for bravery at Magersfontein. They would read the names of the eleven old boys which were to be added to their roll of honour with respect, and think of what the Duke of York's School had done during the war in South Africa.

He was glad to hear that five of the old boys had received commissions, for there were no better non-commissioned officers in the Army than those who came from that school and the Royal Hibernian School in Dublin.

His hope was that the present scholars would, under whatever circumstances they might be placed, endeavour to maintain the high reputation which the sons of the brave had so admirably earned for themselves.

Corporal Lee, who won the silver medal for good conduct, received at the hands of Lord Roberts a silver wrist watch.

Daily Express **1901**

ANSWERS.

CHATELAINE.—A novel way of attaching a thimble to a chatelaine is to have the thimble grooved so that it will screw into a cup, and have much the appearance of an acorn, a ring in the cup attached to the chatelaine.—HAYTOR.

A MAY WEDDING.—It is rather a long time to look forward to, for fashions may change, but at present soft satin, chiffon, mousseline de soie, and lace are the most fashionable fabrics for a wedding garment made with a sweeping train and a transparent yoke and sleeves. Bridesmaids are mostly habited in white, with large hats.—MATRON.

PRESENT FOR BABY.—There are always as suitable presents a pretty coat, cloak, frock, or hat, perhaps; or a bread and milk bowl, which serves for a sugar basin afterwards; a rattle, a mug, and a spoon and fork. But there has recently been invented a very ingenious contrivance in America, called Noel's Nursery Table, which might be imported here with advantage. It is a white enamel table, 2 feet square, with a glass top, having a drawer, a folding leaf on the left, a sliding tray and low shelf on the right, and a feeding outfit, with bottles, matches, towels, soap, a glass measurer, and much beside.—MOTHER OF MANY.

Queen **1901**

The Children's Home

THERE is no more interesting and pathetic work done among the very neediest of destitute children than that known as THE CHILDREN'S HOME AND ORPHANAGE. It has branches in many parts of England, the oldest of which, as our readers may know, is to be found at Bonner Road, London, N.E., quite close to the Victoria Park which the London County Council has made such a delightful playground for that quarter of the metropolis. This great Institution began in a very simple and unpretentious way thirty-two years ago in South-east London, where a young Wesleyan minister, in the course of his ordinary Church mission work, provided a single room as a night shelter for a couple of homeless and destitute street arabs. The Rev. T. B. Stephenson, B.A., himself never dreamed at that time to what his modest deed would grow. The young idea proved a most fertile one, and has now become the Children's Home and Orphanage, through which some five thousand children have passed from destitution, and in many cases the human certainty of a criminal career, into lives of uprightness, and in many cases of devoted Christian service. The illustration printed on this page gives a fair idea of the state of things from which large numbers of children have been rescued. Quite recently a little child of three was rescued by a London police-court missionary from an indescribable house. Both his parents were in prison, and when he was found sleeping in the deserted house and awakened, he coolly asked for a drink, and on being offered water objected, saying, "I want some beer." When the child was first brought to us he asked for a "Ha'porth of fags and a ha'penny 'ot drink." By "fags" we are informed he meant the ends of cigarettes.

THE KIND OF BOYS FOR WHOM THE HOME EXISTS

British Monthly **1902**

800 CHILDREN BURNED A YEAR.

At an inquest yesterday concerning the death of the three-year-old son of a market porter, who received fatal burns from an unprotected kitchen range, Mr. Braxton Hicks said:—

When it was considered that during two years 200 coroners held 1,084 inquests on children who had been burned to death, and that in 1,425 of the cases there were no fireguards, the jury would not be surprised that he almost lost his temper when he came across such cases.

He was not sure that the Government would not make it an offence to leave children in a room with a fire without a guard. The time had arrived when something should be done to class it as carelessness and negligence.

Daily Express **1901**

Should Parents Thrash Their Children?

Dear Sir,—I notice in your paper a letter re "Should Parents Thrash Their Children?"

Yes, they should, Mr. Editor. The only way to bring a child up into a good, honest, and loving Englishman is to thrash him when he deserves it. Many parents do not trouble to punish their belligerent children, and consequently they grow up to be those kind of men which are never appreciated—I mean those kind of men who never have a kind word for anyone, and who think the whole world belongs to them.

No, Mr. Editor, it is not a mistake to thrash children; so let me advise your mother readers (I know there is a considerable number) to spare not the rod. Hoping you will publish this letter in your Parliament,—Yours, &c.,

CHILD.

Wellingborough,
Feb. 25th.

Comic Home Journal **1902**

"I was born about eight o'clock in the morning on May 4, 1825, at Ealing, which was, at that time, as quiet a little country village as could be found within half-a-dozen miles of Hyde Park Corner. Why I was christened Thomas Henry I do not know; but it is a curious chance that my parents should have fixed for my usual denomination upon the name of that particular Apostle with whom I have always felt most sympathy." These sentences occur in the autobiographical sketch prefixed to Messrs. Macmillan's sixpenny edition of Professor Huxley's *Lectures and Essays*. The reprint is very clear, and will be acceptable, we imagine, to thousands of readers.

Academy 1902

A child of fifteen months was rescued last week from almost certain death by the heroism of its six-year-old sister. A married couple named Smith were out on the Saturday evening, when a paraffin lamp caused a fire in the children's bedroom. The little girl Lizzie, awakened by the smell of burning, carried her little brother safely through the flames and smoke to the bottom of the stairs.

Crusader 1904

YES, WHY?

Miss Sweetbit : "Oh, you rude little boy ! How dare you use such naughty, horrid, nasty language ?"
Kid : "Aw, go on ! Wotcher want to stop an' listen for ?"

Illustrated Chips 1904

TEMPERANCE.

A Boy's Influence.

WHEN Mr. Spurgeon was a little boy he lived with his grandfather, who was a minister. One of his members, named Roads, often went to the public house for a 'drop of beer.' This annoyed the pastor greatly. Little Charles saw his grandfather's sorrow. One day he exclaimed, 'I'll kill old Roads, that I will.'

His grandfather reproved him for saying such a thing. Charles said that he would not do anything wrong, but he was going to kill Roads. A day or two afterwards, Charles came into his grandfather's room, saying, 'I've killed old Roads; he'll never grieve my dear grandpa any more.'

His grandfather looked perfectly astonished, but his grandson said he had been about the Lord's work.

Some time afterwards, Roads called at the house and told the following story: 'I was a-sitting in the public house, just having my pipe and mug of beer, when that child come in and says, 'What doest thou here, Elijah? Sitting with the ungodly, and you a member of the church?''

Roads was so struck that he went out of the 'pub' and fell before the Lord, asking his forgiveness. He never touched beer again.

Good Tidings 1903

— Rev. James P. Struthers, of Greenock, keeps a list, to which he is constantly adding, of notable persons who were the children of second marriages. Amongst such were Chaucer, Bacon, Bunyan, and Cromwell. "Take away Bunyan and Cromwell, and you remove the greater part of English history." George Washington was also the child of a second marriage.

British Monthly 1902

OUR COMPETITION COLUMN

ACKNOWLEDGMENT.

DEAR SIR,—Many thanks for prize of book received last Saturday. I am very pleased with it. I am glad I went in for the Children's Competition. When will there be another? I am sorry I missed acknowledging it earlier. Yours faithfully, AMY MARSHALL.
[Another prize was offered in the Children's Corner last week.—ED. T.W.]

The winner of the prize in Competition No. 1 for the best selection of references to psychic matter in Shakespeare is
MISS GERTRUDE WALLWORK,
15, Rectory-road,
Stony Holme,
Burnley.
This lady's work was most carefully written and nicely collated.

The winner of the prize in Competition No. 2 for the best dream experience is
MR. THOS. P. JONES,
6, Craig-terrace,
Dowlais,
South Wales,
for a most interesting and well-authenticated narrative.
We have had pleasure in forwarding prizes to the successful competitors.

Two Worlds 1902

Friendly Talks with British Workwomen.

By Eleanor Boswell.

ABOUT CHILDREN.

A GREAT and good Bishop has told us that the most severe trial to his faith was the spectacle of a suffering child, and that it was his custom after witnessing the death of an infant to retire to his closet and pray fervently for his serenity to be restored. But if the anguish of a good man over the sufferings of youth be so intense, what may be said concerning that of the mother herself? Only the torture caused by crime committed by her offspring can approach to it. On this platform rank disappears, for here the sovereign on her throne may clasp hands with the tenant of the meanest hovel in her dominions. To all those called upon to walk through this fire we would, having endured it, extend the hand of a warm, passionate comprehension and sympathy.

And it is because we would help to spare mothers that bitter trial that the following lines are written. That the loss of a child is what we know it to be, inevitable in many, many cases, is certainly true, but how many little lives are sacrificed yearly to the inefficiency, carelessness, laziness, and selfishness of mothers! Unsuitable food, and insufficient, foolishly chosen clothing of themselves account for many, many victims in the yearly list. Or mothers are seen standing gossiping at draughty corners or on doorsteps in a bitter wind, holding baby in her arms, and children are allowed to sit in a cruel north-easter on stone steps, with no protection against the deadly cold of the stone seat. Then when the inevitable supervenes as punishment and dismay are expressed.

British Workman 1905

STATE MAINTENANCE OF SCHOOL CHILDREN.

Following a week's lectures held under the auspices of the local branch of the Social Democratic Federation, a public meeting was held on Friday night at the Cross on the question of State maintenance of school children. There was a large attendance, despite the fact that the weather was far from favourable. The principal speaker was Mr McLean, of Glasgow, who, in the capacity of teacher, was able to speak with experience regarding the lot of the children. At the close the following resolution was moved, seconded, and unanimously carried :—" That considering the evils arising from the efforts to impart education to underfed and ill-clad children, and the hardship entailed upon the teachers engaged in such work, and further, considering the physical degeneration of the great mass of the people, as evidenced by the number of recruits rejected annually by the Army authorities, as a stepping stone towards the complete State maintenance of all school children, this meeting calls upon the Government to empower local education authorities to provide free meals and clothing for necessitous children."

Carlisle Patriot 1904

FEASTS TO POOR CHILDREN.

Twelve hundred poor children drawn from the St. Luke's and surrounding districts were entertained, through the gift of Messrs. Pearks and Co., to an excellent Christmas dinner on Saturday night in the Drill Hall. After the dinner a ventriloquial entertainment was given.

On Saturday evening the Mayor and Mayoress of Hampstead, Alderman and Mrs. Donald McMillan, entertained four hundred of the poorest children attending the public elementary schools in the borough to a bountiful tea. This was followed by an excellent entertainment, the performers being Graham, the human marionette, from the Egyptian Hall, and the Seltons, the merry magicians.

Daily News 1905

KIDNAPPED CHILD.

With reference to the alleged kidnapping outside the Farmhouse Mission, Harrow-street, Marshalsea-road, of which complaint was made by a widow named Evans on Thursday at Southwark Police Court, the police have issued the following description of the missing boy:

Age, 3 years and 3 months, but looks older; complexion and hair fair, very plump, long scar from a burn on right arm; dressed in green tunic, navy blue trousers, large sailor straw hat, black socks, and laced boots.

The child is alleged to have been decoyed by a dark woman on December 21st. The mother's address is 55, Guildford-street, Southwark.

Daily News 1905

Chic 1904

BABY DISSIPATION.

Then there is the infants' school holiday or outing. Anyone living in the suburbs will have frequently seen these baby dissipations consisting of rows of great high brakes literally swarming with tiny mites, most of whom are reduced to the severest gravity by the solemn dignity of the whole affair. The coachman, having no one on the box to " talk horse " to him, retires into his remotest self, and presents to the awe stricken children the personification of some cannibal goblin who at the most unexpected moment may smell their English blood, and notify that fact to all and several by roaring in foghorn tones, " Fee, faw, fum." This apprehension naturally lowers the tone of their enjoyment, and when the accompanying teacher starts them to sing a pretty little Church hymn there is but a feeble response ; it is not until the journey's destination is reached and the buns and lemonade have freely circulated that the shrill scream of infant delight is heard, and young Adam and Eve are themselves again.

Public Opinion
1903

Several British Army officers hold foreign titles. Mr. Sergius de Bucy, who served with Methuen's Horse in the Bechuanaland Expedition, is the Marquis de Bucy in France, a title granted to one of his ancestors in 1602. Mr. John Melville de Hochepied-Larpent, who was formerly in the Indian Police, is a baron of Hungary, his ancestor, who was the Dutch Minister at the Porte early last century, having obtained the liberation of many Christian slaves from Turkish slavery. Horace de Lousada, who was formerly Lieutenant-Colonel of the 5th Madras Infantry, is the Duke of De Losada y Lousada in Spain, and the Marquis di San Miniato in Tuscany. His ancestors were nobles of Sicily. General Sir H. E. Thuillier is Baron de Malapert in France, and Mr. John Henry Edward de Robeck, formerly a captain in the 8th Foot, is a baron of Sweden, the title having been granted to his ancestor in 1750. His grandfather became a naturalised Englishman eighty years ago. Mr. A. J. Heath holds an Italian barony, his grandfather having been for sixty-two years Consul-General in London for Sardinia and Italy. Master Horace George Butler (born 1898), of Ewart Park, Wooler, Northumberland, is the Count St. Paul in the Holy Roman Empire ; his great-great-grandfather, Horace St. Paul, joined the Austrian Army as a volunteer, and as colonel on the staff fought in the Seven Years' War against Frederick the Great. For his services he was, in 1759, created a count, upon the field of battle, by the Emperor of Germany, Francis I., husband of Maria Teresa of Austria. The little Count's mother, who died in 1901, married Mr. George Grey Butler, J.P., whose little daughters, Hethe (born 1896) and Irene (born 1901), are entitled to be called Countesses.—Condensed from a lavishly illustrated article by J. M. Bulloch in the *Windsor Magazine* for May.

NUGGET FILINGS

Every dog has his day, but the nights belong to the cats.

Bridget would only cook what the policeman on the beat preferred.

"Children," observed the parson, "are the sunshine of our lives." "That's right," rejoined Newpop, with a large sigh ; "and sonrise for me is about two a.m."

Employer (to new office boy) : "Has the cashier told you what you are to do this afternoon?" Office Boy : "Yes, sir. I'm to wake him when I see you coming."

Johnny Geehaw : "Pa, what's the law of gravitation?" Farmer Geehaw : "I dunno. I hain't got time to keep up with all the fool statoots the durn Legislatur' passes."

"The paper says that skirts are to be worn longer than ever." "Well, you needn't be figuring on me wearing mine any longer. I've worn it five years this coming autumn."

"She is beautiful," said the studious girl, "but she is not accomplished." "My dear," answered Miss Cayenne, "there is no accomplishment more difficult than being beautiful."

"Ma," queried little Dolly, "what is a miser?" "A man who thinks his wife's hat should not cost any more than his own," answered the diplomatic mother, as she glanced across the table at her husband.

Willie : "I met our new minister on my way to Sunday school, mamma, and he asked me if I ever played marbles on Sunday." Mother : "H'm ! And what did you say to that?" "I said, ' Get thee behind me, Satan !' and walked right off and left him."

"I should like to look at a nice, fat goose," said the customer, coming into the poulterer's shop, where Johnny had been left in charge for a few moments. "Yes, sir," said Johnny, politely. "Just wait a minute, sir. Father will be here in a minute."

"What are you studying now?" asked Mrs. Newgilt. "We have taken up the subject of molecules," answered her son. "I hope you will be very attentive and practise constantly. I tried to get your father to wear one, but he couldn't make it stay in his eye."

He (reading about the latest society wedding) : "They have a lot to say about what the bride wears, but they have nothing to say about the poor bridegroom." She : "They have no need to, because it is a well-known fact that he usually wears a worried look."

"That's the best I can do for you," said the theatrical manager. "You've been idle all the season so far ; now, will you stay idle the rest of the season or take this small part?" "I'll take it," replied the comedian ; "in this case a small rôle is better than a whole loaf."

A Michigan paper wound up a compliment to a young schoolma'am with a good word about " the reputation for teaching she bears." The next day the young schoolma'am met the editor and chased him down the street with an umbrella, and at every jump in the road she screamed that she had never taught a she bear in her life.

Nuggets 1905

OUR SLUM PARTIES.

FUN FOR THE CHILDREN OF THE STARVING.

WEST HAM'S TURN.

It fell last evening to the poor little children of stricken West Ham to have their turn among "The Slum Parties." Two wonderful gatherings took place—one in Stratford Town Hall, the other in Canning Town Public Hall.

If those of our readers who are so kind as to enable us in this way to brighten the Christmas season for the little ones of those dreary parts of London, where life is always so grey and cold that healthy laughter can rarely get its blessings through the perennial gloom, could but have been present, their gladness must have been as heartfelt as the joy of the children was great.

It was glorious to see the mites so happy. It was splendid to see them almost bursting in the joy of making their voices heard in unrestrained song; splendid to hear their deafening screams of laughter. It did one good to watch their radiant faces and their burning eyes. And all the time the feeling of mingled joy and sorrow crept around one's heart as one recalled the grim reality that every one of these little children, so happy now for these few brief hours, came from homes where want and misery were holding their ghastly feast together, and where the horrors of absolute starvation were being held at bay only by the goodness of those who are so nobly responding to the call of humanity which we sounded just before Christmas Eve. These gatherings were sights which those who witnessed them will never be able to forget.

At Stratford Town Hall there were 1,020 little ones under the care of Councillor Hurry. They had a tea, and the boys' band of St. Paul's played to them meanwhile. Then they sang all together, and afterwards a lady sang to them. How wonderful was that contrast!

Then they had a Punch and Judy show, and then a cinematograph exhibition. And they had laughter all the time. Finally, after cheers of thanks for the kindly unknown hosts and four and a half hours of roaring fun, they had oranges and apples and sweets.

Canning Town's thousand swelled to twelve hundred under the hearty supervision of the Rev. George Hooper, whom every child seemed to know and to hold in such a quaint mixture of veneration and familiarity as they might feel towards Santa Claus himself. Here the children sang all together; some of their number, boys and girls, sang to the rest; and then there was a magic lantern, showing such sweetly pretty, yet genuinely humorous, pictures as Kemble's "Coons," each one of which caused shrieks of merry laughter.

While the willing helpers, whom also the children thanked with cheers, were pouring out the tea and filling the eager hands with cakes and pies, the din from the 1,200 throats was incredible. It had only one sad side. It could be heard in the street and on the pavement around the entrance to the hall. It brought tears to the eyes of scores of other little ones who had not been invited because the hall would hold no more.

Nature is kind. It is not easy to abash the poor little child whose playground from babyhood has been a London back street, and whose wits are the keenest of any children on earth. They came to the party to be happy, and they came in the only way they could come, "as they were." There are thousands of children in West Ham who have no "other clothes." Many at the party were without stockings and boots, and only courtesy—no, not courtesy, but grim necessity—would call their poor little rags clothing. But they were happy, at any rate for the time being. Yet one could see at a glance at the dense brown mass that here and there there were special cases. There was no difficulty in telling the child who had grown used to roughing it, who had known little else from birth, and yet seemed to thrive in a marvellous manner upon it. Here and there were those upon whom the grip of want had fallen only this winter, and who down to a few months ago had happy, comfortable homes. Their great sad eyes, their poor, white, pinched cheeks told their story. The way they sat cuddling together with their arms intertwined brought a grip to one's throat. It, too, told its silent tale of sorrow, of cold, and of hunger.

A HAPPY GROUP

Daily News 1905

*Children under Modern Conditions.

By Aylmer Maude.

ONE of the great difficulties we have to encounter in seeking for our children satisfactory cultivation of mind or of body lies in the fact that our modern world has become so very complex, and is becoming more and more so year by year. In the simpler days of our forefathers the children could, in most cases, see the utility of what their elders were doing. Things were made in a small way. Where a man now goes to a big factory to make the fiftieth part of an article, he then stopped at home and made the whole article, and his children saw him do it. If a man had a business and lived over his shop, his children learnt all about the business gradually from their babyhood. Now the father goes off and is "something in the city" —but whether he is floating bubble companies, or auditing accounts in an honest way, his children see nothing of his work; and when the time comes for them, too, to go into business, it often seems a hateful necessity, taking them away from all that they really understand and really care for.

The advantage of our modern way is that more things are made with less labour, but the disadvantage is that, to "get a living" nowadays, very many people have to do uninteresting work in more or less unhealthy surroundings; and such is the stress of competition that many of them ruin their health in order to provide for themselves in case of sickness.

Vegetarian 1905

FOR UNMANAGEABLE BOYS try old-fashioned methods. On receipt of particulars from parents, experienced Headmaster will write fully or arrange interview London. Great success.—K. 440, *Church Times* Office.

ONE or TWO BACKWARD or DELICATE BOYS received by Vicar of S. Devon parish. Vicarage charmingly situated, near moors. Modern sanitation. Individual attention. References.—O. 588, Shelley's, Gracechurch-street, E.C.

Church Times 1906

EDUCATION.—30 guineas per annum. To fill vacancies. The Principals of a high-class School for Gentlemen's Daughters can receive PUPILS on the above greatly reduced fees, and include-board and thorough tuition in English, French, German, Latin, mathematics, music, drawing, painting, dancing, and calisthenics. Resident staff of certificated English and foreign teachers. Professors attend. Preparation for all local exams. Governess-Student required. Illustrated prospectus and report, and full particulars from Collegiate, White's Library, Stroud, Gloucester.

Church Times 1906

BEQUESTS TO CHARITIES OUT OF LARGE ESTATE.

Property valued at £565,407 gross and £556,807 net has been left by Mr. Edgar Horne, chairman of the Prudential Assurance Company (Limited), who died December 18.

By his will (of which probate was granted to-day) he bequeathed £1000 to Dr. Barnardo's Homes, £500 each to the Refuge for Homeless and Destitute Children, the Westminster Hospital, and the Home for Little Boys at Farningham; £250 each to Princess Alice's Hospital, Eastbourne, and the Church of England Society for Providing Homes for Waifs and Strays.

Evening Standard 1906

The Welsh Flag.

I happened to be in several parts of South Wales at different times during Whitsuntide, and there was one incident that struck me very much. I saw several Welsh Nonconformist Sunday Schools marching out for their treats, and I also saw a High Anglican Church Sunday School marching out on a similar mission. The Welsh Nonconformist Sunday School members were in a district largely Welsh in character, and the High Anglican Church Sunday School was in a district largely Anglicised. In both the Welsh Nonconformist and Church processions, dozens of small flags were carried. And it is here where the striking incident comes in. Whilst all the Welsh Nonconformist scholars' flags consisted of miniature Union Jacks, there were in the Anglican Church School procession not only Union Jacks but a large number of Welsh flags as well—at least, the flag which is now generally recognised as the Welsh one, i.e., a streamer with the red dragon emblazoned thereon.

An Explanation Wanted.

This little incident may appear trivial to those folk who have no sentiment in their compositions, but, to the thoughtful Welshman who loves his native land, and likes to see Wales maintain her distinct nationality, it is a little incident that means much. Childhood is the most impressionable period of life, and ideas of nationality inculcated in boyhood and girlhood days will survive as long as life lasts. In a recent issue of the LONDON WELSHMAN, I remarked that Englishmen who have made Wales their home are often more loyal to Welsh nationality than the native Cymro, and when I explain that the children in that Church Sunday School who carried their little Welsh flags so proudly, were practically all boys and girls born in Wales of English parentage, it looks as if the remark in question finds further corroboration.

London Welshman 1906

It really looks as though every religious body in the country, Churchmen only excepted, had made up its mind as to the school question, and intends to lay its demands before the Government in advance of the Ministerial measure. The resolution framed by the Roman Catholic Education Council is worthy of imitation by Churchmen. It bases the claim to fair treatment on the services rendered to national Education in the past by the Romanist body, and asserts the right of parents to educate their children in the faith they believe to be true—a right which, being given by God, and not by the State, cannot be taken away by the State. If the State establishes a compulsory system of Education, such system must not conflict with the inalienable parental right. Consequently, the Romanist position is that no settlement can be accepted which does not safeguard the distinctive character of Roman Catholic schools, "either by retaining the existing proportion and powers of the foundation managers, or by some equally effectual means," and which does not provide for the continuance of the existing Roman Catholic training colleges. The Council views "with grave anxiety" any proposal to lease, rent, or assign Romanist Schools to the Local Education Authority, and in any case would reject an arrangement that impaired the Roman Catholic character of the school so transferred or leased. We could wish that Churchmen were equally agreed as to their policy, and that they had like courage plainly and emphatically to state their demands.

Church Times **1906**

The apologists of the Government are evidently so conscious of the rank unfairness of their own measure, that they are doing everything they can to raise a "No Popery" cry. Mr. Birrell indicated this by his use of the word "Protestant" in his speech before Easter. Yet Mr. Birrell should know better. Mr. Morley discredited himself in the opinion of hosts of his friends by his reference to the coming report of the Royal Commission in his speech at the Eighty Club. Mr. Perks attempted it in his speech in the House the other night, but to the credit of the Opposition they manifested a strong resentment against such tactics. Mr. Lloyd-George, *more suo*, got on the same line in his speech on Tuesday. Let Churchmen be warned, therefore, and let speakers at the numerous Church meetings never cease to point out that the principles of the Church of England, as expressed in so many trust deeds, have undergone no change. They are the principles set out in the Catechism and other formularies; they remain unaltered, and have to be taught faithfully to the children of Church parents.

Church Times 1906

ANXIOUS TO PLAY THE HARP.

Little Edith was learning to play the piano, but practising was a great trouble to her, and often tears were shed during the half-hour's practice. One day, looking up through her tears into the face of her governess, she said, "Oh, Miss R——, I do wish you would teach me to play the harp." "You must learn first of all to play the piano correctly, then perhaps mother will allow you to learn to play the harp; but why do you wish to play the harp, Edith, dear?" "I have heard that in heaven we shall all play upon golden harps, and I do not want to practise when I get up there."—*Original.*

Sent by K. Read, c/o Mr. Jackson, Market Place, Newbury, Berks.

Crusader 1904

Robert Houdin, the great conjurer, whose marvellous pack of cards is to this day a stand-by to the prestidigitator, was most careful in training his son in the powers of observation. He would take him into a shop and pass out quickly, telling the lad to notice what was displayed in the window, and then both father and son on their return home would write down what they had seen and compare notes. The youthful Houdin, by means of this simple training, became so remarkably quick and proficient that his powers of observation appeared to those uninitiated little short of marvellous. A momentary glance round a room placed him in possession of the position and nature of nearly every article in it. His father put his newly-acquired powers of observation to practical use, and the boy practised as a clairvoyant. He entered a room, was immediately blindfolded, and then gave an accurate list of all the furniture, nick-nacks, persons, pictures, pattern of wall-paper, etc., so that people thought he saw through the back of his head or out of his ears.

Health Resort 1907

OUR HAPPY LAND!

In the course of a High Court action, in which much time and money have been spent in discussing the allegation that the tip had been cut off a kitten's tail, a lady witness proudly stated that she possessed a cat for which she had refused £1,100.

The newspapers reporting the kitten case contain heartrending accounts of the distress caused by the severe weather. "While unemployed fathers tramp the streets, or seek for charity," says one, "tens of thousands of little children, hunger ridden and half-clothed, are in the misery of a continual painful shivering."

Reynolds Newspaper 1907

Unless they are claimed before the New Year, more than 100 children who have been deserted by their parents, will be sent to the Colonies by the Hackney Guardians.

Reynolds Newspaper 1907

A word-building lesson at Hugh Myddelton School, c. 1907.

EDUCATION AT HOME AND ABROAD.

LAST month we dwelt upon the importance of provision being made to enable
some portion of the school life of English
boys and girls to be spent in some
foreign country, and *vice-versâ*.

As was pointed out, such a policy has
the double advantage of enabling a child
to master the foreign language at least
colloquially - and that with an accent
almost indistinguishable from the native
accent—and of enlarging the boy's or girl's
mind by experiencing a change of scene,
manners and customs.

But it may be argued is it not a mistake
to interrupt a child's school life by breaking
the continuity of his or her progress from
the lower to the higher classes? A simple
"yes" or "no" will not answer the question
because it all depends at what stage in the
child's educational course the break is made.

Continuity of study is of great importance, and it is unwise for children to have
their courses of lessons interrupted by
frequent change of school, that is to say,
change from school to school of more or
less the same character. The only change,
save that about to be referred to, which
there should be so as not to break the continuity, is the change from the preparatory
school to the secondary; and, again, where
parents can afford to give their children
higher education, to the universities or at
least colleges affiliated with them.

Continental Express 1908

For the Children

By WINIFRID.

Jim Wolstenholme carries off the boy's prize. He has sent me a photo of his precious little sister, and I do not wonder he is so proud of her:

WHAT I THINK ABOUT BABIES.

Our baby is the nicest baby I know. I did not think babies were so nice before we had one. One night I was woke by my sister. She told me that we had got a baby. I did not believe it at first but when I asked father I found it was true. I got dressed and went downstairs and asked father what kind of a baby it was. When father told me that it was a girl I was not glad because I liked baby boys better than baby girls. Before I went to school I went to see her. She was very red and slept so that you would think she never would wake up. Gradually the redness left her and she became bright. Then I saw my mistake. It was that baby boys are not as good as baby girls. When auntie got her out of bed to wash her down flopt her head. Once when I came from school I asked mother what we were going to call her. Mother said she thought of calling her Margaret Agnes. Then after that we all called her Maggie. Baby gets photographed a lot by father. She was photographed when she was a day old. Now baby is seven months. Most babies are vaccinated but ours is not, and she is not going to be. When she was able to hold up her head she started making little noises. When she is cross she says "Hang it" "Hang it." When she is good she says "Goo" "Goo." Now when mother puts her on the floor she tries to creep. She hunches up her legs but does not know how to move her hands so instead of going forward she goes backwards. Many a time I say I will never change her for any other baby, and now I think I like baby girls better than baby boys.

JIM WOLSTENHOLME.
Age nine years.
79, Burcot Road, Meersbrook, Sheffield.

Clarion 1907

DEAR WINNIE,—I have no little brother, or sister, but I should very much like a little sister, particularly so if they would always remain so small as when they were born, then they would not be able to tell tales to mama you know, like some bigger children do, whom I know. I think babies are very amusing and interesting little creatures. I do think it is funny how they always cry when they want anything. I wonder why God did not make them different so as they could let one know what they wanted in a more pleasing and pleasant manner. I am also surprised, when I think how other babies of animals, such as the cow, horse, sheep, etc., can walk almost as soon as they are born. If babies were only as strong of limb, as of lung, I feel sure that they would be able to walk at once. They are such mysterious delicate mites, that like speaking of the stars I say "How I wonder what you are" or from where do you come. Mama says God makes them like the stars. I can hardly realise that I was such a mite only about nine years ago. I have heard of poor papa's having to get out of a warm bed in the middle of the night to carry the baby round the room, when it has been cross but I think that is all a fable. I will now conclude my first essay; hoping to hear from you shortly. I should very much like a poetry book.

ELSIE WARMINGTON.
Age ten.
129, Gadsby Street, Attleborough, Nuneaton, Warwickshire.

BABIES' COUGHS.

A harmless and sure remedy is VENO'S LIGHTNING COUGH CURE.

The remarkable purity, safety, and freedom from all dangerous drugs of Veno's Lightning Cough Cure has caused it to be called "The Babies Cure." Mrs. Bailey, Providence Place, Ridge Lane, near Atherstone, Warwickshire, writes:—"My two children (twins, just five months old) were very bad with whooping cough, but I tried Veno's Lightning Cough Cure, and it has completely cured them."

Veno's Lightning Cough Cure is guaranteed free from all narcotic and dangerous drugs, is suitable for the youngest child, and is a perfect cure for coughs and colds, bronchitis, asthma, catarrh, whooping cough, and all chest and lung troubles. Price 9½d., 1s. 1½d., and 2s. 9d. of all chemists.

Ampthill and District News 1908

ALLEGED CRUELTY TO WORKHOUSE CHILDREN AT SOUTHMOLTON.

MASTER CAUTIONED.

At the Southmolton Board of Guardians on Thursday, Mr. A. Buckingham presiding, a letter was read from the police with regard to alleged cruelty to certain children at the Workhouse.

In his report P.C. Dergeas stated that from information received, he visited the Workhouse on Monday, the 21st of December, in the absence of the Master. He asked the Matron if he might see two boys named Slee and Tarr, and they were immediately fetched. He asked Slee to show him his legs, and upon the lad doing so he saw a black mark across the left leg 3 inches long by 1½ inches wide. Upon questioning the boy as to how it was done, he replied that the Master did it with a cane. He turned to the younger lad, Tarr, and found his leg bandaged, and under it a place as big over as a penny piece, where the skin had been knocked off, just behind the leg on the top of the boot. He thereupon asked the nurse when she bandaged the place up, and she said on Saturday. About 6.30 the same evening he went in company with Sergt. Newberry, to the Workhouse, and again saw the boys, this time in the Master's presence. The Master then told them that thirteen boys had been caned for misbehaviour, seven receiving two strokes on their hands with the cane, and the other six younger lads one stroke each. The boys were playing outside his office, making a dreadful noise, and that was why be punished them.

Sergt. Newberry, in his statement, added that the punishment was excessive.

Supt. Chamings also wrote that the information had been given the police by townspeople; and with so many rumours about, he thought it his place to have the matter investigated.

The Master (Mr. W. H. G. Pallin) next read his report, and said that these boys had been reported for rowdy conduct in the bedroom, for which he cautioned them. Not long after he cautioned them again, this time for noise in the day-room. After cautioning them three times he caned them. He had no intention to hurt them, and he doubted if the mark on Tarr's legs was ever made by a cane. He had to keep the boys in order, as that was most essential for their own welfare.

Mr. A. E. Shapland said it was a most serious matter. Not long since he had gone to the schools on purpose to see one of the boys. The Schoolmaster then informed him that only just previously a boy had come to school with his hands so hurt that he could do nothing all day. He then went and saw the Master, who said it should not occur again, but here it was again. If the boys could not play about and shout in their play-yard without being thrashed for it, life would not be worth living. He was sure that the hands and legs were not the correct places to thrash lads on. It was their bounden duty to sift the matter thoroughly. He thought the Master's temper was not what it should be towards the boys.

Mr R. Cook said it was nothing more than brutality that boys at the age of five should first have their hands cut, and then their legs either skinned or bruised and marked. If some parents had done this they would have been prosecuted by the N.S.P.C.C., and the Board must do their duty to the people they represented. He thought they should give the master another chance, and inform him if he did not inflict proper chastisement they would have to take other steps.

Mr. H. Smyth moved, and Mr. W. Orang seconded, that the master be cautioned, and that in future, when such punishments as these were necessary, he was to inflict the same in the presence of the industrial trainer and porter.—Messrs. W. Sanders, J. Sanders, and H. Cheriton also spoke on the matter.

The resolution was carried by a large majority. The master was then called before the Board, when the Chairman cautioned him in regard to punishment, and the resolution passed was read to him.

The Master assured the Board that the matter should not occur again. Whatever he had done was what he thought was best for the boys' welfare.

North Devon Journal 1909

Ampthill and District News 1908

Reynolds Newspaper 1907

Apropos of King Edward's visit to Paris, *en route* to Biarritz, the *Gaulois* published an amusing anecdote. Edward VII., while still Prince of Wales, was accustomed to take his morning walk alone in St. James's Park. One day he noticed that he was being followed by two little boys, and turned round to look at them. Although at first much disconcerted, one of them plucked up courage and, taking off his cap, said: "Your Royal Highness, my little friend is French, and I have just made a bet with him that you are the Heir to the Throne of England." The Prince of Wales replied, smiling, "You have won; but what was your little friend's bet?" "He bet that your Royal Highness was a Parisian." "Oh, well, then," said the Prince, again smiling, "he has also won."

World of Travel 1908

The Squeak That Was.

Squeaking shoes are rare now, though, of course, you haven't noticed it. Stop a minute, though, and think. Isn't it true that for some time you haven't come across a squeaking shoe? The thing that caused the trouble was a loose piece of leather in the sole. This, as you walked, worked something like a bellows or an accordion, and great was the unmusical sound thereof. Nearly all shoes are now machine-sewed — the great majority of them used to be pegged — and mechanically accurate sewing does away with any loose pieces of leather in the sole, and, therefore, with the squeak as well.

Scraps 1909

A Short-winded Footballer.

"CONSTANT READER" is one of my chums, who is in training for football. One of his principal drawbacks, however, he finds is his short-windedness. Can I suggest a remedy? he asks. Well, my chum, short-windedness comes from want of condition. There is only one remedy for it, and that is to get oneself into a stronger physical state. Careful, steady training is the one thing needed.

My reader should also pay great attention to improving his lung capacity, and this can be done by practising breathing exercises night and morning.

Let my young friend, when he gets up, stand at an open window, and shutting his mouth, take in a good deep breath—so deep that he finds his stomach pushed out by the force of the air which is being taken into his lungs. Then let him exhale that breath very slowly after holding it for a second or two, as he does so, drawing in his stomach, and tightening the muscles of the abdomen.

Repeat this, and after a while he will find that he can do it twenty or thirty times without any trouble. He will also find that his lung capacity is beginning to increase, that his chest is expanding, and that the short-windedness—if at the same time he takes careful and sensible exercise—is disappearing.

Boys' Realm 1908

At the recent examination held at Barnstaple by the Associated Board of the Royal Academy and Royal College of Music, Miss Mabel Darch (Bideford), pupil of Miss Guerra de Fontoura, passed the advanced grade for singing, also in theory.

CATHARINE HERMIONE WATT-SMYRK, a pupil of Miss Willis, L.R.A.M. (of Barnstaple), has passed with honours the Intermediate Grade Local Centre Examination, for pianoforte playing, of the Associated Board of the Royal Academy of Music, and the Royal College of Music.

North Devon Journal 1909

A LADY wishes to place her daughter in a SCHOOL where, in return for board, laundry, and travelling expenses, she would help with little ones and make herself generally useful.—Address Mrs. Thompson, 3, Anglesea-road, Kingston-on-Thames.

Reynolds Newspaper 1907

This is the age of "Prodigies" and Master Lloyd Shakespeare now performing at the London Pavilion must certainly stand in the list of such. He is only twelve years of age and is a really excellent Cornet Soloist, with a marvellous lip, a born musician and is able to write music and transpose at sight. When but three years of age he was able to play the instrument with ease and produce a good tone. At nine years he started practising in earnest with the result that he has made not only his debut, but has actually appeared at the Queen's Hall Concerts.

Advice 1908

On the Cycle—and Off.

She grasped the bar, arranged her skirts,
With dainty little tucks and flirts;
Posed on the saddle, felt the tread
Of the pedal, and "I'm off," she said.
A whirr of wheels, a swerve and sway,
And from the roadway where she lay
She realized in full degree
The climax of her prophecy.

Scraps 1909

Special Fares for Children.

Children under three years of age occupying the same berth as their guardians for the time being travel free of charge. Two children above three, and not older than seven years, members of the same family, and sharing a bed, pay at the rate of one adult. One child above three pays full Sleeping Car, but only half the railway fare, if within the usual age limit.

Traveller de Luxe 1909

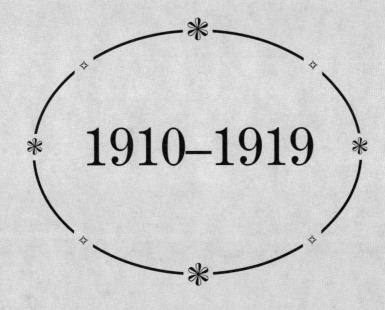

1910–1919

HOW REGGIE TURNED BAD LUCK INTO GOOD LUCK

1 The painters are busy at Dolly Dimple's house; and while they were at lunch, Reggie and Dolly had a fine game with the paint-pots. "I think this is a great improvement — don't you?" said mischievous Reggie, as he painted stripes of bright colour round his humming-top and spots on the horse

2 But, alas! Reggie's fingers were covered with paint by the time he had finished his artistic labours; and somehow or other he must have touched the wall, for there, right before his horror-stricken eyes, were two tell-tale hand-prints! "Oh, dear! you've done it now! We shall never get that off the wall!" cried Dolly

3 "Mother will be dreadfully angry when she sees it," continued Dolly, almost in tears. "Oh, it's all right! Don't worry!" said Reggie cheerfully. "I'll just make some more finger-marks, and then turn them into a lovely wall decoration. Mamma will think it was done intentionally, and we sha'n't get paddy-whacked after all!"

4 And everything turned out just as Reggie had said. Mamma was simply delighted with the artistic effect of the wall-flowers. "Oh, you clever little people! I must kiss you for this," she cried. "Come downstairs, and I'll see if I can find each of you a nice piece of cake!"

Playbox 1910

BABY LORD DE CLIFFORD.

THE infant son of the late Baron de Clifford, who inherits the residue of the estate of £14,443 gross left by his father, after bequests to Lady de Clifford, who was formerly Miss Eva Carrington, the actress. The late Baron de Clifford, who was killed in a motor-car accident, left the "Thanet Pearls" as heirlooms.

BABY IN CHRISTMAS HAMPER.

AN extraordinary Christmas hamper was left on the doorstep of a Slough resident recently. It consisted of a collapsible basket containing a pretty baby girl about three weeks old, neatly dressed, with an infant's outfit, including a bottle of milk, and everything for the comfort of the little stranger. The police took the child to the Eton Workhouse.

Babyland **1910**

CORRESPONDENCE.

EGYPTIAN STUDENTS IN ENGLAND.
To the Editor of EGYPT.

Sir,—Will you allow me to express in your valuable columns some views as to the Egyptian students in England. I feel that the question is vital and some light on it would be of considerable use.

Latterly Egyptian students have been flocking to England in large numbers. Their number has gone up to 300 at least, and the majority of them have come to study at their own expense. But their condition is, I fear, very unsatisfactory, and this is to be attributed to the following causes :—

(1) They come to England without any pre-arranged programme which they are to follow. When they reach their destination they are only at a greater loss what to do. They take up one subject, and, then, perhaps, leave it and take up another, and end in going back without having succeeded in finishing anything.

(2) Some among them are sent here after their failure in Egyptian schools, in the belief that the work here is comparatively easy. Such youths, when they arrive, only take to sport and pass their days in idleness. Their fathers are entirely ignorant of what they are doing, and there is nobody to watch over them. They waste their time and money and gain a bad reputation for the rest of us.

(3) There is a spirit of political opposition to Nationalist views in most of the Universities, especially in Oxford, which renders it a hard task to enter a college.

The second cause is by far the most important. What failure the Egyptians meet with here is mainly due to it. Various remedies have been proposed. One has been to organise a Committee in the Universities, with another in Egypt which would recommend pupils to the colleges and help them to get admitted. But the objection to this is that it would certainly be an anti-Nationalist organisation, and that would be quite enough to condemn it. In my opinion, if the Egyptian Committee would take the matter in hand and get the Nationalist Party and other leading Egyptian public men to appoint an agent to take care of students on their arrival in England it would be the best plan, and would confer a great service on us all.—Yours faithfully,

AN EGYPTIAN STUDENT.

At the headquarters of the Salvation Army, a boy named Cecil Waterhouse, aged 14, fell from one of the upper landings into the basement and was killed. It is said he was sliding down the banisters and lost his balance.

The King's bounty of £3 has been sent to Mrs. Condon, who recently gave birth to triplets, two boys and a girl, in the City of London Lying-in Hospital. All are alive and healthy.

Dunstable Borough Gazette **1910**

How CHILDREN ARE NEGLECTED.

"It is not properly recognized what an enormous effect properly-managed crèches have in checking infantile mortality and physical deterioration," said Mrs. Björkegren, a representative of the National Society of Day Nurseries. "For the whole of England the infantile mortality is 12 per cent., and in the East End of London and the manufacturing districts it reaches from 20 to 24 per cent. And it is simply because the children are so fearfully neglected." The mothers went out to work, shutting the children up for the day with a loaf of bread and a jug of milk. This was devoured as soon as the mother's back was turned. And fire as well as improper feeding claimed many victims. The work in connection with the the crèches was not directly confined to the children ; mothers were given hints as to the preparing of food and various other matters, of which, in the ordinary way, they were often profoundly ignorant. More than once in her experience she had heard a mother say in regard to the mite in her arms : "I can't understand what's the matter with 'im. 'E ate suet puddin' quite early yesterday." The crèche, she said, in no way pauperized the women or robbed them of parental responsibility ; for they paid a fair share towards its up keep. Referring to the work of Brighton's crèche she said that all the children looked the picture of health and happiness.

Babyland **1910**

Always Behind.

A doctor recently died who was the oldest medical man in one of our large Midland towns. The babies he had, in early practice, helped through the perils of childhood had come to be grey haired men ; and one day, as the story goes, he had an engagement with one of these, a well-known merchant. The hour of the engagement was long passed, and the doctor was pacing the floor of his study when the gentleman came in with an apology on his lips. "No matter ! no matter !" said the doctor with an impatient wave of his hand; "you are always behind." "I remember," said he, "thirty years or more ago sitting for ten mortal hours in the little back p'rlour of your father's house waiting for you to be born. You are always behind time."

"PASSERS-BY."

We went to the New Theatre with great expectations of this piece, which ran so successfully in London, and we came away with increased respect for Mr. Du Maurier and Miss Vanbrugh, who had succeeded in making a hit out of such sentimental material—a feat which Mr. Imeson, as *Peter Waverton*, and Miss Amy Ravenscroft, as *Margaret Summers*, could hardly hope to rival. To put it bluntly, they failed, though they failed as ninety-nine out of a hundred actors must have done. Both were, nevertheless really good, they played their parts with restraint and taste, and only failed in neglecting to put into their parts a sufficiency of spontaneous personality to sop up the overflowing and "wishy-washy" sentiment.

It was a play which only a confirmed bachelor, with his well-known weakness for children, could stand. Perhaps that was why the army of London critics forgave the piece. We, for our part, though as yet bachelors, still have hopes.

It is, of course, a child, *Little Peter*, and delightfully played by Miss Marjorie Graham, who acts the *deus ex machina* and brings together this unmarried father and mother, and who rouses the sentimental sympathy of all.

> "Sing me a drawing-room song, darling !
> Bear on the angels' wings
> Children that know no wrong, darling !
> Little cherubic things !
> Sing of their sunny hair, darling !
> Get them to die in June ;
> Wake, if you can, on the stair, darling !
> Echoes of tiny shoon."

But Little Peter does not die, he is merely carried away, and in the hour of general despair, Love shines forth clear and unrestrained.

Granta 1911

HOW TYRE-SOME !

Mrs. Miggs : "How do you account for the fact that I found a piece of rubber tyre in one of the sausages I bought here last week ?"

"My dear madam, that only goes to show that the automobile is replacing the horse everywhere !"

Comic Cuts 1911

TERROR AGED SEVEN.

COMPELLED FATHER TO FETCH BEER AND CIGARETTES.

Amazing admissions were made by a father, at Macclesfield, when application was made under the Children's Act (by Mr. H. E. Smale, on behalf of the N.S.P.C.C.), for a boy aged seven years and nine months to be committed to an industrial school, he being entirely beyond his father's control. "This is a most extraordinary case, and a very sad one," said Mr. Smale. This boy of seven years and nine months is a child over whom the father has lost all control. The boy had only to say to his father, "Go and fetch me some beer and some cigarettes, or if you don't I will give you a jolly good thrashing, or something worse." When in bed the boy had repeatedly kicked his father to such an extent that dry abscesses had formed on his body.—John Thomas Hancell, cotton operative, Bollington, said he had had to fetch beer when requested, because the boy had led him such a life, and threatened him with the brush, tongs, and dolly peg. The lad would not let him get into bed until he had gone to sleep; sometimes he had pushed him out of bed.—Alice Forrest, one of the neighbours, said she had repeatedly heard the boy ill-using his father. When anyone went to the father's assistance the boy locked the door, took the key out of the lock, and so prevented anyone getting into the house. The language the boy used was so bad that she would not like to repeat it.—Another neighbour, Ellen Wood, said the boy used awful and fearful language, and he was not fit to be at large. His father dare not do anything other than fetch the beer and cigarettes when the boy demanded.

JOHN THOMAS HANCELL

HANCELL'S SON.

them.—The boy was committed to the Macclesfield Industrial School until he is 16.

News of the World 1912

BOOKS FOR BOYS

By Sir William Bull, M.P.

I was much interested in Mr. Richard Middleton's article the other week on "Treasure Island," and gladly respond to his request for other experiences of boys' tastes in reading. I am forty-eight years of age, having been born in September, 1863. I could read fairly well before I was seven; consequently my boyhood includes the whole of the 'seventies. The first book I can remember was in our nursery—an immense folio seventeenth-century "History of the Bible," with a picture on every other page. We never read the print, but "Jacob vigorously wrestling with the Angel" and people "Digging the grave for Sarai" represent in my mind's eye those events even now. The first book which was read to my brothers and myself was "Willie's Birthday," a highly proper story, in which Willie asks and is allowed to do anything he likes on his birthday and comes to dreadful grief. The second was "Sandford and Merton," and we naturally had what we called "a sneaking likeness" for Tommy Merton "the wickeder one." There were some excellent fairy stories published in those days, "King Gab's Story-bag and What it Contained," by Heraclitus Grey, with delightful pictures by Walter Crane. Then there was a fat little book, translated from the German, called "A Picture Story-book" (which in 1855 was in its fifth edition); it had 400 quaint illustrations, and contained three capital stories—"Dame Mitchell and her Cat;" "The Adventures of Prince Hempseed;" and the enthralling "History of a Nutcracker," a book which I should have thought it would pay to republish. We read and re-read Louise M. Alcott's books, "Little Men" and "Little Women" and "The Eight Cousins." They were girlish, American, and gentle and simple mixed together in a way we could not understand, but they held us in their sway.

We liked "Alice in Wonderland" and "Through the Looking-glass" fairly well, but thought "The Water Babies" rot, and could see no fun in À Becket's "Comic History of England." We liked the pictures in Surtees' books, but found it difficult to understand the political cartoons in "Punch," even when explained.

I remember buying the first number of "Little Folks" outside the old tin station at Westbourne Park early in the 'seventies. The earlier stories in it were "The Magic Beads; or, Gilbert's Shadow," "The New Mistletoe Bough," "Raggles Baggles and the Emperor;" "Stories Told by some Little Folks around the Nursery Fire," containing one whose title pleased us—"How Polly Patterson took a Dislike to a Little Girl in a Whitey-brown Frock." "The Star in a Dustheap" and others of equal merit followed. A short reading-book called "Nelson's Series, No. 9," had a great influence on us, and by the end of 1875 we could practically recite the whole of it by heart. It consisted of singularly well-chosen extracts from the best authors and some poetry. I could not recite "Beth Gelert" for tears, but I loved Macaulay's "Horatius" and "Armada," and Campbell's "Battle of the Baltic" and "Hohenlinden."

Academy and Literature **1911**

QUAINT SCENE IN A CHURCH.

A picturesque ceremony took place at the old parish church of St. George's, Gravesend, when David Varchell's Charity was distributed. The custom has been observed for 209 Christmases, being interrupted only when the church building was burned down about 150 years ago. Forty poor persons each received a loaf and a new sixpence. The preacher of the anniversary sermon received 10s. under the terms of the will. The churchwardens and the caretaker each received 2s. 6d., and 5s. was spent on candles for the illumination of the candelabra which Varchell presented to the church. Twenty boys who, during the week, had been completely clothed from Varchell's fund, stood up in the corporation pews while the preacher referred to the donor long since gone.

People **1911**

MAD COW CHARGES CHILDREN.

A girl named Rose Baron, 10, and her brother, Eric, 15 months, whom she was wheeling in a perambulator, had narrow escapes from death in West Park, Hull. A mad cow entered the park and charged the perambulator, smashing it to pieces. Both children were picked up uninjured. The cow was subsequently shot.

News of the World **1912**

NATURALLY HE ENJOYED THE PARTY.

"Enjoyed your party, Bobby?"
"Yes, auntie."
"Well, what little girls did you dance with?"
"Oh, I didn't dance. I had three fights downstairs with Billy Jones, and licked him every time."

Comic Cuts **1911**

PICTURE PALACE SCENE.

EXCITING INCIDENT AT CHILDREN'S MATINEE.

Yesterday afternoon an exciting incident which might very easily have resulted in a serious panic occurred during the matinee performance at the Avenue Picture Palace, Rosebery-avenue, Clerkenwell. The audience consisted of 400 children, and halfway through the programme a film became ignited in the operator's box, near the stage. Instantly the man closed the iron door, which is one of the regulation provisions for the safety of the audience, and is intended to shut off the latter from all danger, but this did not prevent smoke belching into the house and out in the street. The manager (Mr. Fred Boustead) instantly took in the situation, and, ordering the exit doors to be thrown open, he directed the marshalling of the children from the building, while the pianist played "We all go the same way home." They went out as orderly as a regiment of soldiers" he said to a "News of the World" representative. "There was no panic, no screaming or pushing, but the youngsters simply trooped out into the street. I told them there was no danger, and they took my word." Outside a large crowd, made up of anxious parents attracted by the smoke, gathered, but, to their relief, saw the children emerge safely. The fire brigade was quickly summoned from the Clerkenwell Station, which is only about 60 yards away. Their services were not required, however, as all danger had passed.

News of the World 1912

News of the World 1912

EAST END TRIPLETS.

OUT OF WORK LABOURER'S FAMILY GROWS FROM FOUR TO SEVEN.

By the birth of triplets the family of an East End labourer, out of work owing to the strike, has been increased from four to seven. The parents are Mr. and Mrs. Baker, who reside in Dorset-street, Commercial-road, and ever since news of the event has leaked out the father has done little besides answering the door to astonished and inquiring neighbours. Nearly a hundred called, unbelievers when they came but quite convinced before they left. A Pressman was shown into the front room by Mr. Baker, where, beside Mrs. Baker, who lay asleep, were peeping above the bedclothes three tiny heads in a row, each with a strangely plentiful crop of hair. All three looked bonny babies, "very much alive and kicking," as their father put it. "The three little ones are all right," he said, "and the doctor says they've come to stop. He's nearly as proud of 'em as the missus and me."

News of the World 1912

Do It Now!

If you have words to say,
    Say them now.
To-morrow may not come your way.
Do a kindness while you may,
Loved ones will not always stay;
    Say them now.

If you have a smile to show,
    Show it now.
Make hearts happy, roses grow,
Let the friends around you know
The love you have before you go;
    Show it now.

If you have hard work to do,
    Do it now.
To-day the skies are clear and blue,
To-morrow clouds may come in view,
Yesterday is not for you;
    Do it now.

If you have a song to sing,
    Sing it now.
Let the notes of gladness ring
Clear as song of bird in spring,
Let every day some music bring,
    Sing it now

Girls' Weekly 1913

SHOULD THEY BE ALLOWED TO MARRY?

STIGMA OF A MURDERER'S NAME.

Is It Worse for a Child Than Illegitimacy?

CHURCH'S POINT OF VIEW

Is it worse for a child to be known as the daughter of a murderer than to be illegitimate?

This delicate problem in connection with the Eastbourne murder has led to a considerable amount of discussion and a marked difference of opinion. It is a case of sentimental and practical views coming into conflict.

The child in question is a girl born on Sunday night to Florence Seymour, whose lover, John Williams, was found guilty and sentenced to death on a charge of murdering Police Inspector Walls

After the death sentence Williams appealed to the Home Secretary for permission to marry Miss Seymour in time to save her child the shame of illegitimacy. This permission has been refused.

The Church of England point of view was put before *The Daily Mirror* by a Canon of St. Paul's:

"Any such marriage might mean reparation towards the woman, but would in no way affect the child. There is no stigma from the Church point of view on an illegitimate child as such.

THE CHILD'S HARD LOT.

"It would, however, be desirable that amends should be done to the woman who has been wronged."

A City solicitor was strongly in favour of the marriage.

"In the first place," he said, "there is the argument brought forward by Mr. W. H. Speed, solicitor for Williams, that there is a possibility of money being left to Williams or his heirs. It would be a cruel wrong, in my opinion, to deprive a child of a father and money at the same time.

"The illegitimate child—more especially if sensitive—has a very hard time of it, as often as not owing to the unintentional cruelty of other children. Apart from this, a marriage would mean much to the woman who has suffered so grievously.

"The fact that her husband has been convicted of murder and may only have a short time to live has nothing to do with the question. The woman undoubtedly loves the man, and such a marriage might mean a moral support for her throughout life."

"BOTH PARTIES MUST BE FREE."

A leading lawyer who has had great experience in criminal cases was strongly of opinion that the marriage should not be allowed. His main reason was that the sentence on Williams might be commuted to penal servitude for life.

"The legal position of Williams is that he is not a free man. Marriage is a civil contract, and both parties must be free.

"The Home Secretary might exercise clemency and allow the marriage, but for reasons that I will give you such clemency would be inadvisable.

"If it were certain that Williams were to be executed on a given date then the marriage might be allowed. Most common-sense people would think it a reprehensible precedent, but at any rate there would be the sentimental consideration of 'having a name.'

"In such a case the woman at the expiration of a certain time would be a widow, and her future existence would more or less be in her own hands. But supposing her prisoner-husband is not hanged.

SOME POSSIBILITIES.

"Williams, as I understand, has appealed against his sentence. That sentence may be altered. Even if the appeal fails, there is always the possibility of the death sentence being commuted for one of penal servitude for life.

"Just think what that would mean. For something like twenty years the woman would, at the same time, be wife and no wife.

"Her whole future is mortgaged. Even supposing that the couple are in love with each other—that does not mean that she will wait twenty years for him.

"As for the child, its position would be exceedingly cruel. At present there is not the slightest reason why she should ever hear of her father's past. She could go through life with tender thoughts of a parent she never knew.

"It may seem hard, but the Home Secretary's attitude is really a kindness towards the woman and her child."

SOLDIER AND HIS DYING CHILD.

Left Without Leave and Arrested as Deserter.

AN ESCORT DESERTS.

Thomas Rule, aged 48, the soldier who left the depot of the 5th Middlesex Regiment without leave in order to visit his dying child, was again brought up at Highgate to-day on the charge of being a deserter.

Rule had been remanded for the arrival of an escort, which, it was now stated, had also deserted. A second escort was on the way.

Rule explained that he heard that his child was dying, and left the depot as he could not rest. He arrived home, to find that the child had died in hospital. He had telegraphed for permission to attend the funeral, but had got no reply.

He would like to attend the funeral of his child to-morrow.

The Magistrate (Mr. Burfield): Shall we remand him so that he can do so?

The Clerk said he was afraid it was impossible, as the escort was on the way to take him back.

Rule said he would be satisfied if he could look on his dead child. She was lying at New Southgate.

Mr. Burfield asked that arrangements should be made for him to go to New Southgate.

Mr. Graves said that a policeman in plain clothes should go with him.

Rule: Thank you.

A Pretty Tunic

IT is an important event in the life of every small boy when he is put into wee knickers for the first time. Laid aside for ever are the petticoats and skirts that have clothed him from infancy, and who so proud as he at his first approach to masculine attire.

It may perhaps prove useful if we give here a table of necessary garments.

(1) Combinations, worn with or without Jaeger belt at discretion.

(2) Knickers, either buttoned on to a bodice or held up by soft, loosely woven braces.

(3) A blouse or tunic.

When he goes out the small boy will, of course, in winter time, wear a warm overcoat of some description or another. Many mothers prefer a man-o'-war reefer coat to any other style.

Hearth and
Home 1913

DOG GUARDS WANDERING BOY.

Police Unable To Approach Lost Child.

WHAT THE ANIMAL "SAID" AFTERWARDS.

Duke is a proud Great Dane.

He kept guard for six hours over a three-year-old boy who strayed from home and wandered for ten miles. Such care did he take of the little one that he defied a policeman who was on the look-out for the child.

The story of Duke was told to the *Daily Sketch* yesterday by his master, Mr. White, of Clarendon-road, Notting Hill.

"Shortly after noon on Good Friday," he said, "it was reported that Eric Lennard, the three-year-old son of a neighbour, was missing from his home. My dog Duke was also away, but no one connected the two, though they were fond of each other.

"The matter was put into the hands of the police, Hyde Park being especially searched. As nightfall approached nothing had been heard of the lost boy.

"But about seven o'clock as a group of neighbours were discussing the disappearance the youngster and the dog came round the corner. Eric was holding on to the collar of the dog, not an easy thing, considering that Duke's back is some inches higher than Eric's head.

"How can I explain it? Well, all I can think of is that Duke knew by instinct that something was wrong, and trotted off, 'picked up' the scent and kept guard over the mite from that moment

"In fact, a policeman who spotted the lad near Marble Arch was unable to approach owing to the threatening attitude of the dog.

"When Duke returned with the child his manner was almost human. He looked up at me, wagged his tail, looked down at the boy, and then up again at me as much as to say 'You see I've taken care of him all right, master!'"

Daily Sketch **1914**

Queen 1912

[Daily Mirror Studios.

MISS MEYER AS HOP o' MY THUMB AT THE DRURY LANE THEATRE.

Photo by Stearn & Sons, Cambridge.

THOSE IN AUTHORITY.

MR. A. C. TELFER (SELWYN COLLEGE).

CAPTAIN, C. U. H. & H. C.

ON March 8th, 1893, there arrived at Faversham a phenomenally light but tremendously energetic baby, who a few weeks later was christened Andrew Cecil Telfer. Fate had decreed that this child was some day to become a great runner, for did not his father long ago run seven miles to school and home again every day amid the mountains of Fife ? Cissie, as the infant soon was to be called, developed rapidly, and at the age of three, imagining that jumping was his vocation, tried to emulate his brother, and landed at the bottom of three stone steps in the most approved fashion, wrong way up. Thanks to the good Scotch blood in his veins he survived this downfall of all his hopes, and finding that high jumping was not quite so pleasant as he had imagined, he took to hurdling. He had many miraculous escapes from fences and walls, but in spite of this he was not satisfied with the sport, and finally decided to disregard the goadings of his vaulting ambition and to essay the safer pursuit of running.

Granta 1913

FIRST INSURANCE BABY.

Earliest Birth Under New Act Occurs One Minute After Midnight!

One minute after midnight !

This was the exact time at which the first baby in London to be born under the new maternity benefit of the Insurance Act—which became payable only at midnight last night—arrived in Queen Charlotte's Lying-in Hospital, in Marylebone-road, Paddington.

The first Insurance baby was a girl.

She was born as near after midnight as she well could be, and no other baby in the country is likely to beat this record.

The mother is Mrs. Golding, of 23, Senior-street, Paddington.

The Act sets forth that the wife of an insured person who gives birth to a child after midnight

MRS. GOLDING.

last night is entitled to a benefit payment of 30s. in respect of each confinement.

If insured herself, every mother giving birth to a child is entitled to 30s. maternity benefit and 7s. 6d. per week while ill, up to a limit of twenty-six weeks. The insured parent must have been in insurance twenty-six weeks and have paid twenty-six full contributions.

In order, however, to obtain the maternity benefit it is necessary for the doctor or midwife attending the confinement to certify the time of birth.

The husband, or, if he is not insured, the insured wife herself, should make the claim and send it to the approved society. The claim may also be made on her behalf by any other person whom she may depute.

Daily Mirror 1913

The Punishment of " Joy " Riders.—The Divisional Court of the King's Bench have dismissed an appeal by the father of a lad named Radley against a decision in favour of the London County Council at Westminster County Court. A car conductor mistook Radley for one of the boys who annoyed him by " joy " riding on the car, and cuffed him. The boy fell, and it was stated that the conductor fell on him and broke the boy's arm. A claim was made, and the County Court judge held that the conductor was not acting within the scope of his employment, and non-suited plaintiff.

Tramway and Railway World 1913

Enjoyable Dance in Aid of the Soldiers' and Sailors' Help Society.

A most enjoyable dance for children and young people was organised in the Exhibition Hall, Belfast, on Tuesday last week in aid of the Soldiers' and Sailors' Help Society, and through the kindness of Brigadier-Gen. Count Gleichen, K.C.V., and Countess Gleichen, under whose patronage the dance was given, prizes were awarded for the best fancy costume, the judging being undertaken by the Lady Mayoress (Mrs R. J. M'Mordie), who was assisted by Mrs J. C. Payne and Mrs Shoveller. Countess Gleichen, who was gowned in mole cloth and velvet, presented the prizes, the first being won by Miss Doris Wallace as Bo Peep, in a dainty dress of blue and white. The second prize was awarded to Miss Maisie Mallon, in a Red Indian's costume, Master Sam Hughes as a Cowboy winning the prize for the best boy's costume. There were many dainty and pretty costumes worn by the children, amongst them being Quaker Girls, Swiss Peasants, Pierrots and Pierrettes, a Chinese Mandarin, a Geisha, Chinamen, &c. At eight o'clock the younger children went home while the elders than danced, supper being served about 9.30. Much praise should be given to those who kindly assisted in making the dance a success, amongst them being Mrs St. Clair Boyd, Miss Dorothy M'Gonigal, Mrs J. C. Payne, Mrs George Jameson, Mrs Archdall, Mrs Wilson, Mrs David Watson, Mrs Shoveller, Miss Edwards, and Mrs Clarke, &c. The music was supplied by the band of the Dorset Regiment under the conductorship of Mr Richards.

Queen 1914

SPECIMEN OF THE CONVERSATION BETWEEN DR. BIRCHER AND ARTHUR.

" Sit down, my dear boy," said the Doctor rising from the chair where he had been seated. " It is with with great pleasure, my dear boy, that I welcome you to St. Clement's. I hope you will be one of its most popular inmates. We will do our best for you, Arthur, I assure you.

"Always, my dear boy, say your prayers ; and remember that cleanliness is next to godliness. I have given instructions to the matron to air you a pair of pants for Sunday. You had better not change your vests till May is ended. You will doubtless remember, my dear boy, the old adage,

" ' Change not a clout
Till May is out.'

" And now good-bye, my little man." So Arthur went out to the noisy whirl of school-life, much cheered by the kind words of his future chief.

Granta **1914**

QUEEN ALEXANDRA.
Queen Alexandra was enthusiastically cheered as the Royal carriage drew up at the covered way to the porch and her Majesty stepped out. Her Majesty's arrival was marked by an interesting incident. As the Queen passed on her way into the church a group of children, obviously of the poorer class, and some of them shoeless, in their eagerness to see what was going on behind the awning, pushed their little heads through an opening just as the Queen passed. Her Majesty instantly noticed them, and bending towards them with a smile, patted them gently on the head before passing on.

Pall Mall Gazette **1915**

A PICK-ULIAR OCCURENCE.

1. Just as Percy the navvy was going to biff the road with his pick a Zeppelin dropped a bomb from the sky.

2. But, luckily, Percy's pick caught a water-pipe a nasty one, and a jet of water spouted up and met that bomb half-way.

Butterfly **1914**

EXPELLED FROM ETON.

Boy of 15 Who Broke Out for a "Lark."

HEADMASTER AND MOTHER.

Sympathetic Movement by Old Etonians.

A sensation has been caused at Eton by the expulsion of a boy, Edward Broughton-Adderley, and still more by the energetic championship of his mother, the Hon. Mrs. Broughton-Adderley, who has addressed a strong letter to Dr. Lyttelton, the headmaster, on the subject.

It appears that the boy and a companion got out of Mr. Booker's house at Eton on Monday night and went to Maidenhead for a "lark."

They were caught, and next day were both expelled. The way these things are done at Eton is illustrated by the fact that the first news Mrs. Broughton-Adderley received of so momentous a decision, was a telephone message from her son.

He is a boy of 15, and this is his first serious fault during three years at Eton College.

Mrs. Broughton-Adderley, who is a daughter of the fourth Lord Castlemaine, and sister of the present peer, comes of good fighting stock, and she declined to acquiesce quietly in this decision.

HEADMASTER'S LETTER.

She went to Eton and interviewed the "Head," but without avail. A correspondence has since taken place which we publish by permission of Mrs. Broughton-Adderley:—

The Cloisters, Eton College.
June 24, 1914.
Dear Mrs. Broughton-Adderley,—It is quite impossible for you to be anything but very angry unless you take in the following facts which, up to the present, you have forgotten:—

1. It is not from caprice or because I enjoy doing it that I have to send your boy away, but because I am quite convinced it is my duty.

2. When this is the case no amount of worrying will make me relax my decision.

3. Your view that a young boy's life is spoilt from a mere escapade is entirely wrong. His age makes it perfectly easy to get him into any profession, and I have promised him a leaving book after six months, if he can get a character from some responsible person.

4. As there has been no vicious conduct it is quite easy for you to state the facts without qualification or concealment and everybody will understand.

5. The boy is so flighty and unsteady that it is very doubtful if he could have remained at Eton without risk of a far more serious collapse.

6. This being so, you may rest assured that the shock will do him permanent good if you do not spoil it all by taking his side against authority. Please remember that every violent speech you make in his presence will encourage him in resisting law, to which he is already dangerously prone.

7. If, as I am told you threaten to do, you put the whole matter into the paper, the only result will be to damage the boy's reputation very seriously. There is not a right thinking man in the country who would not see that I could not do otherwise.

Under these circumstances I must ask you to refrain from seeking an interview in order to shake my decision, as it would only be a waste of time, and I have none to spare.

If you are willing to abide by what I have said, you may reckon on my doing all I can for the boy and seeing him safe into the Navy. And in two years' time you will wonder that the matter ever appeared to you so disastrous as it has.—I remain, yours very truly,

E. LYTTELTON.
P.S.—I have just seen the parents of the other boy, and they were quite consoled and fully in accord with what I said.

MOTHER'S REPLY.

To this letter Mrs. Broughton-Adderley sent the following reply:—

Granville-place, Portman-square, W.
June 24, 1914.
Dear "Head,"—I have been reading and dissecting your letter most carefully, the tone of which I do not like. I am not angry, but suffering from what I consider a gross injustice, a most cruel punishment for a first offence, and especially as he was not the ringleader.

However, I am glad to see (immaculate as you think yourself) that you own there has been no "vicious conduct"; the chief sin seems to be the sin of being found out. You have been able, I note, to console the other parents.

I am glad for their sake, but I am incapable of taking such a case of injustice lying down, and perhaps I have gone too deeply into life to care for your consolation. I never remember having made a violent speech in the presence of any of my children, and have always tried to enforce strict obedience on them.

I do not wish to use any threat, but merely to state facts through the medium of the Press, and so remove the likelihood of any stain resting on my son's name in after life. Unless it is widely known in to-day's hurry through life one only hears "That chap got the sack from Eton," and no one stops to ask why, and for a small offence the worst constructions are oftentimes put upon it.

I refuse to allow this in my son's case, for perhaps I feel more strongly than most women the great difference that lies between a small boy's naughtiness and an unnatural offence.

Your panacea for your harsh treatment is no use to me. I want my son neither to have the leaving-book nor your valuable help in his future life. At the age of fifteen you have not given him much courage to go on with.

I hope to put him to a college in Canada, and let him work and make his living there, and as long as I live inculcate into him always the necessity of never forgetting the three greatest things in life: Love and faith in God, to try and be ready at any time to face death fearlessly, and to be ready whenever called on to serve his King and his country.

No doubt rests in my mind that he will do well some day. I fail to see how my boy's reputation will be damaged very seriously by having his case put into the papers.

Nor do I agree with you that every right-minded man will see that you could not have done otherwise. You must remember that there are many right-minded men who are the fathers of sons, and by living again in them have made them remember that they, too, were once boys, and the old adage "Boys will be boys" remains green in their memory and keeps them human and just.

You have doubtless long ago forgotten. You have treated two children as criminals. We will leave it at that, as you are incapable of understanding.—Yours faithfully,

FLORENCE BROUGHTON-ADDERLEY.

We understand that Mrs. Broughton-Adderley, as her son's guardian, has determined to face even the disadvantages of publicity in order that her son's real offence shall be widely known for what it is, and no more.

OLD ETONIANS' SYMPATHY.

Her son has left Eton, and is in London with her. She has already received many messages of sympathy from friends, and one well-known peer, an Old Etonian, has expressed a desire to meet her in order to seek to arouse the sympathy of Old Etonians in the case.

This would be a direct challenge to Dr. Lyttelton's statement that there is "not a right-thinking man in the country who would not see that I could not do otherwise."

Star 1914

"What's the child's name?" asked the priest of the grandfather at the christening.

"I dunno," the grandfather replied. And he turned to the father and whispered hoarsely, "What's the name?"

"Hazel," replied the father.

The grandfather threw up his hands in disgust.

"What d'ye think av that?" he asked the priest. "With the calendar av the saints full av gur'rl names an' him namin' his after a nut!"

In Love At Sixteen.

E. D. B. wants me to say if it is advisable for her to accept the attentions of a young man who is nineteen years of age, she being only sixteen.

Sixteen, admittedly, is an early age at which to start a love affair, but, provided that E. D. B. is assured that the young man who has fallen in love with her is a good and straightforward chap, and that he has the full approval of her parents, I see no great objection to the arrangement; although I would point out that she is far too young to commit herself to any definite engagement to marry.

The understanding she should form with the young man in question should be of such a character that she or he should be able to withdraw honourably from it at any time.

Our Girls 1915

TWO SOLDIER BOYS.

Two soldier boys, one aged 16 and the other 15, were charged at Crewe, on Monday, with being absentees from their regiments. Pte. Albert Edward Froggatt was charged with being an absentee from the 17th Battalion King's Royal Rifles, Paddock Hurst, since May 25, and Pte. Charles Stock was charged with being an absentee from the 3rd Battalion, 17th County of London Territorials, since the same day. When asked by the magistrates their civilian age and their War Office age, Froggatt gave his as 15 and Stock 16, both smiling. It appeared that they had been wandering about London nearly three weeks and left then for Manchester. Detective Inspector Rogers found them detained in the guard's van of the London train at Crewe. They admitted they were absentees from their regiment and had no railway pass.—They were put back for an escort.

Crewe Chronicle 1915.

YOU MUST ALL ENTER FOR THIS COMPETITION.
WILL YOU ASK YOUR FRIENDS TO DO SO TOO?

Try this Competition

The other day I came across Queenie writing to you to wish you a Happy New Year, so I asked her if she would let me have her letter to turn into pictures for the competition. She did, and here it is.

I am keeping the letter quite safely, and shall not look at it again until you send me *your* letter.

※ ※ ※

It is quite simple, and all you have to do is to find out what these pictures stand for, and write the letter out neatly in *ink*.

When you have done that, write your name and address underneath, cut out this picture and pin it to the piece of paper. Then send them to "Letter" Competition, MOTHER AND HOME, Gough House, Gough Square, London, E.C., to reach there not later than Wednesday, January 5.

I shall give a sovereign as a prize to the girl or boy who sends me the correct answer, and if more than one of you does so, I shall divide the prize between you.

You can send in as many entries as you like if you keep to the rules, but no one will be awarded more than one share of the prize.

Also my decision must be accepted as final, and you must only take part in the competition on that understanding.

Don't forget to tell your little friends to enter for the competition, so that they can read Queenie's New Year wish to them.

Mother and Home 1916

BE POLITE TO YOUR CHILDREN

Example is better than any amount of "preaching." If we want our children to grow up well mannered and considerate to others, we must be polite and courteous to them.

"Y OU silly child ! *You'll* never be able to write stories. Take it away ! I haven't time to read it ! "

Those were the words I heard as I walked into a friend's drawing-room the other day. They were addressed to the small daughter of the house, who slipped out of the room with her face scarlet with self-consciousness and hurt pride.

" Isn't Elsie a little goose ? " my friend remarked, as I approached. " She has a great ambition to be a writer when she grows up. But, of course, as I tell her, she'll never be any good at that sort of thing."

" How do you know ? "

" Why, I've read one or two of the things she's written, and they simply made me roar with laughter. I had some friends here at the time, and we had great fun out of them."

" But what about Elsie ? "

" What do you mean ? "

" I mean, how did Elsie like being laughed at ? "

" Why, of course, she didn't like it at all. But she's only a child ! "

" Only a child ! "

Respect their Confidence

A ND my friend considered herself a good mother ! So she was, as far as material things went. She saw to it that her children were well fed and decently clothed, but she did not understand that if she wished to exert a beautiful and lasting influence over their lives she must respect their confidence.

Nothing hurts a sensitive child so much as being laughed at. To come to its mother, as a little child does, with the absolute confidence of ignorance, and, after expressing all the inmost thoughts and ambitions that seem so important to the young mind, to be ridiculed—no doubt, quite kindly—why, don't you see what happens ?

That little child thinks twice before venturing on any further confidences, and, in time, learns to keep its hopes and fears and ambitions to itself.

And in later years the parent who has thus in the early days checked the confidences of the child very probably complains that the growing—or grown-up—daughter " keeps things so much to herself."

Only the other day I was talking to the mother of two nearly grown-up sons.

" They're quite good boys," she said, " but, you know, I can't help feeling that I am growing out of touch with them.

" They so very rarely confide in me now, as they used to do. When they were little, they used to tell me everything, but very often I hadn't time to listen."

Then I understood why this particular mother had lost her children's confidence in these later days.

When they were young, and had looked to her to share their innermost thoughts and ambitions and desires, she had checked the childish confidences with a distracted " Yes, yes, dears ! But mother can't listen now. Run away and play ! "

Bad Examples

W HY should we be less polite to our children than we are to people of our own age ? And how can we expect them to grow up polite and considerate to others if we offer them such a bad example of rudeness and want of consideration by our manners towards them ?

It is so often the really kind, well-meaning parents who are inconsiderate and thoughtlessly unkind to their children. I have known little children whose lives have been made almost unbearable for them, simply because their parents—quite good parents, too—have not tried to understand the miseries they are going through.

Unnecessary Humiliation

O NE instance I have in my mind of a little girl whose mother would go out shopping and come home with the weirdest garments that she had purchased cheaply, and which she insisted on making her daughter wear.

She never listened when the child protested, but simply insisted that they were good and useful clothes which had been honestly paid for. Quite right and true ! But what a one-sided argument !

The child was not allowed to put forward *her* side of the question—that the other children at the school made fun of her, and everyone turned and stared at her.

You see, with a little thought, and a little effort to put herself in the child's place, that mother would have realised that she was submitting her child to totally unnecessary humiliation.

The mother was not particularly rich, certainly, but she could have procured quite serviceable, pretty, and up-to-date garments for as small an outlay as she spent on the ugly and abnormal clothes that she made her little daughter wear.

Mother and Home 1916

The Children's Hour

The hour that ought to be the sunniest and best to children and parents alike; the hour in which an understanding sympathy is only to be obtained by those who share a common happiness on equal terms.

THE relations between parents and children in our own country are popularly supposed to be the happiest the world over.

Yet as in so many instances where we laud ourselves to the skies, and thank Providence piously that we are not as others, we might do well to imitate our Japanese Allies, and by the introduction of more mutual playtime into the lives of parents and children, benefit both to an almost like degree.

Blase Superiority

POSSIBLY, as a nation, we do not take our pleasures *quite* as sadly as our Continental neighbours delight in believing. But it is an undoubted fact that a leaven of the old Puritan spirit still dominates our parenthood, almost entirely excluding the tender playfulness that, making them as children with children, would gain childish confidences and childish hearts to an extent never possible to the parent who persistently maintains his attitude of grown-up and more or less blasé superiority.

It is by deliberate intention that the masculine gender is used in the previous sentence. Mothers—during the first years of their infants' lives, at any rate—are infinitely more alive to the necessity of mutual play than parents of the opposite sex. To see a father really romping with his small son or daughter is as rare a sight as it is delightful!

True that in most families the rule of "children's hour" holds good—an hour, supposedly devoted to infantile amusement, but in what that hour *really* consisted most of us darkly remember! The astonishing thing being that our remembrance does so little to lighten its darkness for the babies of to-day.

Heart-Sinking Moments

WHO does not remember the terrible rigidity of the starched frills that chafed our chubby limbs? The heart-sinking moment when nurse opened the drawing-room door, to discover, at *worst*, a circle of grown-ups prepared amicably to talk down to our level; at *best*, a mother and father so bent on being improving that we perforce lived up to our stiff perfection of attire, until even the sometime hated prospect of bed seemed to loom quite pleasantly upon the horizon of our youthful imaginations?

Such a Sunny Hour

THE children's hour! The hour that ought to be the sunniest and best to children and parents alike; the playtime in which the trials of the day are put aside and forgotten; the hour in which an understanding sympathy is only to be obtained by those who share a common happiness on equal terms.

It is something worth securing, this children's hour.

The father who can throw aside all memory of the tasks and anxieties of the day and *play* with his boys and girls gains infinitely more than a pleasant hour of childish happiness.

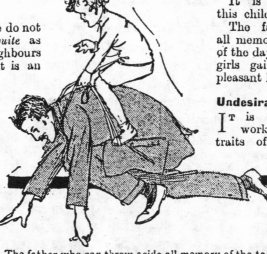

The father who can throw aside all memory of the tasks and anxieties of the day and play with his boys and girls gains infinitely more than a pleasant hour of childish happiness.

Undesirable Traits

IT is in playtime rather than worktime that little, undesirable traits of character stand revealed and may quietly and unobtrusively be corrected.

The girl or boy who learns by unconscious imitation always and above everything to "play the game," to do their very best to win, yet accept defeat good-temperedly — success with modesty—has assimilated lessons in honour and good-fellowship that will go with them through life.

It is in the *home* playtime that the small boy grows chivalrous and gentle in his dealing towards all things feminine.

Father and Mother

FATHER—quite as a matter of course—assumes that "a fellow" makes certain allowances, gives way gracefully to "the girls"—just because they *are* girls. Mother's pleasure and theirs is consulted *first*. That any other course of conduct should be possible never dawns on the little lad until it is forced upon him in later days, and unhesitatingly condemned as "caddish." Things—lessons—not easily inculcated in school, however good the master.

The mere fact that, for one hour of the day, at any rate, mother is "just a girl," and father "another fellow," gives them a position in childish eyes that no amount of kindly sympathy, differently expressed, could give.

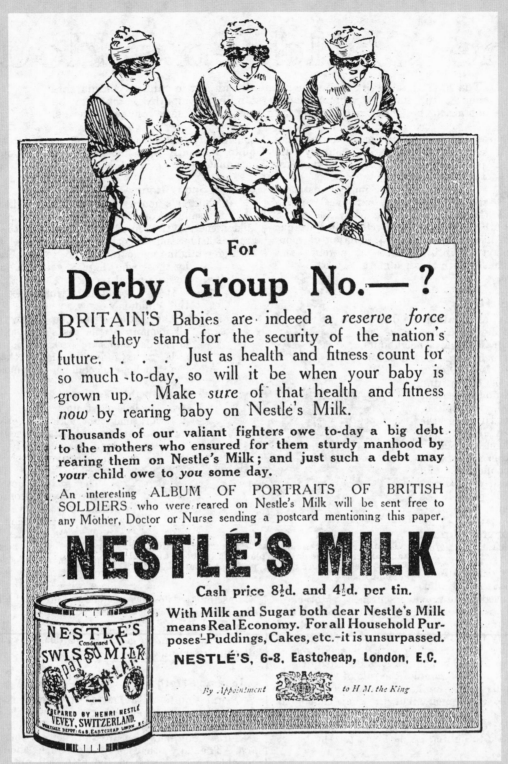

For

Derby Group No.—?

BRITAIN'S Babies are indeed a *reserve force* —they stand for the security of the nation's future. . . . Just as health and fitness count for so much -to-day, so will it be when your baby is grown up. Make *sure* of that health and fitness *now* by rearing baby on Nestle's Milk.

Thousands of our valiant fighters owe to-day a big debt to the mothers who ensured for them sturdy manhood by rearing them on Nestle's Milk; and just such a debt may *your* child owe to *you* some day.

An interesting ALBUM OF PORTRAITS OF BRITISH SOLDIERS who were reared on Nestle's Milk will be sent free to any Mother, Doctor or Nurse sending a postcard mentioning this paper.

NESTLÉ'S MILK

Cash price 8½d. and 4½d. per tin.

With Milk and Sugar both dear Nestle's Milk means Real Economy. For all Household Purposes-Puddings, Cakes, etc.-it is unsurpassed.

NESTLÉ'S, 6-8, Eastcheap, London, E.C.

By Appointment to H.M. the King

NESTLE'S
Condensed
SWISS MILK
PREPARED BY HENRI NESTLE
VEVEY, SWITZERLAND.
WHOLESALE DEPOT: 6&8, EASTCHEAP LONDON E.C.

Mother and Home 1916

CHRISTMAS TOYS FOR YOUNG HUNS.

HORRORS OF WAR IN LEAD AND PICTURE BOOKS.

The Christmas gifts to the German children this year do not bring any suggestion of love and goodwill towards others; on the contrary, they tend to teach the German little ones to gloat over the miseries and hardships of the small folk of the enemies of the German Fatherland.

Reuter's correspondent has had a private view of a collection of toys intended for distribution in Germany at Christmas and the New Year, specimens of which have just reached France by a roundabout route. Most prominent among the "playthings" for little Germans were models in lead of the ruins of French and Belgian villages laid to waste by the German troops. In addition are picture books filled with illustrations of military operations, in which, of course, the German troops always have the upper hand, and their enemies are annihilated.

These "documents of the great war" form but a small part of the collection now being gathered in the Library and Museum of the War founded under the auspices of the French Ministry of Public Instruction.

Among the most interesting features of the library-museum are the medals struck by order of the German Emperor in honour of German "victories," such as the sinking of the Lusitania and the Sussex. M. Camille Bloch informed the correspondent it was his intention to make it absolutely international. He is issuing an appeal to all the Governments of the Allied Powers to furnish him with "documents" connected with the war.

The French Government has asked the Chamber for £10,000, and various private persons have promised gifts in kind for the furtherance of the work.—Reuter.

Nottingham Evening Post 1917

HEALTH IN THE SCHOOL.

THE local education authorities, through their school medical service and their teaching staff, have established a system under which education committees, doctors, nurses, teachers, school attendance officers, and voluntary workers have built up, in a handful of years, a co-operative system of machinery on behalf of child welfare. The need for this work is shown in the mass of defect and diseases, " most of it preventable," discovered by the School Medical Service in the past eight years. Sir George Newman's statement that out of our six millions of school children a million " are so physically or mentally defective or diseased as to be unable to derive reasonable benefit from the education which the State provides " has been challenged in some quarters, but not by those best acquainted with our elementary schools. As he says, the figure means, apart from the suffering involved, that a portion of the public money spent on education is practically wasted. Last year, in the groups of children inspected (about two-fifths of the whole number at school), more than 17 per cent. suffered from defects of vision, 11 per cent. from defective hearing, 13 per cent. from malnutrition, 20 per cent. from disease of the nose and throat, 13 per cent. were uncleanly, and almost 70 per cent. required dental treatment. These figures need to be reinforced by understanding and sympathy in their readers. The " Report " reminds us, for example, that " for the child uncleanliness is dis-ease, irritation, and disablement. Infection follows it like a shadow, and maladies of the skin soon arise. Thus the child becomes a victim of dirt, its sleep is disturbed, and its education largely nullified." In the same way, dental decay is not merely a source of present pain, but it prevents proper mastication and so causes indigestion, and if the teeth are neglected too long the poison is absorbed into the system, setting up serious internal troubles. Those who question the value of dental clinics for school children have little idea of the real conditions.

Common Sense 1916

EDUCATION IN THE NURSERY.

FROM THE POINT OF VIEW of the nursery, the chief interest in the Educational Conference being held at the Imperial Institute probably centred in the discussion on the Montessori method of training which formed the theme of a most interesting afternoon on Friday, last week.

Lady Plunkett presided over the meeting, which was arranged by the Montessori Society, Lance-corporal E. A. Claremont and Miss Muriel Matters being the principal speakers. In opening the proceedings, Lady Plunkett described the Montessori Society as having great aims and high ideals, amongst which self-development played an important part. She hoped to hear from authorities on the subject that self-control, too, was another prominent feature, for she feared that in these days it was a virtue too little impressed upon the young, and yet it was one of the most important assets in connection with the · well-being of humanity.

Lance-corporal Claremont spoke upon " Dr Montessori and the Future," and claimed that the method summed up the sources of new ideas, reflecting and in some cases transforming them so that they were woven into an harmonious whole. The fundamental principle of the method was freedom and an appeal to the child's natural interest. We made an ideal of play in the present day, and play was, or should be, an important factor in education. It has, indeed, been described as an instinct which Nature implants in a young creature by which it can seek self-development. It brought out the personality, skill, and knowledge, on which the Montessori child worked with avidity. Lady Plunkett had voiced a feeling by no means uncommon, that in the permission of complete freedom self-control might be cold-shouldered, the realm of freedom allowing no room for duty and discipline, but he maintained the Montessori School offered full opportunities for both these, while allowing a freedom for the inner important things to advance and develop on their own lines. The great inspiration of Dr Montessori was the introduction of science to education; this meant that education would become attractive to the scientific mind, to those who had a real love of education; and, therefore, a great advance in the child's welfare might be expected to take place. He hailed Dr Montessori, indeed, as the Darwin of education.

Miss Matters spoke in interesting fashion on Dr Montessori and social reconstruction, insisting as a basic truth on the value of personality and individual growth in a favourable environment. The aim of education should be not merely to fit an individual for a livelihood, but to fit the individual for life, to enable him to live at his highest, and to her the most inspiring thing about Dr Montessori was her attitude towards life, the fact that she realised that all she was privileged to do was to assist in the unfolding of life. It was not surprising that the great thinkers of to-day were turning their thoughts towards the little child, for they were realising that they would have to come nearer to the source of life, and that " where there is nothing growing, one former is worth a thousand reformers."

Queen 1917

Queen 1917

9208   9209   9210

247   248   249   250

Full-size Pattern of any Garment cut to any breast measure
7d. each. 2 garment suits 1/2. 3 garment suits 1/9.

The John Williamson Company Limited, 42 Gerrard Street, London, W.

Children's
Clothing
Illustrated
1916

FATHER VAUGHAN'S EAST END PARTIES.—On Thursday and Friday last Father Vaughan gave his annual treats to East End children. For the 500 boys there was a play, and, of course, refreshments; for the 500 girls a pantomime and dainties. The festivities were held in Our Lady's Hall, presented to the parish by the Father. Every child had a special invitation card for the party from Father Vaughan. Some of the children keep these yearly souvenirs framed upon the mantelpiece. This is the fourteenth year of Father Vaughan's connection with Commercial Road. During that time he has, besides doing other work, catechized the tribe of children weekly. He calls his catechism class his Power House which keeps him young, and gives him strength to carry on like a house on fire in the interest of Jesus Christ.

The Tablet 1917

ADVENTURE ISLAND!

A Splendid New Serial Story,
Dealing with the Adventures
of a Shipwrecked Circus
Party.

– :BY :–

HARRY REVEL.

THE FIRST CHAPTERS.

Jim, Harry, and Ted, three chums, acrobats in Bunker's Circus, and Tom Toddy, the clown, are wrecked on a desert island, and are the only human survivors of the great liner s.s. Empire City. They call the island Adventure Island.

The chums manage to land several of the circus animals, including Gerry, the gorilla, and Charlie, the elephant.

Later, two natives whom they discover on the island, and name Wiggy and Gilbert, and Johnny, a Chinese boy, are added to the party.

Mick Doolan—whom they have rescued from the rocks off Adventure Island—with the help of the boys, builds a steamship which he names the Alligator. On her trial trip they discover a Solomon Islander on the reef, who turns out to be Wiggy's brother, who has escaped from a pirate ship. He is nicknamed Ginger.

One day the chums are attacked by pirates at sea. They are assisted in the fight by a number of Chinese whom they had captured in a previous battle. They emerge victoriously from the desperate encounter, and Tom congratulates them on their bravery, and declares that they have all earned a few days' holiday. He suggests that they spend them in climbing Mount Columbus, the peak in the centre of the island.

The next day the expedition, accompanied by Charlie, the elephant, starts. After travelling some distance the boys are attracted by the twittering of a small bird, which, Wiggy tells them, is a honey-bird, and which evidently wants them to follow him. The reason why this small bird was so friendly was that he wanted his human friends to disturb the earth about the bees' nests, so that he could get at his favourite food.

After swathing their heads in gauze, the boys, with Wiggy, follow the honey-bird.

There was a rumble and a big fall of dry sand, followed by a dismal howl from Wiggy. The boys were horrified, for Wiggy was dancing madly in the midst of a black cloud of infuriated wild bees.

Chuckles 1917

The Church Army asks help for the two following cases :

G.—A little motherless girl who needs training for service has been sent to us. Her father will pay a little towards her keep, but there is the cost of her outfit. We would like to train her as a competent nursemaid, for she is devoted to children and is a nice-looking girl, but it is useless to place her out without training, for she has not yet learnt to be clean in her work, and it is so important that the caretaker of our little ones should be in every way worthy of their charge. Who will help in this? £5 would go far in giving her a real start.

H.—A child of theatrical parents, who leave her to make her way alone, has kept in touch with a worthy Canon, who thinks well of her. She lives alone in lodgings, where she owes £2 10s. She has tried to get employment on the trams, but had a very bad cold, and lately she tried for a milk round, but again her cold was too bad. She is a very honest girl, who lives straight, and tries to stand alone. She has heard of a place as servant (she is really superior to this), but will go, only the lady will not advance anything for clothes, enable her to pay weekly, or meet her in any way. She is longing to discharge her back rent. £5 would help her to do this and prepare for service.

Queen 1917

KITTY FROM CORK.—*Diet for child of two.*—The child should certainly be having something more than the milky farinaceous food you mention. You say she was a splendid baby, but now is pale and heavy looking, constantly suffering from indigestion, "in spite of the great care you take in her diet." Unless I am much mistaken, it is really this over-care which is the cause of the mischief, especially as the delicacy of digestion did not manifest itself until well after infancy. I expect also she has a tendency to an enlarged abdomen, although you naturally do not know enough of probable symptoms to mention this. It all goes back to too much farinaceous food—potatoes, bread, milk puddings, and so on. It is not uncommon to find mothers distressed at threatened tubercular trouble or internal mischief when nothing at all is the matter but conditions resulting from such food as this. As a matter of fact, a child, normally, should have fish, eggs, and meat in proper form from the time it is certainly fifteen months old; and it is want of this which causes the very common condition which is worrying you in your little girl. I should put her promptly on an "ordinary" diet, suited of course to her age, in which lightly cooked fresh meat, eggs (you are lucky living in the country, with your own fowls, to be able to give her these nowadays!), fresh vegetables, suet pudding, and so on. Drop the invalidish food, potato and gravy, and so on, let milk puddings only take their proper turn with other kinds of sweet things, and stop the little feeding-up meals at odd times, and I feel sure you will soon notice an improvement. Will you let me hear how she goes on after a few weeks of this treatment? I should be so glad to hear. Of course, I am going on the assumption that she was quite a healthy and normal baby, as you say, otherwise there might be some reason for your fears which, from your letter, I have no grounds for assuming.

MEGAPHONE.—*Bread for children.*—Wholemeal bread is far better for children than the white variety, which up till now has been almost universally used; so your apprehensions are quite unnecessary. Next week a little article on the knowledge which should determine the choice of bread for children in different cases is appearing, and this will help you in your indecision, I hope. The value of the wholemeal variety lies in the fact that it contains the whole grain after the removal of the husk; whereas white bread had only the inside of the grain and was practically all starch, with very little of the protein which finds its place on the outside of the grain, and therefore is removed in the whitening process. Brown bread contains the husk or bran as well as the whole grain; this is of no nutritive value, but it is very good in providing a sufficiency of bulk in the food, a point sometimes overlooked, especially with people who have given some thought to dietetics and endeavour to fix their minds on the constituent parts of food overmuch. This need of bulk is very decided where many growing boys and girls are concerned, and often the substitution of brown bread for other kinds in their cases does a great deal of good. It has also benefits in cases of constipation or its tendency, because the bran present sets up a healthy mechanical irritation in the bowel. The sufficiency of bulk also help matters in this respect, another fact which is only too often ignored.

Queen 1917

DR. BARNARDO'S ARMY.

For over fifty years the Barnardo Homes have been saving children, fashioning out of the raw material of utter destitution tens of thousands of capable citizens. Out of the 86,747 children helped by the homes 10,715 men have been provided for the Great War. With the coming of Peace the need of the nation for healthy, upright and honourable citizens is greater than before. Every year, however, the work of the Homes grows bigger, every year come fresh admissions and fresh developments and greater expense. Food, clothing and bare necessities cost more, and help is urgently needed. Readers may send contributions for this most deserving cause to the Honorary Director, Mr. William Baker, M.A., LL.B., Dr. Barnardo's Homes, 18 to 26, Stepney-causeway, London, E. 1.

The Editor's Corner.

"PUCK" EDITORIAL OFFICE,
THE FLEETWAY HOUSE,
FARRINGDON STREET,
LONDON, E.C. 4.

My Dear Boys and Girls,—

Did you like the "Ping-Yang" code? I hope so, and that you will find it useful.

I have ideas for all sorts of jolly things for "Puck" in my head, and shall do my best to get one "extra-specially" nice thing in each week.

I am busy at the moment upon a new competition; it is quite different from anything you have ever had in "Puck" before, and I'm sure you will all like it ever so much.

If possible, I shall get it in the paper next week, but I *may* not be able to have it ready until the following week. I tell you this so that you won't be disappointed.

The other day a little boy I know came home from school chuckling to himself.

"What are you so merry about, Jeff?" asked his father.

"Oh," laughed Jeff, "I caught teacher *so* nicely in class to-day!"

"How did you do that, Jeff?" his father asked.

"Why, teacher was giving us a lesson on the different parts of the body. She said: 'The trunk is always the middle part of the body. You all understand that, don't you?' Everyone said 'Yes, ma'am,' but I.

"'You understand that, don't you, Geoffrey?' teacher said.

"'No, ma'am; because the trunk is not always the middle part of the body,' I said.

"'What do you mean?' asked teacher.

"'Why, teacher, what about the elephant?' I said.

"Teacher *did* laugh, and so did the other boys."

Your sincere friend, *The Editor.*

Puck 1918

British Weekly 1918

— At Edmonton it was discovered late in the evening that a girl of 9½ years was on the register, and on inquiry at her home it was found that she was in bed. When her parents were told that she could vote, the little girl was hurried out of bed and rushed off to the polling booth. At Bush Hill Park polling station, Enfield, a child four years old who was on the voters' list registered his vote.

Jewish Chronicle 1918

LADY GLENCONNER'S BOOK.*

Is it wrong for mothers to write down the quaint remarks of their children? The reviewers are discussing the question, apropos of this delightful collection, "The Sayings of the Children," brought together by Lady Glenconner. Why should it be wrong, provided that the child has no idea that the mother keeps a record, and so does not get conceited or self-conscious? This dainty volume, with its charming snapshots of the five Tennant youngsters, will be read over and over again. The children's adoration for their mother is delightful. "Now I'm praying for mummie that God should love her and give her a divine heart. She shan't die at all. Not at all." "You're Heaven and the North Pole to me." We could fill columns with quotations, but it must suffice to give a few :—

"Sometimes when I'm saying my prayers I see God so plainly that I jump up quickly, because I feel if I didn't I should *have* to go with Him."

"You know, I see them quite plain— the angels—when they come in the night. They look like red fire. I know them by their little eye of golden."

"I'm a tiger. Yes, a tiger." And his mother : "And I don't think I want a tiger in my bedroom."

"But this is only a kind one. He won't hurt you. Quite a kind tiger, with your name on it."

We have rejoiced over every page of this winsome book.   M. R.

* *The Sayings of the Children.* Written down by their mother, Pamela Glenconner. (Oxford: Blackwell. 3s. 6d.)

British Weekly 1918

MID-CORNWALL JUNIOR VOCAL FESTIVAL

CONTESTS AT BUGLE.

The second annual Mid-Cornwall Junior Vocal Festival, promoted by members of the Bugle Silver Band Committee, with Mr. Tom Brokenshire as hon. secretary, was held at Bugle Cinema Hall on Wednesday week.

The event included a contest for a Challenge Shield presented for annual competition to promote the advancement of junior vocalists by the firm of Messrs. John Lovering and Company, and open to choirs of singers not exceeding 16 years of age, who were required to sing as a test piece a two part song: "May Bells" and "Flowers' (Mendelssohn). Own choice vocal competitions were also held. The adjudicator, Mr. E. A. Russell of Lostwithiel, said he found some of the singers to be exceptionally good, and conducted the massed choirs in a rendering of the test piece. His awards were:—Choir competition: Bugle Junior Choir (Miss Meta Hawke), 86 points; Indian Queens Council School Choir (Mr. Husband), 86; St. Austell County School Mixed Choir (Miss Helena Parry), 85; St. Austell County School Girls' Choir (Miss H. Parry), 77. The Bugle and Indian Queens choirs having an equal number of marks, were requested to sing again, when the award went to the latter, who received the Challenge Shield, and a special prize for conductor. Solo singing—Class 1: 1. Elsie Marks (Bugle), "The Better Land," 88 marks; 2, Ida Bice (Indian Queens), "There's a Land," 86; 3, Vera Wedlake (St. Austell), "Your England and mine," 69. Class 2: 1, Gwen Higman (Bugle), "Little Gray Friend," 90 marks; 2, Janie Phillips (Bugle), "Sing me to sleep," 81; 3, L. Sharpe (Indian Queens), "Perfect Day," 79. Class 3: 1, Howard Reed of St. Austell, who gained 93 marks the highest awarded in the competition, and so pleased the audience that he had to repeat his rendering of "In an old fashioned town." Class 4: Duet singing, 1,Lily Phillips and Ruby Jacob (Bugle), "Hush me to dreams," 84 marks; 2, G. Higman and Violet Heard (Bugle), "Whisper and Hope," 82; 3, Harold Sincock and Elsie Marks (Bugle), "O'er the dreamland sea," 74.

The successful competitors were awarded certificates of merit, and special prizes of books. In the unavoidable absence of Col. Sir William Serjeant, C.B., and Col. William Lovering, the prizes were given away by Mr. T Brokenshire, who said through competing at such an educational festival, those taking part would in the future thank their trainers for the tuition given which would greatly assist them to develop into good and proficient members of choirs for the benefit of their respective districts.

Selection were rendered by the Bugle Silver Band under Mr. J. Kessel.

Cornish Guardian 1919

The British Weekly 1918

NEWQUAY'S MEMORABLE DAY.

SERVICE MEN WELCOMED HOME.

CHILDREN AND PEOPLE ENTERTAINED

The Newquay Peace celebrations programme was carried out with great success thanks to the good work of the various committees and the host of helpers. In spite of a threatening morning the weather proved fine, with a nice breeze which blew out the hundreds of flags displayed, and made a rare show. Every street had its decorations, and strings of flags across the roadway and many of the houses and business premises were most tastefully and elaborately adorned, whilst some, too, were illuminated at night.

THE CHILDREN.

The parade of the school children which was the first item on the programme, was one of the prettiest sights of the day. Headed by the Newquay band, under Bandmaster B. Opie, they marched to the sports field at Trethellan, kindly lent by Mr. J. V. Rowe, where sports were held and tea provided. Nearly every child carried a flag, and as they stepped proudly along marshalled by their teachers, they called forth great admiration from the spectators. The elder girls wore headdresses of the national flag, and some of the children carried flowers. Arrived at the field the sports were quickly set going, and were got through with wonderful celerity by Capt. Peters, headmaster of the Council Schools; Miss Stevens, head mistress, and the other teachers. After the sports, which were much enjoyed by a huge crowd of about 2,000 persons, the children were each presented with a bun a pound in weight and tea. All the old people over 70 years of age were also entertained to tea, and the general public joined in.

Cornish Guardian 1919

Telegraph Messengers and Overtime Pay.

The following correspondence is published for information:
44552/18.   General Post Office, E.C. 1.
                                                October 8, 1918.

OVERTIME AND SUNDAY DUTY RATES FOR BOY MESSENGERS AND TEMPORARY GIRL MESSENGERS.

SIR,—I am directed to inform you, with reference to that part of your letter of November 16 last (No. 9036/17), which relates to the subject mentioned above, that with the concurrence of the Lords Commissioners of the Treasury the Postmaster-General has given instructions that the minimum hourly rate of Boy Messengers and Temporary Girl Messengers for overtime and for duty performed on Sunday, Christmas Day and Good Friday shall be raised to 3d. as from the 1st instant. This is, the Postmaster-General understands, the general rate of overtime pay for Boy Messengers throughout the Civil Service.

Certain other aspects of this subject are still under consideration.   (Signed) ARTHUR H. NORWAY.

We did not understand this, and so I wrote to the Post Office on the subject. No reply coming, Mr. Robinson sent a reminder, and now we get the following:

                                    General Post Office, E.C. 1.
                                                January 9, 1919.

SIR,—Mr. Robinson wrote to me on the 10th ultimo (No. 10454/18) about a letter from you, dated October 9, regarding the overtime rates for Boy Messengers, &c. Your October letter had unfortunately been mislaid.

We propose to apply the decision as regards inclusion of bonus in overtime rates to Boy Messengers, &c., by making additions to the normal rates as indicated in Section (b), page 498, of the Post Office Circular of December 17 last. The increased minimum rate communicated in Mr. Norway's letter of October 8 will, of course, be operative as from October 1.   (Signed) E. RAVEN.

The sections referred to provide that messengers eighteen years of age and over will get an addition to their present overtime rates of fourpence an hour, and to those under eighteen years of age an addition of threepence an hour. This applies to both boys and girls. It is a pity the decision has been hung up so long.   G. H. STUART BUNNING.

Postman's Gazette 1919

Militarism and Education.

Unfortunately we have had to hold over Miss T. W. Wilson's account of the meeting held Saturday, Dec. 6th, at Trinity Presbyterian Church, Camden Town, on "Militarism and Education." Late though it is, we feel we must find space for it.

The Conference on Militarism and Education turned in the main into a serious realization of the needs, the hopes and the oppressions of boys and girls who have to face an immoral social order at the moment of their awakening to life.

I pass over Mr. Coltman's wonderful picture of the tragedy of the "van boy," for we may get his paper at length later.

But Miss Lester first brought before us vividly what it means in the days of adolescence when boys and girls, awakening to their own personality are failed by the grown-up world.

For a wonderful hour of life they may hope for the great, the wonderful, the beautiful—then they lose it, never to regain it, or it is regained with terrible difficulty.

Three pictures, given as only Miss Lester can give them, remain with me.

Miss Lester, entering a sordid home—only the children there, for parents have to work. The children rush out in excitement, and cry out "Look—our Bob's nail!" What is the meaning? Bob—just feeling himself—realizing that he is a separate personality—had awakened. He demands something personal—of his own. The only possible expression of his yearning crystalizes into one rugged nail, to be his own upon which he alone may hang his cap.

Crusader
1919

1920–1929

NIBBLING AT THE CHILDREN'S CHARTER

A Bad Sign of the Times

GIVE THE CHILD ITS CHANCE

There are signs in many parts of the country that Mr. Fisher's Education Act, the Children's Charter, is being nibbled at all round to keep children at work. Even the London County Council is giving way to those who cry out for school children as wage-earners.

There are plenty of grown-up people to do all the world's work, if all of them who can work will work. What is needed for the child, and for the nation through the child, is that it shall grow up healthy, strong, and good, and be fully prepared to take up the world's work. But putting the child too soon to fritter away its strength on odds-and-ends of work that lead to nothing is bad for it and for the nation, and for all.

It is saddening to see that even Education Committees often do not observe these plain truths. Teachers see them. The leaders of the Labour Party see them. All who have thought long about education see them. The doctors see them. Let all who do see them make clear to Mr. Fisher that they are his supporters against the shortsightedness that would stunt the young growths which will be the future British race.

Children's Newspaper 1921

BABY "STEERS,"—BUT YOU CONTROL THE TINY-TOT

52/6 BABY CAR

Here is the jolliest car for every baby between 18 months and 4 years of age. The controlling rod turns the handle in front of the delighted little occupant, and

HE THINKS HE IS STEERING!

The "Tiny Tot" is ideal for parents too, because it **folds** when not in use. Over-all measurement 21 in. long, 13½ in. wide, 20 in. high. Weight 13½ lbs. Strongly made. Compact. May be taken into shops or carried in train or bus. Obtainable from all general stores and dealers.

THE POLIVIT MANUFACTURING CO., LTD., 43 Old Queen Street, Westminster, London, S.W.1

FREE! Every mother who wants her baby to be happy while riding should send for the "Tiny Tot" leaflet.

He thinks he is steering

"Tiny Tot" folded for carrying.

Good Housekeeping 1920

MOTORING FOR BABIES

The Cradle in the Car

Babies can now indulge in the pleasures of motoring in safety and comfort by means of an invention known as the motor crib.

This is a neat cradle strapped to the back of the front seats of the car. By an arrangement of springs all shocks of the road are absorbed.

There is a protective hood on the wind side, and the crib, weighing only ten pounds, folds up flat when not in use.

Children's Newspaper 1920

CAN YOU FIND MRS. BRUIN?

"Hip, hip, hurrah!" shouted the Bruin Boys as they all came flying down the slope in their sleigh.
    What a jolly time they were having! I don't think they would have looked so pleased, though, if they had known that Mrs. Bruin was watching them not far away. And she had her slipper with her, too! You can guess what that was for!
    You see, those naughty boys had slipped out without permission, and should really have been doing their lessons!
    Can you see Mrs. Bruin in the picture? If you look very carefully in all the corners and all ways, you will be sure to find her hiding there—and her slipper, too!
(Do you like these jolly pictures? There is a fine one in "Tiger Tim's Weekly" each week.)

Rainbow 1921

£565 FOR CIGARETTE CARDS.

Cash for Tram Tickets.

A CERTAIN brand of cigarettes are giving picture cards away again as before the war.

Some of these collections are to-day quite valuable, for most of the "sets" of cards are now unprocurable, at least in their entirety. Fifty guineas is no uncommon price for a really good one, and not so very long since one was sold for the record price of £565. It comprised no fewer than one hundred thousand separate varieties of "fag" cards, collected from all over the world, and it filled twenty large albums.

IRISH SCENERY.

The "gem" of this unique collection consists of a complete set of cards depicting six hundred separate views of Irish scenery. These were specially photographed by the cigarette-manufacturing firm that issued them, the operation taking several months.

Other valued sets deal with sports of all kinds, exploration, natural history, botany, arboriculture, railways, and so on. In fact, these hundred thousand tiny pasteboards constitute in their entirety a miniature illustrated encyclopædia.

TRAM TICKETS WANTED.

The craze for collecting tram and bus tickets, which preceded the cigarette-card one, is even now not quite extinct. Every now and again there appears in a London evening newspaper an advertisement offering to buy these seemingly useless pieces of pasteboard.

The advertiser is a gentleman living at Reading, who was led to take an interest in the hobby by his little son. He now possesses a collection numbering over ten thousand specimens, and is still adding to it. In an interview recently he described the hobby as "a most interesting one."

Boy's Pictorial 1921

Good Housekeeping 1922

THE proposal of the Geddes Economy Committee to exclude children from the State schools until they are six may benefit the tax-payer, but infinitely more it will benefit the children who escape the " deadening influence " school life exerts on the very young child. The personal care of its mother is the child's first right, yet one of the reasons advanced by the Education Department for sending a child of five to school is that its presence at home prevents the mother from going out to work. If public opinion were healthy, any able-bodied man who let his wife turn bread-winner would be treated with the contempt he deserves. While the woman who would let any outside work prevent her giving her personal service to her children would be regarded as the unnatural freak she is

A GOOD TURN TIP.

ONE of the most frequent Good Turns that Cubs are able to do is that of carrying a person's bag.

If, however, the bag is heavy and bulky, this is none too easy a task, as the bag will jolt against your leg.

By trying the little dodge shown in the sketch you will get over the difficulty. Make a compact pad of newspaper, a hand-

WAD OF PAPER

kerchief, or your cap, and place this under your arm.

You will be surprised to find how much easier it is to carry a bag with one of these pads under your arm—you try it !

Scout 1921

BOYS' BOTTLE BOMB.

Quarter-filling a lemonade bottle with calcium carbide, four Grimsby boys added water, fixed the stopper, and placed the bottle in the porch of the house of John Blow, where it burst with a loud explosion. The door, porch, and windows of the house were damaged, and the old man's cheek was cut open. At the local police court Cyril Moulds was fined 40s., and Horace Norton, Royce Norton, and William Alvey were fined 30s. each.

Illustrated Sunday Herald 1922

SEVENTEEN CHILDREN.

All But Three Died at Birth or Shortly Afterwards.

(FROM OUR OWN CORRESPONDENT.)

BRIGHTON, Saturday.

An inquest was held at Brighton to-day on the newly born child of the wife of Harry Brown, a fishmonger.

It was stated that she had seventeen children in seventeen years, and fourteen had died at birth or lived only a few hours.

The present child lived only thirty-eight hours, and Dr. Hillshaw said death was due to inanition.

Evening News 1922

Baby should live in his TAN-SAD these bright days

69/-

Your Baby will grow bigger and bonnier every day if he spends all the sunny hours out of doors. In his Tan-sad he will be as comfortable as in his cot, and when you push him out for walks will never feel the slightest jolt, however uneven the pavement or country lane, because every Tan-sad is so wonderfully sprung. The bumps and jars a Baby suffers in an ordinary Pram are a terrible shock to the tender nerves—see that you buy a Tan-sad.

There are Tan-sad Prams at 37/6, 69/-, 75/- and in Rexine Leather-cloth, 115/-, and Tan-sad Push Chairs for Toddlers at 21/- and 25/-.

Visit the TAN-SAD Exhibit at the British Empire Exhibition at Wembley....Stand No. F201.

TAN-SAD
Super Sprung Folding Prams

TAN-SAD PUSH CHAIR. Price 25/-. Fitted with reclining back. A strong, serviceable car, suitable for children of two years and over. Sprung on the back wheels by our patent method. Folds and stores in a very small space. Ideal for travelling & holiday use.

WARNING.—*Many cars are sprung to look like TAN-SADS, but our method is patented and cannot be infringed.*

Write to us NOW for illustrated leaflets and name of nearest agent (Post free).

TAN-SAD Ltd., Pine Works, Albert Street, BIRMINGHAM.

CHOIR OF 5,000 CHILDREN.

Eight thousand vocalists from Sunday Schools in the London district took part in the revived annual festival of the London Sunday School Choir at the Crystal Palace yesterday. The Barnard Shield was won by Kew Road Wesleyan S.S. Choir, Richmond, and the Founder's Shield by Homerton District Permanent Choir.

A junior festival concert was given by 5,000 children, the oldest being about 13 years, and an adult choir of 3,000 voices sang selections from Mendelssohn's "Elijah" and Sir Edward Elgar's "Caractacus."

National News 1920

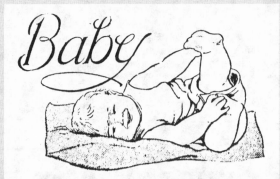

THE VALUE OF TRAINING.
by NURSE MARGARET.

BABY'S training should start from the day of his birth. He must be taught to become automatically obedient a long, long time before he knows anything about voluntary obedience. Automatic obedience quickly resolves itself into habit, and good habits have an influence that stretches beyond babyhood into adult life.

Thus you see what wonderful opportunities a mother has of moulding not only the life of a baby, but the life of the man of years to come.

The sleep habit is the first that must be developed with the new baby and then good feeding habits. The first one is not very difficult to establish, because the healthy new-born baby wants to do nothing else. But what should be aimed at is the waking at regular intervals for food and the sleeping throughout the night *without* food. This system may need a little perseverance and firmness at first, for the baby is rather apt to interpret it as meaning that whenever he wakes he must be fed. Don't burn a night-light, the dark quiet room will impress itself upon the baby that waking in such circumstances is not associated with feeding.

During the day when the baby has been fed, it should be laid down at once in its cot. To sleep after food is most important for every infant and should continue till about eight or nine months old. Never rock the baby to sleep and never stay by its side.

Everywoman's Weekly 1922

"I want you to read my little story below,"

BIRTHDAY ROSES.

A Very Short Story by Ellaline Terriss.

LITTLE Frank, aged nine that very morning, his eyes bright as stars, and his hot little hands tightly clutching a small bunch of wild roses, burst into the one room that was "Home."

"Look, Mummy, what a lady gave me—she must have known it was my birthday," he cried. "I watched one of those big motor 'buses come in from the country, and the lady told me she picked these herself. Oh, Mummy, do you know what I'd like better than anything else in all the world? I'd like to go to the country and pick lovely flowers like this myself!"

"So you should, sonny," replied Mother, looking up from her sewing, "if only Daddy were alive."

Daddy had been a soldier, and his name had early appeared in one of those dreadful lists that brought despair to the hearts of wives and mothers. And Frank knew "for positive certain" that he had been brought home and laid in Westminster Abbey. The "Unknown Warrior" was his great secret.

If only Daddy hadn't died, he'd have gone to the country again!

He didn't know that there is a big institution called The Fresh Air Fund, that only requires a sufficient number of fifteenpences collected from a public that doesn't forget, and they will find him out and make his wish come true. But there are such a lot of soldiers' kiddies to look after, about 375,000 left fatherless by the Great War.

Last year the Fresh Air Fund took 151,370 for a day in the country, and 6,933 of the most needy from a health point of view, for a whole fortnight to country or seaside.

Perhaps Frank's turn will come this year. It will "for positive certain" if every single person who reads this, my appeal to you, will be generous and send a donation to the F.A.F., the cheapest charity in the world.

Fifteenpence will send one child to the country, and this will pay for fare, food, and somebody to look after him or her.

If you should collect twenty shillings, that would pay for a whole fortnight's holiday for one child. The cost of a complete party for a day's outing, with the necessary adult attendance, is £13, and those who give this amount may have the outing known by any name that they wish. Donations, by the way, are spent entirely on the children.

Please address your contributions to me, care of PEARSON'S MAGAZINE, 18, Henrietta Street, W.C. 2. Amounts received will be acknowledged in this magazine.

Pearson's Magazine 1921

Jack grasped Walford by the hair and dragged him away from the frightened fag, sending the bully sprawling on his back!

Champion 1922

TUBERCULOSIS.
by NURSE MARGARET.

TUBERCULOSIS is one of the commonest diseases to which children are liable, and it is during the first two years of life that they are *peculiarly* liable to its ravages. It may attack the internal organs, the skin, the joints, or the glands. The living tubercle bacillus finds access in many ways, but there is a consensus of opinion among experts that the most frequent way is via the air passages and thus into the blood. Then it attacks the part or organ that has the least power of resistance at the time. Dust contains dried tubercle bacilli, and a tiny child should always be guarded very carefully from it.

Another means of attack by the germ is by infected food. This germ is far too frequently present in our milk supply, which is notoriously unclean and germ infected. Unless a mother is satisfied that her milkman serves her with milk beyond suspicion, such as Grade A. certified, which is sold under licence from the Ministry of Health as being taken from cows free from tuberculosis, and which, moreover, is produced under sanitary conditions, she had far better avail herself of dried milk.

Every-woman's Weekly 1922

THE ETERNAL FEMININE.

First Critic. "THAT'S THE ONE I'D LIKE TO HAVE."
Second Critic. "ME TOO."
Third Critic (contemptuously). "THAT SHAPE AIN'T BEING WORN NOW."

Footnotes to History.
From a schoolboy's essay :—
"After the Diet of Worms, Luther exclaimed, 'Thank God! I can take no other course.'"

Punch 1922

HOW HE RAN AWAY
Darted Into Taxicab to Visit His Old Haunts.
CHILDREN SPOTTED HIM
"Here's Charlie," They Cried When They Saw Him Strolling.

Charlie ran away after lunch yesterday. It was peculiarly a Chaplin "stunt."

When the hubbub outside the Ritz had subsided, he suddenly determined on a walk, "just to quieten me down," as he put it.

So with Mr. Donald Crisp, chief producer of the Famous Players, and Mr. Garretty, another film chief, Charlie left the hotel by the staff entrance.

Those Early Days!

"We walked along Piccadilly and down Regent-street," said Mr. Crisp, relating the incident to the *Illustrated Sunday Herald*, "and as we approached Trafalgar-square Charlie was talking wistfully of many places down Kennington way associated with his early days.

"'I want to visit those places, and especially the house where I lived until I was three years old, alone,' he said.

"Then, without warning, he darted into a taxi-cab and immediately made off, leaving us as surprised as you can imagine."

"It's Marvellous."

Mr. Crisp stated that Charlie was in a terrible state of nerves following the happenings of the past two days. He had not slept for two or three nights, and had scarcely eaten anything.

"He expected only a few children to meet him," Mr. Crisp added.

"What happened has taken all his breath and nerves away. He could hardly talk at lunch, and when thinking of the events of the previous few hours could only ejaculate, 'It's marvellous.'"

CHARLIE FLED AGAIN.
Boisterous Welcome by Kiddies.

Although Charlie attempted to see the sights of Kennington by stealth, he soon found himself famous.

Leaving the taxi-cab in Kennington-lane, he strolled round the by-streets of the district, followed by the taxi at a short distance.

But no sooner had he made his way out into the main Kennington-road than a group of children spotted their favourite at once.

"Here's Charlie," they cried, and thereupon the quiet street became a scene of loud confusion.

It was too much for the already overwrought comedian, and within a few moments he had scrambled out of the mob into the taxi, which was never far away.

"Good-bye, Charlie, come again soon," was the Kennington children's farewell.

"The Bailwyd river, Blaenau Festiniog, overflowed on to the Festiniog railway yesterday morning. A train stuck fast in two feet of debris, while the water entered the coaches full of children going to school. After some trouble the river reversed and managed to get back to Tan-y-bwlch."—*Welsh Paper.*

It wass ferry unusual, yess, inteet.

Punch 1922

THE JAMBOREE
Boy's Great League of Nations
SHOWING THE STATESMEN HOW TO DO IT

While prime ministers and statesmen generally are talking of the foundation of a League of Nations the boys of the world have started one. The League holds its first international rally at Olympia from July 31 to August 7, and its official title is the Boy Scouts' Jamboree.

Representatives of 24 nations are coming to London. Boys have already started from places half the world away.

When the Jamboree starts more than one hundred thousand Scouts will be present. Among the 1100 foreign troops staying at Olympia as guests of the British Boy Scouts will be representatives of America, Argentine, Belgium, Chili, Czecho-Slovakia, Esthonia, Denmark, France, Finland, Greece, Holland, Italy, Japan, Latvia, Lithuania, Luxembourg, Norway, Poland, Portugal, Rumania, Spain, Sweden, Switzerland, and Serbia. America is sending her 250 on a warship, the Minnesota, the finest use to which a warship can be put.

Pageant of John Smith

There is to be a great camp of 5000 Scouts in Richmond Park, and other camps will be dotted all around London, for many troops from the provinces are taking Jamboree week as their Scouts' camping holiday, and, pitching their tents somewhere near London, will journey daily to Olympia.

The great feature of the week will be the pageant of the life of John Smith whose marvellous story was told in the April number of the mother of the C.N., My Magazine. The part of John Smith will probably be played by the Chief Scout, Sir Robert Baden-Powell, and he will be assisted by 250 English Scouts.

The Jamaican troop is giving a tribal display of the Arawak Indians, the French troop the daily life of an old-time cavalier, the Scottish troop will picture a Highland gathering and an episode, "The Lady of the Lake." The Italian troop is portraying the landing of Columbus, the Dublin troop an incident in the life of St. Patrick, and the Ulster troop the story of the flax from field to aeroplane-wing.

Children's Newspaper 1920

A NOTABLE EXPERIMENT IN THE FEEDING OF CHILDREN.

Dr. Geo. A. Auden, M.A., M.D., D.P.H., F.R.C.P., School Medical Officer for the City of Birmingham Education Committee, in co-operation with Dr. James R. Mitchell, has recently carried out at the Alcock-street Council School, Birmingham, an experiment in which a pint of milk was given daily to thirty under-nourished school children for a period of four months. It is well known that malnutrition generally results from a deficiency in either the quantity or the quality of the food taken, and these experiments were designed to test the value of milk in making good the deficiency in either event. Fifteen girls and the same number of boys, all aged from seven to eleven years, were selected, who showed the greatest deficiency in weight for height, age, and sex, as well as a low proportion of the red colouring matter of the blood, and these children were ascertained by medical examination to be free from any active disease, and were also found by the head teacher to be making poor progress in their school work. The experiments were duly controlled and scientifically conducted, and the conclusions arrived at by the two doctors, as stated in their report, are as follows:

There was an improvement in the rate of increase in weight and in nutrition, as calculated by different methods of investigation, a notable improvement in mental and bodily vigour and alertness, and an improvement in the amount of the red colouring matter of the blood.

In the report a touching fact is recorded. It was found by the examination of the same children one month after the issue of the milk had ceased that a general slight loss in weight had taken place.

A copy of the full report will be sent free on application to the National Milk Publicity Council, 27 Southampton-street, Strand, W.C.2.

Schoolmistress 1923

"DOLE" FOR BOYS AND GIRLS OF 14.
7/6 A WEEK WHEN THEY LEAVE SCHOOL.
SWEEPING SOCIALIST PROPOSALS.
BENEFITS FOR WORKERS THROWN IDLE BY STRIKES.

STARTLING changes in unemployment insurance are proposed by the Government. They are as follows:—

Extension of the scheme to boys and girls of fourteen. At present only boys and girls of sixteen are insurable.

Unemployment pay for workers thrown out of employment by strikes in which they are not taking part.

Agricultural workers to be insured against loss of work.

The purpose behind the proposed lowering of the insurable age of boys and girls is to give the labour authorities power to compel them to attend juvenile education centres when they are unemployed.

Daily Express 1924

A PRESENT FROM ROBIN

Last week the daily Press published an account of a robin. who approached and dropped a treasury note in front of a poor woman and her children The bird had taken it from a milk can on which it had been left in payment. The house was 200 yards away.

Children's Zoo Pictorial 1921

Good Housekeeping 1924

Home and Country 1925

CHILDREN AT MEETINGS.

Dear Editor, I often demonstrate to Institutes and although there is much to praise and enjoy in the meetings, there is one thing that seems to me wrong. There is a growing expression of opinion that Institute members do not want children brought to the meetings. I think the Institutes will die a natural death if they do not have the young mothers as members. How are we to get fresh blood in without them? It stands to reason a cottage mother must bring her children or stop at home. I am glad to say that in our own Institute we make a great deal of our babies. But there! as some of us get older we forget we were once children ourselves.

Yours faithfully, Mercy Leigh,
Blackheath-Guildford.

OH, HARK!

" Now, having learnt about the rhinoceros, what other monster has a horn and is dangerous to mankind ? "
" Please, sir, a—er—motor ! "

Miss Oldmaid: Do you know what becomes of little boys who use slang when they are playing marbles ? "
The Boy: "Yes; they grow up and play golf ! "

Comic Cuts 1923

A boys' school had been taken to a performance of "The Virgin Queen" at the local cinema, and the following day's lesson was an essay on the reign of Queen Elizabeth. The boy that did not go to the top of the class wrote : "Queen Elizabeth was known as the Virgin Queen because she was such a great success as a Virgin."

Films 1923

THE DUTCHESS OF ALBANY AND THE MOTHERS' UNION.

The members of the Mothers' Union in the diocese of Winchester have heard of the death of her Royal Highness the Duchess of Albany with special feelings of regret, for she was patron of the Mothers' Union in this diocese and always full of sympathy with our aims and objects.

Those who were present in the Guildhall at Winchester on March 16th, 1911, will remember with what earnestness she addressed us, urging us to do all in our power to protect our boys and girls from evil influences. "I would plead," her Royal Highness said, "that every mother should make it her duty to know her child's friends and companions, whose influence is brought to bear on that child, for that is the principal factor in the forming of character, and in the end it is character, well trained and strengthened, which is a woman's, and a man's, best safeguard. . . . Is enough stress laid on the sacredness of womanhood with boys, as well as with the girls themselves? Is duty and its fulfilment taught and insisted upon as a paramount necessity? Let every child grow up with a clear understanding that it is a responsible being to whom are spoken the old Bible words, 'Thou shalt be holy, for I am holy, saith the Lord.' The evil of our age seems to me to be a want of balance and impatience of control of any kind, and an unwholesome craving for excitement, and we mothers have to face the fact that we can no longer control our children as we ourselves were controlled. We cannot control them, but we can do what is better—teach them to control themselves. Self-control we must teach them if we would save their lives from shipwreck, and ours from misery and self-reproach. The lesson must be begun in the cradle and should not be forgotten till life's end. We are living in serious times, and a heavy responsibility lies on this our Mothers' Union, that it may play its part well in the work for our beloved country, for the honour, nay, for the very existence of our Empire depends on the character of the men and women of the future, our children and grandchildren."

These stirring words of her Royal Highness will come to us with fresh power now, and we can thank God that "she being dead, yet speaketh," and try with greater earnestness to carry on the work she upheld so splendidly.

L. M. A. GORE-BROWNE.

Hampshire Herald 1922

THREE NAMES FOR THE TUBE BABY.

MARIE ASHFIELD ELENA.

The "Tube" baby born at the Elephant and Castle Station of the Bakerloo Railway is to be christened Marie Ashfield Elena.

Lord Ashfield, chairman of the Underground Railways, acting on the suggestion first made in the "Daily Express," will stand as godfather.

Marie has been chosen because the birth of the baby coincided with the date of the Queen of Rumania's arrival in London; Ashfield comes from her godfather; while Elena is the nearest approach possible to the Elephant, the place of her birth.

Her first present is a beautiful silver christening cup given by Lord Ashfield. Mr. G. H. Hammond, the proud father, wishes to thank the railway officials, who were so considerate to Mrs. Hammond in her trying ordeal, and also the numerous readers of the "Daily Express" who made kindly inquiries.

The date of the christening has not yet been fixed, but it will take place at Wealdstone.

Daily Express 1924

COMIC CUTS Office, 145, The Fleetway House, Farringdon Street, E.C.4.

MY DEAR READERS,—The football season is now well advanced, and I expect by this time you are all getting used to one another's play in your respective teams.

There is nothing like combination to make the team a social success and a match-winning side.

I have known many teams who have numbered several fine players in their ranks, but have been unable to defeat another team which on individual form should have been hopelessly beaten.

The reason for this is lack of combination. You should always remember that you are a team of eleven players, and although an individual effort on the field is pretty to watch, it is useless to your side if you are ultimately robbed of the ball.

Don't be selfish; if there is another player in a better position than you are to score a goal, 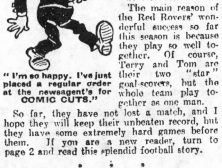 don't hesitate to pass the ball to him. Just as much credit is given to the man who makes the opening for the goal as to the man who scores it.

The main reason of the Red Rovers' wonderful success so far this season is because they play so well together. Of course, Terry and Tom are their two "star" goal-scorers, but the whole team play together as one man.

" I'm so happy. I've just placed a regular order at the newsagent's for COMIC CUTS."

So far, they have not lost a match, and I hope they will keep their unbeaten record, but they have some extremely hard games before them. If you are a new reader, turn to page 2 and read this splendid football story.

* * *

Here is a conversation I overheard on my way to the office this morning.

Servant: "Your milk looks very watery."

Milkman: "Yes. You see, we took the calf away this morning, which upset the cow, so she started crying, and some of the tears fell into the milking-pail!"

* * *

I was standing waiting for a bus the other day, when I saw a little boy sitting on a doorstep, crying bitterly.

"Hallo, my little man!" I said tenderly. "What are you crying for?"

"Please, sir," sobbed the little lad, "I've been tossing up this coin to see whether I go to school or play truant, and it's come down fifty-nine times on the wrong side. Boo-hoo!"

Comic Cuts 1923

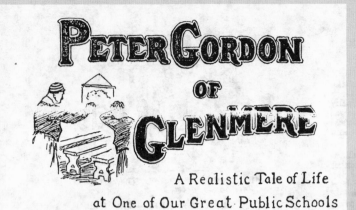

PETER GORDON OF GLENMERE

A Realistic Tale of Life at One of Our Great Public Schools

PART I.

Granta 1924

CARRIAGE doors banged, the guard's flag waved, there was a cheery "Good-bye, old son ; keep your pecker up !" and the train steamed out of the station, slowly at first, then faster and faster, until it turned a distant bend and was gone.

The few passengers who had got out at Glenmere busied themselves with their belongings, hailed porters, hurried to and fro. But of these few there was one who stood with misty eyes watching the train until it was out of sight. He was a small sturdily built youngster of fourteen. He had an honest open face, clear blue eyes and a mass of curly hair ; as clean a figure of young boyhood as one could wish to see. He stood on the edge of the platform in his new Eton suit trying to choke back a lump that *would* rise in his throat. His right hand, buried in his trousers pocket, gripped the pound note his father had given him in the carriage as they drew into the station. Now his father had gone and he must face the world alone. He thought of all the jolly times he had had at home, the Christmas pantomimes and the parties ; he thought wistfully of the spiffing Conductor's Set he had got in his stocking (all *that* would have to stop now he was at a big Public School), and he recalled, with lips twitching at the corners, that day when his Mounted Life Guards (supported by his Teddy Bear, who didn't *really* belong in the fort, but who had to be used because some of the Life Guards were broken) had completely routed the Uhlans on the nursery floor, and how Uncle Clarence had come to tea in the evening and brought him some Transfers.

CORRESPONDENCE

CHRIST'S COLLEGE,
CAMBRIDGE.
November 21st, 1924.

DEAR SIR,

In future I shall not subscribe to *The Granta.* Nor, I hope, will any other decent Briton, since you have thought fit to publish so gross a misrepresentation of Public School life as "Peter Gordon of Glenmere." I presume your contributor (who, understandably, prefers to deliver his vile attacks anonymously) hopes, like H. Dennis Bradley, to leave his readers "hot and gasping." But he will not succeed. WE BRITISH ARE TOO SANE. We know that the British Public School is *sound to the core ;* and will continue so, in spite of infamous libels such as this—and I have every reason to believe that this is but one of a series of organised attempts to undermine the finest of our British institutions, financed, need I say, *by Bolshevik gold.* The British Public School spirit is sane and healthy, and no Britisher brought up in its atmosphere would dream of assisting at any such disgraceful, un-British scene as is described in this foul propaganda. I particularly object to the passage, ' "Yes, break him, smash him up !—the little swine !" chorused the crowd, enjoying the sport immensely.'

I trust you will follow the excellent example of *The Daily Mail* and *The New Statesman* and publish this letter, in common fairness.

Dare I hope that I may prevent you from publishing a second instalment of this outrageous libel ?

Yours, etc.,
PRO LUDO PUBLICO.

(No, Sir.—ED.).

Granta 1924

AN AGED BUN !

Mrs. Quack : "How dare you say that bun I gave you is hard ! Why, I made buns before you were born !"
Dicky : "Yes, perhaps this is one of them !"

Tiger Tim's Weekly 1925

Romance

Some have told the truth about Rider Haggard—some have not. Newman Flower in the *Sunday Times* does justice to a great romancist, for that Rider Haggard most certainly was. What impertinence it is to belittle "King Solomon's Mines" and "She" and "Allan Quatermain" and the rest. They thrilled when they first appeared—they still thrill those who have ears to hear the call of romance. Here is a touching story I heard the other day. A schoolboy, overworked, had a touch of brain fever, which threatened to become very serious. He had recently read "King Solomon's Mines," and in his fever was convinced that the story was true, and was determined to start at once to visit the mines. The parents and the doctor were concerned, for the fever grew; till at last they wrote the circumstances to Rider Haggard. He without delay came from a distance to the bedside of the boy, and patiently set to work to convince him that the mines were only of a novelist's imagining; nor left the house till the boy had dropped satisfied into dreamless sleep. So many legends grow up round popular novelists that I cannot vouch for the literal truth of the story; but it is doubly characteristic of Rider Haggard, of his genius and of his kindliness.

British Weekly 1925

Champion 1922

PICCADILLY CHASE.

BOY'S FIREWORKS AMONG THEATRE CROWDS.

Considerable alarm was caused among the crowds leaving theatres in Piccadilly-circus last night when a flash was seen and a report was heard which caused men and women to scatter in all directions.

The police saw two men running towards Shaftesbury-avenue and shouting "Stop that man!"

The "man," it appeared, was a boy who had ignited some fireworks just as the crowds were leaving the theatres and had thrown them in their midst. Two constables chased the boy but he was lost sight of in Dean-street. No damage was done.

Daily Mail 1926

CHILDREN'S READING.

More than 1,400 boys and girls, aged 10 to 15, who belong to the Croydon junior libraries, were asked recently to name the books they like best, and the census has shown that while Dickens holds second place in the girls' preferences, he stands only fifth in the liking of the boys.

The familiar giants in juvenile literature, such as Rider Haggard, Ballantyne, Jules Verne, and Charles Kingsley, appear to be suffering an eclipse—with the exception, however, of Henty, who comes third on the list of the boys' favourites. Their first favourite is P. F. Westerman, and that of the girls A. Brazil.

The test indicated that girls develop a taste for "adult" literature much earlier than boys, for the names of many acknowledged modern masters appear among their "preferences."

Daily Mail 1926

QUITE SO!

Teacher: "I'm afraid you are not trying enough, my boy!"

Billy Bear: "Why, mother says I am the most trying boy she has!"

Rainbow 1924

Preparing for Christmas

Hamleys have it!

Dolls—Motor-Cars—Trains—Bears —Footballs—Toys and Games of every description to please the hearts of children of every age.

HAMLEY'S toys are all stoutly made, yet inexpensive—designed for the hard use that kiddies give them, and Hamley's century-old experience in designing unbreakable toys ensures the little ones perfect satisfaction.

BOY'S MODEL MOTOR-CAR

Stoutly constructed and suitable for boys from 4 to 10 years. A most realistic model, with adjustable wind-screen, driving-mirror, horn, stop-and-go mechanism, tool box fitted with tools, four lamps, hood-cover, enamelled dashboard, and starting-handle. Rubber-tyred wheels and pedals. May be had in various colours. Price £4:19:6

DOLL'S PERAMBULATOR

The most delightful present of all for girls. The inexpensive model illustrated has plated fittings, with long tubular handles, leather-lined hood, apron, and outside Cee springs, and is in every way an exact model of an up to date baby carriage. Price 52/6

Good Housekeeping 1924

A BEAR, however hard he tries,
Grows tubby without exercise.
Our Teddy Bear is short and fat,
Which is not to be wondered at;
He gets what exercise he can
By falling off the ottoman,
But generally seems to lack
The energy to clamber back.

Punch 1924

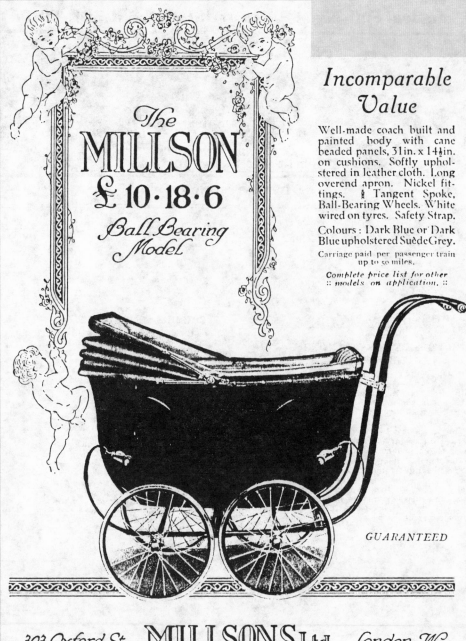

The MILLSON £ 10·18·6 *Ball Bearing Model*

Incomparable Value

Well-made coach built and painted body with cane beaded panels, 31 in. x 14½ in. on cushions. Softly upholstered in leather cloth. Long overend apron. Nickel fittings. ⅛ Tangent Spoke, Ball-Bearing Wheels. White wired on tyres. Safety Strap.

Colours : Dark Blue or Dark Blue upholstered Suède Grey.

Carriage paid per passenger train up to 50 miles.

Complete price list for other :: models on application. ::

GUARANTEED

303. Oxford St. MILLSONS Ltd *London. W.*
Telephone :- Mayfair 1722 .

Ideal Home 1924

"The Young Britons."

The Imps of to-morrow are the children who to-day are approaching the age of fourteen. Communists and Socialists are doing their best to capture these youngsters, and to fill them with an unhealthy contempt for duty, patriotism, law, and order.

The Unionist Party is awake to its duty in this matter. It is urging the formation, in all parts of the country, of "Young Britons."

The main purpose of the "Young Britons" is to instil into the minds of the children love of their country and pride in the traditions and ideals which have made the Empire. The organisation also suggests the duties of citizenship and of working together unselfishly for the good of all.

*Imp
1925*

Playing Ninepins

On the Lawn

IF you have six ninepins, set three at one end of the lawn and three at the other; if no ninepins, find some empty vinegar or lime-juice bottles. The game is played by two people and a judge.

At a signal from the judge, one child starts from one end of the lawn and the other from the opposite end. Each has to fetch the ninepins opposite to him, separately, and the one who reaches the point he started from first, after his three, swift, breathless journeys, is winner. If more than two play, they should be timed, and the one who is the quickest wins. Each ninepin must be made to stand up; it must not be thrown down.

*Good
Housekeeping
1926*

'NOT EQUAL IN GOD'S SIGHT.'

AMAZING SPEECH ON ILLEGITIMATE CHILDREN.

"COPEC" STORM.

FRANK SPEECHES ON BIRTH CONTROL.

"Daily Express" Correspondent.
BIRMINGHAM, Tuesday.

"I DO not believe that the twenty illegitimate children of the woman who was recently before the London magistrates are worth as much in the sight of the Lord as, say, Paula, the daughter of Dean Inge. I do not believe that children born in sin and wickedness and iniquity are as valuable in the sight of the Lord as children born in God-fearing Christian homes."

This amazing speech was made at the "C.O.P.E.C." conference (Conference on Christian Politics, Economics, and Citizenship) in Birmingham to-day by Mr. Arthur Black, of London.

He was criticising a resolution asserting that it is fundamental to Christianity to regard every person as of equal value in the sight of God.

BIRTH CONTROL.

A frank discussion on birth control provided the most remarkable debate which the conference has yet had.

"The real question is to control birth control," said the Rev. G. Studdart-Kennedy ("Woodbine Willie"). "The present conduct of the business is a damnable scandal, and is playing the very devil with the nation. If you wish to ask for celibacy within the marriage bond between people who adore each other, for God's sake, be careful. Do you believe," he asked, "that the bringing of children into the world as they are to-day is in accordance with the law of God. Is the population of China in accordance with the law of God?"

Daily Express 1924

"At a Standstill" till given Virol

MOLLIE KATHLEEN WALKER.

69, Southfield St., Arboretum,
WORCESTER. 18/6/24.

" I feel it my duty to let you know the results of Virol. When one month old, my little girl was at a standstill, and nothing seemed to satisfy or suit her.

We tried different sorts of food, but did not get one to suit her until we tried Virol. After a fortnight's trial we could see the difference. She began to put on weight and seemed satisfied. Now (at 15 months) she is a big bonny baby, as you can see by her photo.

Thanking you for your wonderful food, which brought my little girl to what she is now, and assuring you of my recommendation for your food always."

(Sgd.) CECIL WALKER

There are literally thousands of children—many of them now grown up—whose lives have been saved by Virol. Babies that do not thrive on—cannot even take—other foods, absorb Virol, and, with it, strength to fight *and win* the battle of Life.

VIROL

40,000,000 portions of Virol were given in Hospitals and Clinics, etc., last year

In Jars, 1/3, 2/-, 3/9.   VIROL LTD., HANGER LANE, EALING, LONDON, W.5.

Good Housekeeping 1924

PURCHASER OF "BLUE BOY."

DEATH OF GREAT AMERICAN COLLECTOR OF PICTURES.

Philadelphia, Monday.

Mr. Henry E. Huntington, the well-known railway magnate and company director, died this morning. Mr. Huntington was a great amateur collector, and had one of the finest private collections of English and American literary works in the world. He was also famous as the purchaser of Gainsborough's "Blue Boy," which he acquired for £150,000.—Reuter.

Yorkshire Post 1927

MISS SYBIL CAVENDISH.

Lord Desborough, at an informal meeting of the women members of the Bath Club, Dover-street, W. yesterday presented a silver medal to Miss Sybil Cavendish, aged 11, daughter of Lord Richard and Lady Moyra Cavendish, of Holker Hall, Lancashire, for saving a nursemaid from drowning last summer.

The nursemaid, who could not swim, was sinking for the second time when Miss Cavendish, fully dressed, entered the water and brought her safely ashore after swimming some distance.

Daily Mail 1926

What Makes a Jolly Party?

Jean Stapleton tells you in this
article how to plan a really
successful Children's Christmas Party

IF a children's party is to be a great success a few outstanding points must be kept in mind. A programme of entertainment must be worked out beforehand, the right sort of nice things to eat chosen, and the help of two or three grown-ups who love children (and parties) enlisted. The invitations should be written on pretty party cards, stating the times of arrival and leaving; these should be sent off ten days or more before the day of the party.

All easily reached ornaments and breakables should be put away on the great day, fires should be safely guarded in case of accident, and the rooms should be well lighted and made to look as gay as possible. All kinds of inexpensive paper decorations can be bought now, as well as balloons, airships and animals to "blow-up" and hang from the walls and light fittings.

On arrival the children's outdoor wraps should be taken off in a warm room, and the little guests may be told each other's names and started off on the path of happy-friendliness that is the keynote of a jolly party.

"To break the ice" for shy children, the fun should start immediately. Musical chairs for the first game is usually a success, for what child can be shy during such noisy performance? That finished, each child might be asked to name his or her favourite game, and the most popular chosen in turn.

About an hour after the party begins comes tea, and the children may be allowed to choose their own order of sitting down, as by this time a general friendliness is sure to have manifested itself. Instead of one large table, several small separate ones are a pleasant change, but each must have exactly the same main point of attraction.

On the tea-tables have one gaily coloured cracker and a pretty paper serviette for each little guest, nothing more, except the food and decorations. At children's parties very often the wee tots are so excited with small gifts and other surprises on the tea-table

that they eat little or nothing, and consequently grow very tired before the evening is over. For tea it would be well to have milk, tea, and thin chocolate, served not too hot; plenty of little scones well buttered, tiny cakes with coloured icing; good sweet biscuits and sponge fingers of various kinds; jellies in small glasses, some plain, others with chopped fruit in them, such as grapes, cherries and bananas; orange compote; half peaches filled with whipped white of egg and cream, and last, but by no means least, a centre cake, iced, and decorated with tiny flags, sugar birds or animals, one of which should go with each piece of cake. Sometimes small sandwiches, made with minced ham or tongue, are appreciated, especially by schoolboys.

After tea comes the great event of the party—a treasure hunt. This is the modern version of a bran-pie and is invariably a great success. It should be advertised on large coloured cards in the hall, on doors, and on the staircase. Each child is given a small coloured card with a pin through it, and his or her name written on it. Then one of the grown-ups, dressed up as a pirate, explains that in a certain place treasure waits for the first four explorers who pin their cards nearest the spot where it is hidden. This should be in the largest room or space available. Ten minutes might be allowed for the pinning of the cards, then a bell is rung and the treasure exposed by the "Pirate."

After it has been handed to the four fortunate ones, a distribution of other little gifts might be made, each having the recipient's name written on it, as consolation prizes, so that every child has a little souvenir.

The party could end with some dancing, or the old happy game of Blind-Man's Buff. On leaving, in the room where the children put on their wraps, it is nice to have a tray with sponge biscuits and small glasses of warm milk and sweet lemonade, and for each child a tiny gift or fancy basket of chocolate or sweets as a parting gift.

Modern Woman 1926

THE CHILD AND HIS PROBLEMS

"The Child and His Problems." By Dr. Alice Hutchison. (Williams and Norgate. 5s.)

This book by the well-known physician of the Tavistock Clinic, Dr. Alice Hutchison, breathes a very gentle, understanding, motherly spirit. Dr. Crichton Miller, in a foreword, speaks of the author's record of successes with different children. The real experience given for the benefit of others in these pages is precious. "I know a little boy of three in a good working-class home, who daily washes down a flight of twelve linoleum-covered steps for his mother, and does all her messages, handing a paper up to the counter in each shop." It is a certain quality of tone which invites to obedience, a look in the eye which seems to say, "I love you and I know you are going to do it." Dr. Hutchison gives the much-needed reminder that it is necessary to put an end to all punishment while we study the difficult child. The chapter on "Children Seeking Limelight" is valuable. A child eating little, screaming, biting to attract attention, should have his energy switched off into a more useful channel. Can he excel in tidiness at home or at lessons? Dr. Hutchison discusses the fear of darkness. Would she give a child who asked for it a light at once? Her personal experience of arguing away fear before Alpine climbing by holding a conversation and argument with herself in her own room is deeply interesting. Perhaps she will remember how the youthful Goethe would climb the Minster Tower again and again till he conquered his giddiness, and how he haunted churchyards at midnight till he became indifferent to fright. Talking out fear is one way to banish it, suggests Dr. Hutchison. When a child is brought to her, sleepless and unhappy, she tries to break unhappy associations with a certain bedroom by ordering it for a holiday.

M. R.

British Weekly 1925

As I write I have before me a pamphlet entitled "The 'Red Menace' to British Children." This can be obtained from G.H.Q., British Fascists, 297 Fulham-road, London, S.W.10, price 1d., and deals exhaustively with the various Communist organisations working amongst the children of this country—Socialist Sunday Schools, Communist Sunday Schools, The Young Socialists League, Red Boy Scouts and Girl Guides, to name but a few. There are many others, but the aim in every case is the same. To quote their own leaders' statement, "To teach the children the ideal (!) of revolution should be the primary aim of a Socialist Sunday School. All other teaching is of no avail." They are also taught to ridicule the Christian religion.

One of the greatest objects of the British Fascists is to fight these movements by means of Fascist Children's Clubs which are being formed wherever necessary.

1. "Oh dear!" cried Patsy. "I feel so tired, Pinkie. Let's have a rest under this tree!" "Oh, yes!" cried Pinkie. "I could just do with a sleep!" "So could I!" gasped Jim the Jackdaw.

2. They had been playing with their balloon all the morning and were feeling very tired. Soon they were fast asleep. "Oh dear!" cried Jim, who was on a branch. "Here comes cousin Percy!"

3. Yes, that naughty boy was just going to shoot some peas at Pinkie and Patsy. "I'll break the balloon and wake them up!" cried Jim. And he drove his beak into it. *Pop!*

4. "Quick!" cried Patsy, awakening. "Percy is shooting peas; let us hide behind this tree!" And soon those children were safely hidden from Percy's pea-shooter. "Ha, ha!" laughed Pinkie. "He cannot get at us now!" Wasn't it clever of Jim to wake them?

Tiger Tim's Weekly 1925

Brighton and Hove
Illustrated Weekly News 1927

A LITTLE SHIVERING BOY OF FIVE

WHERE IS HE TO PLAY?

Everybody's Chance for a Golden Deed

ROOM FOR A BIT OF FUN

One cold night there came into a pleasant room in Clerkenwell a little shivering boy of five.

The room was one of the London Play Centres, cheery and warm. Outside a bitter wind was raging, and the child had no protection against it but a thin, ragged coat. The superintendent smiled at him.

"Hullo, sonny, have you come to play? You look cold. Won't Mother give you a warmer coat?"

"I ain't got no muvver," was the child's reply.

"Then Father will have to, won't he?"

"Oh, farver! 'E don't want me!" said the mite.

"Well we do. Come in and get warm."

Always in Somebody's Way

Afterwards the superintendent made inquiries and found that the child's report was true; his mother was dead, the father indifferent. The misery of his so-called home had sent him wandering in the streets; he drifted into the Clerkenwell room.

Since then he has come many times. He is one of the thousands of slum children who look on the Play Centres as something between the Kingdom of Heaven and one of the magic places told of in the Arabian Nights. In those rooms these little ones are welcomed; they can be warm, shout, and play games, and they are never in anyone's way.

This last phrase can only be appreciated when we remember that the majority of these children come from homes that consist of two rooms in which somehow a large family has to be housed. They are always in somebody's way. The street is their only playground. Hundreds of them have never played a real game before, or owned a real toy, or seen a green field. Only those who know East London know in what a barren area the children have to pass their days.

Little Mothers of Eight

The little girls have a worse time than the boys. Little girls are expected to turn to and help, and be mother to two or three younger than themselves. Little boys can go and play—do anything so long as they get out of the way. The Play Centres welcome them all, but they keep a tender heart for these pathetic little mothers of eight on whom the shadow has fallen so soon.

Now a child who is happy and carefree and can jump about in healthy conditions has a chance of growing up into a healthy and good citizen. This development is impossible in East London. That is why reformers for two generations have been dreaming of Play Centres, fighting for them, writing to the papers about them, talking in public places about them, struggling to get the sympathy of great bodies and powers like the London County Council and the Board of Education.

Evening News 1923

Chinese and English children in Limehouse, East London, c. 1928.

CAUSE OF LOW BIRTH RATE.

HUDDERSFIELD DOCTOR AND THE LAWS OF NATURE.

For the first time for many years deaths exceeded births in the Huddersfield district during the first quarter of the present year. The figures of the Registrar General show that births numbered 405, giving a rate of 14.53 per 1,000, and deaths numbered 559, the rate being 18.97.

Interviewed concerning the figures yesterday, Dr. S. G. Moore, medical officer of health for Huddersfield, said that the death rate for the quarter was unusually high. "Unfortunately," added Dr. Moore, "the birth rate has to be regarded as about normal. A generation ago the birth rate was about thirty per 1,000, but it has gradually sunk to the present deplorable figure, and has not yet reached the bottom. The cause of this decline is notorious.

"Whoever idsobeys the laws of nature pays for it inevitably. He can no more escape the consequences than he can escape his own shadow. And so it is with nations, which are merely aggregates of individuals. the days of men are short, but the days of nations and empires are relatively long. Speaking with these facts in mind, it is correct to say that, a few years before the fall of Rome a phenomenon similar to the present fall of the birth rate in this country was observed."

Yorkshire Post 1927

The Duke of York has asked this week for a million pounds to provide playing fields for the nation. Belper, like many other provincial centres, has long cried out for recreation grounds for her children. Adults are already well supplied with hockey, cricket and football fields. The demand is by no means so acute for the children as a few years ago, and some half-dozen playing grounds for various parts of the town are, or soon will be, available. The latest acquisition, the old Acorn Ground, should prove an immense boon for the many children swarming in the neighbourhood, though a smaller plot in the vicinity has long been available. The recreation ground problem is something like that of garden allotments, the difficulty being to obtain sites near to the houses, which often enough means the yielding up of land that should be available for building purposes. But at present recreation grounds do not appear to solve entirely the street playing problem, especially in the evenings of autumn and winter. Despite the heavy motor traffic children still persist in assembling near some street lamp to race about and shout lustily when the provided playground remains in darkness. It is during the dark evenings from seven to nine o'clock that the recreation ground fails, and the tired householder wishing for quietude requires heroic patience.

Belper News 1927

BOY VIOLINIST MOBBED.

AMAZING ALBERT HALL SCENE.

WOMEN RUSH PLATFORM.

FRENZIED ATTEMPTS TO HUG HIM.

YEHUDI MENUHIN, the 12-years-old violinist whose genius has astounded the whole of Europe and the United States, was the central figure in amazing scenes at the Albert Hall, Kensington, S.W., last evening.

At the close of his recital, which was listened to rapturously by an audience of many thousands, hundreds of women and girls surged excitedly towards the platform and struggled to reach him.

Yehudi stood smiling nervously and bowing awkwardly, and when, with some difficulty, he escaped to the

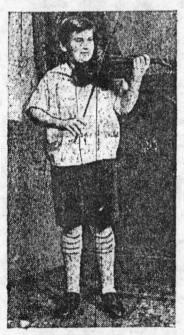

Yehudi Menuhin.

artists' room, the audience burst into clamorous cheering.

Presently Yehudi reappeared and played again, while his audience crowded thickly about him on all sides. With the last note the clamour once more broke forth. A second time he came back and played, and a third time. This last time he found himself hemmed in on the platform, people packing themselves so closely round him that he had barely room in which to wield his bow.

Daily Mail 1929

THE PETER PAN STATUE TARRED & FEATHERED.

Queer Mystery of Kensington Gardens.

SACK OVER THE HEAD.

The famous Peter Pan statue in Kensington Gardens was to-day found to have been tarred and feathered.

The outrage was discovered by a keeper who reported it at once to the Office of Works. The statue, happily, has not been damaged, and it was being cleaned this afternoon.

The Peter Pan Statue in Kensington Gardens. Another Picture on PAGE THIRTEEN.

Evening Standard 1928

CHILD VICTIMS IN WEST HAM

£1,000,000 " Economy " and More to Follow

MORE INFANTS DIE

FROM A CORRESPONDENT.

The three Commissioners appointed by the Ministry of Health to usurp the elected Guardians of West Ham have just issued their report, in which they proudly claim to be reducing the annual expenditure on poor relief, etc., by a million pounds a year (that is by nearly half). They have reduced the number of " able-bodied " on relief from 16,000 under the elected Guardians to 6,000; and this despite the greater numbers thrown off the Labour Exchanges under the Tory Government.

The Commissioners also promise that " by steady administration," it will be possible still further to reduce the numbers and cost.

With a million pounds " economy " it should be possible to reduce rates. And so it is. Ratepayers in West Ham will be happy to know that the Commissioners in the last half-year have made a reduction in the rates of twopence in the pound.

The effect on the workers of this policy of the Tory Government's officials **can be given** by figures:

In 1925, under the elected Guardians, the infantile mortality was 65.9 per 1,000.

In the very first month of the new regime it rose to 82·4 per thousand.

In December last year it was 90·7, and in January it was 104.

At the same time the hours of nurses in the infirmary have been increased from 48 to 56 per week.

Worker's Life 1927

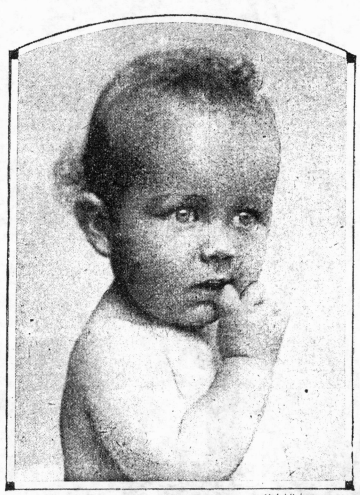

It's not sensible to disturb a perfectly good wide-awake baby just to make him smile. A baby's "long, long thoughts" should not be interrupted

Modern Woman 1926

A BOY LOSING HIS VOICE

THE SAD CASE OF ERNEST LOUGH

Nature Has Her Way and Disappoints Us All

THE GRAMOPHONE TO THE RESCUE

Thousands of listeners-in all over the world are saddened to hear that Ernest Lough's voice is breaking. It can never have happened that so many people have been interested in such a thing before.

Ernest Lough, the choirboy of Temple Church, has sung for years as only an excellently-trained chorister with a marvellous voice can sing.

Since 2 L O sent out his voice across the country and the world from a gramophone record made in Temple Church, especially with the rendering of Mendelssohn's " Hear My Prayer," in which he was soloist, he has become world-famous. People from far and wide have written him. A gold medal has come from Vienna.

Exquisitely Pure Notes

Men and women in remote parts of the Empire can sit and listen to those exquisitely pure notes rising and falling in " O For the Wings of a Dove " and think they are at home again in an English church. The chorister's voice is singularly pure. He hits the note perfectly, and his attack shows what a master he has had.

Lough, now about seventeen, is still a schoolboy. The choirboys of the Temple Church and the Chapel Royal are given education at that splendid house of learning the City of London School. Many a boy whose name has been famous has passed through that school (Mr. Asquith among them), leaving boyhood with its glorious memories behind him, as Ernest Lough soon must.

Children's Newspaper 1928

LOST GIRL PUZZLE

Riddle of 'Phone Call to School and Telegram to Mother

FROM OUR OWN CORRESPONDENT
Chertsey, Friday.

Police are investigating the disappearance in unusual circumstances, reported to-day, of a fifteen-year-old Chertsey schoolgirl, Clare Chester, who lived in a bungalow called " Quite-at-Home."

While at school yesterday she received a telephone message from someone—stated to have spoken with a foreign accent—who told her that her mother had received a telegram and had gone away.

When the girl arrived home she found her mother absent, for the mother had meanwhile had a telegram saying: " Meet me Victoria Hotel one o'clock. Jack."

On the assumption that an uncle had returned from Australia, Mrs. Chester went to London, but failed to find anyone she knew. She returned to Chertsey to discover that Clare had packed all her belongings and disappeared.

It is thought that the telegram to Mrs. Chester may have been a subterfuge arranged by the girl or some friend.

To-day Mrs. Chester received a few lines from the girl bearing the postmark, " London, N.W.1," saying that she was " quite all right " and asking her mother not to worry.

Police describe the girl as 5ft. 3in. in height, of medium build; with dark brown bobbed hair; large brown eyes; pale complexion

Empire Mail 1929

Seventh Child Superstitions.

Quaint healing superstitions of the remote Highlands and the adjoining islands are recalled by the visit to Lewis Island, in the Outer Hebrides, of Major W. E. Elliot, Parliamentary Under-Secretary for Scotland, who opened hospital and sanatorium extensions there last month.

The islanders still believe that the seventh child of the seventh son can cure all bodily ills. For such a child to dance with its bare feet on the bare back of a person suffering from lumbago is regarded as a certain cure for that ailment. Surgical tuberculosis, known to the islanders as King's Evil, is also believed to be curable by the seventh child, although here the superstition insists that a daughter must have preceded the first line of sons. The seventh child of the seventh son is also supposed to be gifted with clairvoyant powers. There is one Scottish Member of Parliament who is the seventh member of his family.

Highlander 1928

There was a little girl who wore a little curl,
Right in the middle of her forehead;
When she was good, she was very, very good,
And when she was bad, she was horrid.

FABRITIUS, OSLO

The habitually bad=tempered child, the difficult girl, the naughty boy—are you yourself not to blame for their bad behaviour? Are you certain that they are not suffering from malnutrition, or that their distressing conduct is not simply Nature's danger=signal against what may in effect be chronic underfeeding?

See your Doctor about it. He will probably recom= mend more vitamins. Get them bottled — in the form of Norwegian Cod Liver Oil, the most economical source of Vitamins A and D, without which healthy childhood is impossible.

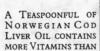

A TEASPOONFUL OF NORWEGIAN COD LIVER OIL CONTAINS MORE VITAMINS THAN

ALL THE BUTTER AND MILK ANY INDIVI= DUAL CAN EAT AND DRINK IN A DAY

NORWEGIAN COD LIVER OIL

National Committee for Promoting the Consumption of Norwegian Cod Liver Oil, Bergen, Norway.

Good Housekeeping 1929

1930 – 1939

Rainbow 1930

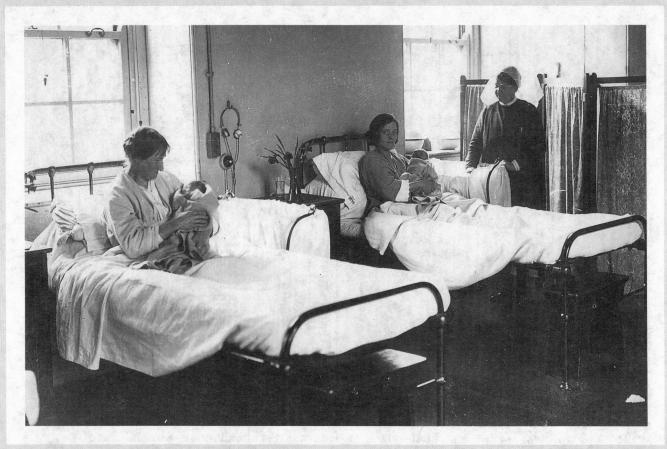

New mothers in a general lying-in hospital, 1930.

FOR HEALTH ASSURANCE USE WRIGHT'S

PROTECT YOUR CHILD'S HERITAGE

DON'T TAKE RISKS

The biggest asset any child can have is health– and that depends on you. See that right from babyhood your child is regularly bathed with Wright's Coal Tar Soap. Wright's will protect him from dangers that are unseen—dangers that nevertheless can have serious consequences.

The cause of most illnesses of childhood is infection. Wright's kills germs and so safeguards health. Doctors, knowing this, have recommended Wright's for Nursery use these past 65 years. You will be wise to follow their advice.

use **WRIGHT'S COAL TAR SOAP**

6d. per tablet.

USE WRIGHT'S AS A REGULAR HEALTH POLICY

Good Housekeeping **1930**

Keep Baby in "HIGH-GLEE"

In the downy softness of High-Glee Nappies baby's comfort and contentment is assured, and they are so easy to wash and dry. Airtight transparent wrapping gives full hygienic protection to their absorbent texture.

Awarded Certificate of Institute of Hygiene.

HIGH-GLEE REGD *Hygienic* **NAPPIES & TOWELS** ETC.

Everything softer and safer for baby.

Tubular Nappies **9/6** 24" × 24"   Doz.

Nappies 30½" × 30½"   Doz. **12/9**

Bath Towels 2/6 each. Cot Pads, 18" × 27", 3/3 each.
HIGH-GLEE FABRICS LTD., 66 Mosley St., MANCHESTER 2.

Good Housekeeping **1930**

HORNBY TRAINS ARE BETTER THAN EVER NOW!

Even last year's Hornby Trains have been eclipsed by the wonderful new models! The locomotives are fitted with stronger mechanisms that give still longer runs, with still greater hauling power. The Rolling Stock is greatly improved, and many new models have been added to the range. The Accessories are more numerous and more realistic.

Hornby Trains, Rolling Stock and Accessories are supreme! Always the leaders, always the best, they are better than ever now! The Locomotives are the longest running locomotives in the world. In a recent test a Hornby No. 1 Locomotive, running light, covered the amazing distance of 182 ft. on one winding! Hauling three No. 1 Pullman Coaches, the same locomotive ran 150 ft. on one winding. This wonderful performance could only be accomplished by a Hornby!

For every boy who is keen on model trains this **must** be a Hornby Christmas! Get your boy a copy of the Hornby Book of Trains described here and let him make his choice now. If he prefers to have an ordinary price list, he may obtain a copy of catalogue No. 6 from any dealer, free of charge, or direct from Meccano Ltd., price 1d. Ask him to write to Department C.

THE 1931-32 HORNBY BOOK OF TRAINS

Better even than last year! Read how our railway track has developed from crude rails laid on stone sleepers; how the modern passenger coach has grown from an open truck! Other articles tell about the special features of the four British groups. Page after page of fascinating information, and every page illustrated! All the splendid Hornby Locomotives, Rolling Stock and Accessories are depicted in full colour. There are details and prices of every item in the Hornby System.

Your boy must have this book! It can be obtained for 3d. from any dealer, or post free from Meccano Ltd. for 4½d. in stamps.

PRICES OF HORNBY TRAINS		
M0	Goods Set	5/-
M0	Passenger Set	5/9
M1	Passenger Set	9/3
M1	Goods Set	10/-
M2	Passenger Set	10 9
M3	Tank Goods Set	15/-
No. 0	Goods Set	18/6
No. 0	Passenger Set	17/6
No. 1	Goods Set	25 -
No. 1	Tank Goods Set	25 -
No. 1	Passenger Set	28/6
No. 1	Special Goods Set	32/6
No. 1	Special Passenger Set	35/-
	Other Models up to 85/-	

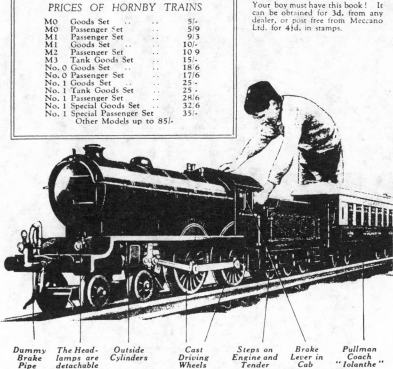

| Dummy Brake Pipe | The Head-lamps are detachable | Outside Cylinders | Cast Driving Wheels | Steps on Engine and Tender | Brake Lever in Cab | Pullman Coach "Iolanthe" |

HORNBY TRAINS

BRITISH AND GUARANTEED

Manufactured by

MECCANO LIMITED (DEPT. C) OLD SWAN LIVERPOOL

Discipline and Fear.

Guidance, Not Punishment.

Need for Expert Handling of Adolescent Problems.

At last evening's meeting of the Halifax branch of the Child Study Association, Miss W. Hindshaw, M.A., M.Ed., of the Faculty of Education of the Manchester University, spoke on "The Psychology of Discipline."

The Rev. Gwilym Rees, M.A., who presided, said that it was generally realised that most of the cutural trend of the times was in a state of fluidity and we did not yet know exactly where we were, politically, industrially, or even educationally. In the development of thought on all vital problems psychology was playing an important part. Principles of education had been greatly altered by discoveries in psychology and if they wanted to help the generation and exercise a healthy influence and control over children and young people it was necessary to know something about the mechanism of the mind.

Training the modern view of discipline as meaning guidance—formerly it frequently stood for reproof and often punishment—Miss Hindshaw dealt at length with the psychological aspect of the question as it affected young people.

In the case of the young child, said the lecturer, strict discipline in the sense of much ordering and punishment had almost disappeared and a period of carefully formed habits had taken its place. Habits of cleanliness, order, good manners and give and take had their starting point in the fundamental human instincts and the association with companions. The instinct which usually gave most trouble, if it appeared at all, was the instinct of fear. The speaker did not think that generally the motive of fear was used to the little child any longer, but sometimes children were pulled, pushed and frightened in some way into doing something of which they were really terrified. With good fortune and foresight, however, this should not be necessary.

Turning to the children of from seven to eleven or twelve years of age, a period of active adventure in life, the lecturer said that the new way of classifying children in the educational plans and the formation of junior schools were turning out pretty well. In the old days this was regarded as the period for drilling the memory, but now, with the new classification, we were seeing that memorising was not the only capacity of children of these ages and they were given opportunities for assuming responsibility and self-activity and tasks which they could carry out as individuals. At this stage the power to secure and hold the attention of a group of children was a great asset and might often be the means of averting danger.

With the early adolescent the prefect system had long been in use. It was perfectly true that many matters should be left in the children's hands, but when it came to a case of stealing, or any other out of the way matter in which the motive was obscure, the trouble should be the concern of the head teacher, the medical man or the psychologist. Sex trouble required expert handling. In a certain sense they were all the time meeting the sex troubles of adolescents frankly but, when the matter came to something rather important, the case required the attention of the expert, and the individual giving trouble should be removed from the scene of the difficulty and attention diverted in another direction.

Good Housekeeping 1930

Halifax Courier and Guardian 1931

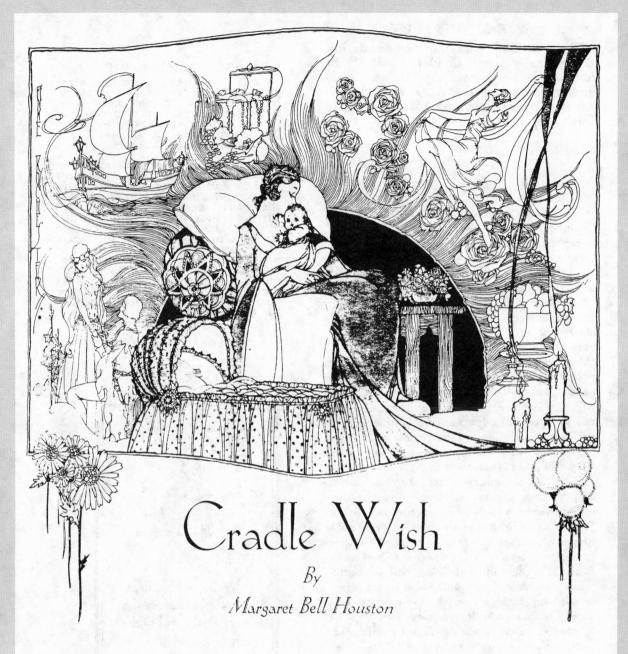

Cradle Wish

By

Margaret Bell Houston

Illustrated

by

Anne

Rochester

What do I wish for you,
Little New=born?
Hair that is yellow
As silk of the corn.

Eyes that are blue,
Lips that are red,
So you'll be wooed;
So you'll be wed.

Seas you may sail,
Roads you may roam,
So you'll be happy
To come back home.

Gold a=plenty
To come at your touch,
So you'll not think about
Gold too much.

Roses to walk on,
If you choose;
Music to dance by,
Silver shoes.

Life is a moment,
A bite and a sup.
Full be your plate,
Brimming your cup.

Bright be the lights,
And when they are low,
May you be sorry,
Sorry to go.

Good Housekeeping 1931

WORK THIS OUT

The farthing collection made during the year by the " Childer Chaine " in aid of the Belgrave Hospital for Children, presented at the At Home on Saturday, amounted to £93 13s. 6d. (89,928 farthings).

South London Press 1933

A former President of the Manchester Chamber of Commerce, Sir Ernest Thompson, is reported to have said recently that " the great tragedy of most young people's lives is the terrible inequality of opportunity offered between the important ages of 14 and 18." All of us who work in secondary or elementary schools can endorse that statement out of the bitterness of our experience. We watch our boys develop, we know their worth and their abilities and their potential usefulness, but we have to see them pass to work which is unworthy of them, work which offers neither scope for their abilities nor prospects of advancement commensurate with those abilities; and we know that from the moment they leave us there is no hope that they will go as far as they might.

For the secondary school boy who has ability, energy and character there is one straightforward path to a career of usefulness. If he can acquire a matriculation certificate he gains a ticket of entry to a large number of professions; if he adds a higher school certificate the value of that ticket will be somewhat increased. Should he win an open scholarship, make his way to a university, and there obtain a good degree, his chances will be improved. But, though straightforward, this path is by no means an easy one. The holder of the matriculation certificate has to compete with many thousands of others with the same qualification; the holder of the higher certificate has reached a dangerous age, at which few employers will consider him without special and personal recommendation; the degree man has to compete against those who have enjoyed a relatively far richer and fuller social life.

But if the path is difficult for the bright boy without means it is far more so for the less bright; and, now that secondary education is being offered to the more practically minded of our children, this problem is going to become more acute. So far such children have usually passed into employment at 14; now they are to be kept at school until 15 or 16, or even later; their general education is to be prolonged, and their special powers are to be developed; so that it will be even more unfortunate if they cannot secure suitable employment.

Times Educational Supplement 1930

ANOTHER £10,000 GIFT.

Sir Thomas Lipton has made another gift of £10,000 for the benefit of the poor in Glasgow. When Lord Provost Kelly was in London, on Wednesday, on public business, he, with Sir John Samuel, called on Sir Thomas Lipton at his residence at Soutgate to report on the manner in which the gift of £10,000, which Sir Thomas made last January, for the benefit of the poor, mothers and children had been distributed. Sir Thomas was so gratified at the report that he spontaneously asked the Lord Provost to accept a further gift of £10,000 to be devoted at the Lord Provost's sole discretion for the benefit of the poor of Glasgow in memory of his mother. On the occasion of the previous gift Sir Thomas, when handing over the cheque remarked. " That won't be the last." The gift was distributed by means of tickets entitling the recipients to fod and coal.

Halifax Courier and Guardian 1931

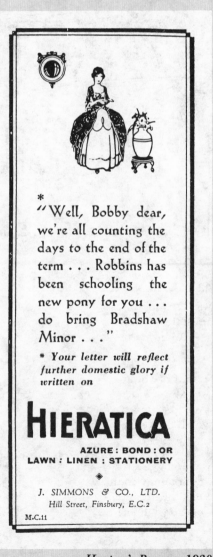

* "Well, Bobby dear, we're all counting the days to the end of the term . . . Robbins has been schooling the new pony for you . . . do bring Bradshaw Minor . . ."

* *Your letter will reflect further domestic glory if written on*

HIERATICA

AZURE : BOND : OR LAWN : LINEN : STATIONERY

◆

J. SIMMONS & CO., LTD. Hill Street, Finsbury, E.C.2

M·C·11

Harper's Bazaar 1930

REGISTERED ADOPTED BABY AS HER OWN.

WOMAN BOUND OVER AT MIDDLESBROUGH.

"VERY FOOLISH, BUT SHE MEANT WELL."

The story of how two women registered the birth of the same baby each claiming to be its mother, was told at Middlesbrough yesterday when Emily Charlton or Sharpe, of no fixed abode, was charged with perjury.

She was bound over for 12 months, the Stipendiary Magistrate (Mr. H. S. Mundahl) remarking that while she had been very foolish, he thought she had meant well.

It appeared that another woman had a baby born to her last December, and advertised for someone to adopt it. As a result Charlton agreed to adopt the baby without any payment being made for its maintenance.

SAID SHE WAS ITS MOTHER.

That was in January. Charlton then went to the Registrar and registered the baby, saying that it had been born in January and that she was its mother.

Later on, the Registrar made inquiries and went to a hospital where the real mother was lying. She, too, afterwards registered the baby, this time correctly.

The Registrar-General was communicated with, and the prosecution resulted.

The defendant, who cried almost throughout the proceedings, said that she had not meant any harm to the child, but, being childless, she wished to deceive the man with whom she was living.

Northern Echo 1931

YOUTH ON THE SCAFFOLD.

A great change in public opinion is indicated in Mr. Laurence's record of juvenile hangings. In the days of George II. it was a common thing for children under the age of ten to be hanged, and on one occasion ten were strung up together as a warning. As late as 1831 a boy of nine was publicly hanged at Chelmsford for setting fire to a house. In 1808 Michael Hamond and his sister, aged seven and eleven respectively were hanged at Lynn for felony. Yet in 1890, as many will remember, when Richard Davies was hanged for the murder of his father at Crewe, there was a great outcry at "the barbarity of inflicting the extreme penalty of the law on one so young." Richard Davies was nineteen.

Rhyl Journal 1932

Our Children's Column.

THE STORY OF A NEW FROCK.
(Concluded.)

Mrs. Franklin was very puzzled as to why Erica was so strangely quiet with regard to the great prize-giving day. At first she had been tremendously excited, in fact, it had occupied all her conversation, and she wondered what had brought about the sudden change.

It was only on the night before the event that Erica said as casually as she could, "Oh, by the way mother, I have decided not to wear my green frock to-morrow. You won't mind, will you?"

Mrs. Franklin was surprised but she tried her best not to show it. She knew that Erica was really disappointed, so she just answered, "Oh no, dear, of course not, but what is it you do not like about it?"

Then Erica told her mother the whole story. Mrs. Franklin listened very quietly. Erica pretended that she did not care, but it was quite evident that she was only acting. When the explanation was made, Mrs. Franklin just said,

"Well, dear, I am very glad that you have thought of Ella before yourself. I quite agree with you that it is very hard on the poor child that she should not be able to take her prize. I can assure you of this, you will enjoy the prize-giving because you have learnt the true meaning of unselfishness.

Erica did not answer. She did not like to be praised. Surely any sporty girl would do the same for a school-fellow.

Mrs. Franklin's words proved to be true. The prize-giving was a great success and I am certain among the girls there was not one who felt happier than Erica did, unless it was Ella herself.

(The End.)

Halifax Courier and Guardian
1931

"THANK-OFFERING" FOR ELECTION RESULT.

DOUBLE SUBSCRIPTION FOR YORK ORPHANAGE.

At the opening of a sale of work in the Assembly Rooms, York, in aid of St. Stephen's Orphanage, yesterday, Dr. W. A. Evelyn said that he was prepared to double his subscription to the Orphanage as a thank-offering for the result of the General Election.

Sir William Worsley presided at the opening.

Sir William said that they should be thankful for the unprecedented expression of loyalty and common sense which the people of the country had made during the last few days.

Mrs. V. Holt, of Kirbymoorside, opened the sale, and said that children of the Orphanage were being trained to play useful parts and must claim their support.

Northern Echo 1931

3OO FAIL TO GAIN ORDINARY B.A. DEGREES

BUT 1,100 ARE SUCCESSFUL

FACTS OF LAST YEAR'S EXAMINATIONS

UPWARDS of 1,400 undergraduates were examined in subjects for the Ordinary B.A. degree last year, of which number approximately 1,100 were successful in passing the examinations.

A drop of 67 on the previous year is shown in the numbers of those attending the courses in Subsidiary subjects, the total last year being 775.

Of the Principal subjects in Group I. the most popular was History, accounting for 173 of the total, although Law was chosen by 138 members of the University.

Other subjects in this group which were read by considerable numbers were:

Economic History	81
Psychology	79
Economics	72
French	54
English	87

By far the best attended course in Group II. was Engineering, which claimed over 200.

Only one undergraduate out of a total of 97 failed to gain the approval of the examiners in "Law and the Layman," the most popular of the various Subsidiary subjects, while the numbers of those who attended the other courses of lectures with success were as follows:

Peoples of the British Empire	82
The Sun, Stars, and the Universe	76
Everyday Science	72
Modern Social Problems...	55
India	53
The History of English India	46
Man and his Environment	46
English Life and Literature	38
History of Cambridge ...	36

The Board of Examinations, whose 58th report has just been issued, add in conclusion that they are following the practice of recent years in not printing extracts from the remarks of the examiners on the work of each paper

Varsity Weekly 1932

SERIOUS OFFENCE AT ACLE.

LABOURER AND YOUNG GIRL.

At Norfolk Assizes, on Tuesday, before Mr. Justice Avory, Edward William George (22), farm labourer, was sentenced to six months in the second division on a charge of having committed criminal offences against a girl under the age of 16 years at Acle between August 20th, 1930, and October 12th, 1930.

Mr. Gordon Clark, for the prosecution, said that at the time of the alleged offences the girl was just over 14 years of age. She lived at Acle with her grandmother. Accused lived next door. He had known the girl's family for some considerable time, and about 1929, with her grandmother's permission he used to take the girl out in the evening to cinemas and other places. This went on until, in January, 1930, the girl's grandmother spoke to accused and said the girl was too young to be going out in the evening, and that she desired the association to stop. It did not stop, and in June, 1930, the grandmother saw George again and to'd him he had not done as she requested. She added, "If she has to be sent away through you it will be a criminal case." Accused replied, "I know it." In spite of these warnings accused continued to go out with the girl in the evening, and at the end of August or beginning of September, according to the story of the girl, the first of the offences was committed. The girl was expecting a baby.

Accused, on oath, denied that he had ever interfered with the girl, although he admitted that he had taken the girl out on several occasions and had been up lanes in the Acle district with her. When the girl's grandmother told him she did not wish him to take the girl out any more he tried not to do so, but the girl used to wait for him and run after him, as all the village knew. He had not been out with the girl since August. He had a young lady of his own. "I might have had one before if she had kept out of my way—one of my own age," he added.

The jury, after a short retirement, found prisoner guilty.

Mr. Linton Thorp, for the defence, said he had a letter from George's employers saying he was trustworthy and reliable. Mr. Thorp added that accused had an absolutely unblemished character. "Your Lordship knows better than I do," said Mr. Thorp, "the temptation to men in our villages. There is nothing much e'se to do. I ask your Lordship to deal as leniently as you can."

The Judge, in passing sentence, said: "This offence, as I have had occasion to observe, is so prevalent in this part of the country that it is absolutely necessary that it should be punished when brought home." Addressing prisoner, the Judge said, "You have aggravated the offence in this case by the perjury you have committed in the witness box, and you have burdened this unfortunate girl with an illegitimate child, of which she is about to be delivered. You must go to prison in the second division for six months, where you will be treated as a young offender."

Norfolk Chronicle 1931

MILK IN SCHOOLS
Agricultural Committee Discussion

It was reported at to-day's meeting of the County Agricultural Committee at the Shire Hall, Gloucester, that active assistance had been given to Gloucestershire Education Committee in making arrangements for the supply of clean, fresh milk to children in elementary schools.

Mr. A. H. Chew, chairman of the Agricultural Education Sub-Committee, said the supply of fresh cow's milk to schools was suffering from competition with malted milk, which was delivered in tins at a cheaper price. In order to guard against impurities which might creep in through the use of cups, the bottles of cow's milk were provided with straws, through which the children sucked it.

Gloucestershire Echo 1932

SCHOOL ATTENDANCE in the St. Asaph elementary school district was last month affected to some extent by the prevalence of influenza, and the schools that suffered most were St. Asaph National Infants' and Bodfari National. There are now, however, welcome signs of improvement in both these parishes. Tremeirchion National School heads the list of attendance returns for the district with a percentage of 96.2, and the order of the others is as follows :—Rhuallt Council School, 94 per cent; St. Asaph National Girls' School, 93.4 per cent; Bodelwyddan National School, 92.8 per cent; St. Asaph National Boys' School, 92.7 per cent; St. Asaph Roman Catholic School, 92.6 per cent; Bodfari National School, 78.3 per cent; St. Asaph National Infants' School, 74.8 per cent. The scholars of the St. Asaph, Bodelwyddan and Tremeirchion Schools attending the manual training centre made every possible attendance last month, as did the Bodelwyddan scholars attending the domestic subjects centre. The average attendance at the St. Asaph evening class for woodwork is 11, the number on the register being 15.

Rhyl Journal 1932

SCHOLARSHIPS AND ECONOMY.

A correspondent writes :—The entrance scholarship examination to the various Intermediate Schools in the county will be held on June 3 and 4. This examination has been the subject of a series of conferences between representatives of the teachers and of the Education Committee as the teachers have on several occasions expressed the definite view that the present method of examination is not the best form of test for selecting children who are mentally and intellectually qualified to follow a continued course in secondary schools. In previous years the regulations allowed scholars between the ages of 10 and 12½ to compete for scholarships, and pupils who exceeded the age of 12½ on August 1st to attend the examination, and their successes to be classified for the purpose of application for a maintenance grant, commonly known as a Bursary. This year, owing to considerations of economy, the regulations allowing children over 12½ years of age on August 1st has been withdrawn, and such pupils will not be allowed to attend the examination. Therefore, as far as Flintshire County Schools are concerned, no child over the age of 12½ will be admitted next September. The Head Teachers of the Primary Schools are very disappointed that the Education Committee should consider it necessary to insert such a condition in their regulations, as it will deprive many of the county's children of the opportunity of securing secondary education. There are several instances of boys and girls who have entered the Intermediate Schools at a later age than 13 and have later become distinguished in their different vocations. The Head Teachers resent the clause, and are making arrangements for representations to be forwarded to the County Education Committee. The Head Teachers strongly feel that they are in duty bound to oppose very strenuously any attempt at economising through the curtailment of the child's opportunities for continued secondary education. If any further economies are found to be necessarry in education they must be obtained through a reduction in the cost of administration and not in the reduction of admissions to the secondary schools.

Rhyl Journal 1932

SCHOOLMASTER'S ROADSIDE DEATH

On Thursday, a middle-aged cyclist was seen to dismount at Fobbing and sit on the roadside, apparently resting. Later he was found to be dead. When some scholars of the Southend High School for Boys came along in a motor car they recognised the dead man as their English master, Mr. Francis E. Jope, who resided at Madeira Avenue, Leigh. Mr. Jope had been to Grays, and it is thought he had a heart attack. He was a well-known speaker at Brotherhood meetings.

Essex Herald 1932

EIGHT TO A ROOM
Workless Father's Plea of Poverty

The Willesden Magistrate yesterday made an order for ejectment against a father, mother and six children living in one small room at Kilburn.

The father said he was out of work and could not afford proper accommodation for his family, and the mother said the children were ill owing to overcrowding.

They were allowed 28 days to find other accommodation.

Reynolds Illustrated News 1933

THE PRINCESS'S RABBIT

Duke Of York Makes Kind Inquiries

The Duke of York to-day made careful inquiry regarding the health of a rabbit.

The inquiry was made on the strict instruction of Princess Elizabeth, when the Duke visited the Disabled Soldiers' Exhibition in London.

The "little rabbit"—as the Princess referred to it—is named Madame Butterfly, and it was presented to Princess Elizabeth some time ago by the workers at the British Legion village, Preston Hall, near Maidstone.

While the Duke and Duchess are in town Madame Butterfly surveys the beauties of the grounds of Preston Hall, where it receives every care. At the exhibition to-day the Duke went to one of the stallholders and asked how Madame Butterfly was progressing.

When he was told she was quite well and happy he replied that "Elizabeth will be delighted to hear it."

The Duke and Duchess made many purchases, among them a large family teapot in green china.

The stallholders were amused when the Duke chaffed the Duchess about it. "You can't make tea in a silver pot," he said, "so we'll see what you can do with a china pot."

Gloucestershire Echo 1932

GROVE-ST. MISSION

Poor Children's Party On Leckhampton Hill

Children of Grove-street Mission enjoyed their first annual outing yesterday when they went to Leckhampton Hill. More than 100 sat down to tea in Mr. Le Feuvre's tea gardens.

During the afternoon the children climbed the rocks or played cricket and other games. After tea between 30 and 40 of the young people took part in the wild flower competition. A large variety of flowers had been gathered on the hills as well as wild strawberries. In the evening races were run. The party returned home at 8 o'clock.

Mr. J. W. Manning (pastor) and his band of workers express themselves as being exceedingly grateful to the "Echo" for kindly allowing an appeal for the mission to appear in the paper. As a result a gift has been made of an American organ and several parcels of groceries. Anyone desirous of bestowing further gifts on the mission should send them to Holt View, Sandford Mill-road, Cheltenham, or write a postcard to that address and the gifts will be called for.

Gloucestershire Echo 1932

TRIPLETS FOLLOW TWINS

Mrs. Grace Reed, aged 34, wife of Mr. James Reed, a foreman at Courtauld's Works, Braintree, gave birth to triplets—two boys and a girl—during the week-end. Nearly four years ago Mrs. Reed presented her husband with twins. She has five children under the age of four years and eight under thirteen years. Mrs. Reed's grandmother was one of triplets.

On Monday at Braintree Parish Church a special service was held, in order to have the triplets baptised to qualify for the King's Bounty, for which application has been made. The Rev. G. R. Woodhams officiated, and Mr. A. M. Silcox, the Braintree representative of THE ESSEX CHRONICLE, was invited to be Godfather to the triplets, in addition to an uncle, and he consented. The triplets, aged two days, were brought to church by Nurses Fenwick and Walsh in a large perambulator, and were christened Rex, Roy, and Rita Reed. They "chirped" when the curate sprinkled them with water over the font. They were in the arms of Nurse Fenwick and two aunts, and the two Godfathers faced them. There is no record of such a unique baptismal service at Braintree Church before.

Mrs. Reed is the eldest daughter of Mr. W. Melbourne, the well-known newsagent of Braintree.

The last triplets were born at Braintree 15 years ago to Mr. and Mrs. Goodwin, of Rayne Road. They were girls, and were baptised at Booking. Nurse Fenwick attended both mothers.

Harwich and Dovercourt Newsman 1932

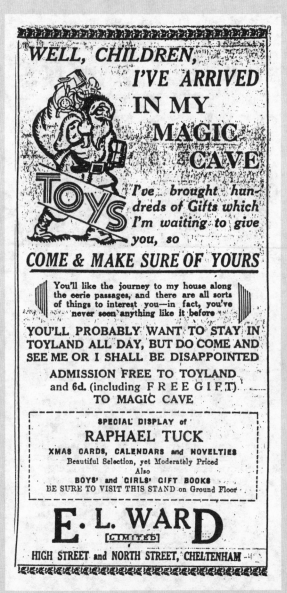

Gloucestershire Echo 1932

AMBULANCE CADETS

IN UNIFORM AT BOSCOMBE.

The Southbourne Cadet Division of the St. John Ambulance Brigade paraded in uniform for the first time on Monday at the headquarters in Palmerston-road, Boscombe. Their ages run from 10 to 16, and they are fully qualified.

A concert was arranged by the members of the St. John Ambulance, with the object of raising funds towards the cost of the uniform, and the event proved very successful. Major F. O. Chappell, Corps Superintendent, inspected the new division, and complimented all, including Mr. W. J. Bromfield, Divisional Superintendent, upon the smart appearance of the Cadets, considering that they had only recently been organised.

Among those present were Dr. J. R. John, Divisional Surgeon.

The concert was contributed to by Messrs. Len Davis, J. Dunford, Les Davis, Noel Rawson, Aldridge Cast, Jack Norris, Private Short, Misses Rebbets and Needham. The Revels Concert Party gave a voluntary performance.

There was a large attendance.

Bournemouth Daily Echo
1932

MURDERED BY BANDITS.

British Woman's Fate in China.

ATTEMPT TO KIDNAP HER CHILDREN.

HARBIN, Wednesday (Reuter.)

A British woman, Mrs. Woodruff, was this morning attacked and murdered by four bandits, who also attempted to kidnap her three children.

Mrs. Woodruff was the wife of the chief accountant of the British American Tobacco Company here.

Two Russians pursued the bandits, but the latter fired and wounded both seriously.

Chinese policemen then took up the chase and fired at the bandits, killing two.

The other two escaped, while the children were rescued and brought back to safety

Bournemouth Daily Echo 1932

Good Housekeeping 1933

The Children's Charter

An explanation of the important Children and Young Persons Act of 1933

The Sections of the Act

I. The Prevention of Cruelty and Exposure to Moral and Physical Danger.

II. Employment.

III. Protection of Children and Young Persons in relation to Criminal and Summary Proceedings.

IV. Remand Homes, Approved Schools, and Persons to whose care Children and Young Persons may be committed.

V. Homes Supported by Voluntary Contributions.

VI. Supplemental.

The section on Employment first places many restrictions on the employment of children. It has, so I read, already caused it to be an impossibility to include a baby as a character in any film shot in this country. No Jackie Coogans here! Opinions will differ as to the entire good of such a limitation.

The following are the prohibitions:

Children under twelve must not be employed :—

(a) Before close of school hours on school days.
(b) Before 6 a.m. or after 8 p.m.
(c) For more than two hours on any school day.
(d) For more than two hours on any Sunday.
(e) For lifting or moving things heavy enough to injure them.

Local authorities may, by by-law, modify certain of the above provisions. The bad feature of the powers entrusted to them is that they may differentiate between the sexes. One knows of yore that by-laws ostensibly protecting girls work out to their economic disadvantage. Women town-councillors, etc., should be extremely vigilant upon these matters.

Good Housekeeping 1933

A CHILD OF TWO DRUNK

When Blodwen Parker (45) pleaded guilty at Cardiff to-day to being drunk in charge of a child aged two years eight months, and with unlawfully giving the child intoxicating liquor, it was stated by Constable Collins that the woman was holding the child's hand. Both were staggering, and the child was unable to stand without support. The child smelt strongly of alcohol.

A doctor stated that when he first saw the child he thought it was dead, but it was only drunk. Parker, who was fined £4, said the child took a sip of port wine from her glass when she was having supper. It was stated that the child was in hospital and was recovering.

Edinburgh Evening News 1934

FORTITUDE OF A SCHOOL MISTRESS

Southwark Pupils Unaware of Her Suffering

The funeral took place on Saturday at Elmers End Cemetery of Miss Winifred Smith, a schoolmistress, of 27, Westow-st., Upper Norwood.

For six months Miss Smith had struggled against the advance of an incurable disease and in spite of great pain she had continued her work and none of her pupils knew of her suffering.

She died at her home on January 24 at the age of 48 as a result of influenza and pneumonia.

Miss Smith had been the headmistress of Gray-st. Infants' School, Southwark, for the past ten years.

She had taught in South London schools for 30 years and started her career as a pupil-teacher at Woodland-rd. School, Upper Norwood. She had also been headmistress of St. John with All Saints' Infant Department, Waterloo-rd., and assistant mistress at Waterloo-rd. L.C.C. School.

The funeral service was conducted by Canon Wilson at Christ Church, Gipsy Hill.

The school was represented by the acting headmistress, Mrs. D. Rees, and the headmaster of the boys' department, Mr. E. H. Betts.

There were many floral tributes.

South London Press 1933

Era Of Wonder

THEIR CIVIC DIGNITY FORGOTTEN.

Darnall's New Playground.

LORD MAYOR AND LADY MAYORESS ON "MERRY-GO-ROUND."

The unusual sight of the Lord Mayor and Lady Mayoress of Sheffield (Alderman and Mrs. Ernest Wilson) and Alderman J. G. Graves taking a ride on a merry-go-round, in company with highly delighted youngsters, was one of several pleasing incidents at the opening of a new playground yesterday.

This little unexpected episode was thoroughly enjoyed by the civic dignitaries, and by the 500 children from the five schools in the Darnall area, who had assembled to listen to the speeches at the opening of a fine open space in Surrey Road. and to give audible thanks to Alderman Graves, the generous donor. Children of Darnall will now be able to play in perfect safety, and, judging by the enthusiasm witnessed yesterday, there will never be vacant places on the whirling platforms, swings, rocking-horses, merry-go-rounds, and other popular amusement devices. The very tiny tots have not been forgotten, some of the swings being provided with cradle seats.

City's Fairy Prince.

This particular district of Sheffield has been brightened by the latest gift by the city's fairy prince. Alderman Graves, and as the youngsters pass the summer hours in healthy play they will forget the drabness of their surroundings.

Gaily-coloured flags at the entrance to the playground and on the various devices greeted the civic party. There were hearty cheers from the dense crowd, as the Lord Mayor and Lady Mayoress and members of the Council took their seats on the platform erected near the shelter close to the entrance to the ground.

The Lord Mayor said that Alderman Graves was a particularly beneficent citizen. The playground had an area of 1,500 square yards and was originally part of land purchased by the Highways Committee for the extension of Greenland Road. It was transferred to the Parks Committee at a cost of £100, which had been defrayed by the Graves Charitable Trust. The cost of the gift, including equipment, was £1,300. Sheffield was fortunate in the number of parks and open spaces that it possessed. There was a total acreage of 2,557, of which 1,100 had been provided through the generosity of Alderman Graves and the Graves Charitable Trust.

Sheffield Daily Telegraph 1933

SCIENCE GIFTS FOR 1933

PARENTS WILL SOON CHOOSE—BOY OR GIRL

INCUBATORS!

Man can make of the world just what he wishes.

That is the burden of the declarations made to the "Sunday Dispatch" yesterday by two distinguished scientists, Sir Richard Gregory, the chemist, and Professor A. M. Low.

"I ANTICIPATE in the near future an increasing attention to the voice of science," said Sir Richard Gregory.

"Man is beginning to learn that he is in truth master of his fate and that we are not mere creatures of circumstance, subject to disease, poverty, want. We can control these evils if we will.

"**It will soon be possible for a man, in fact, even to control the sex of his children, and where muscles and nerves are lacking to build them up in incubators.**

"We shall discover in 1933 fresh means of combating the pests that destroy the plants and animals upon which we depend, and processes for the conversion of inorganic substances into foods in the laboratory.

HOPE FOR BLIND

"A new hope is promised for the blind and deaf in the new experiments in electrical stimulus of the brain.

"The internal-combustion engine is on the road to being displaced by a new method of storing power. New textiles will compete with cotton and wool, and man will mould the vagaries of nature to his will.

"**I think, too, we shall see a return to books, not only for entertainment but also for education. The talk-film and the radio talk are too transitory for educational purposes.**"

Professor Low declared that prophecy was now quite a scientific process. He added:

"**I believe the time is now ripe for some new feat of invention. We have seen aeroplanes, radio, talking pictures and motor-cars alter the aspect of the whole country within a few years, but detailed improvements are now becoming increasingly difficult.**

"I do not think 1933 will produce a death ray or commercial television by some new radio process, but I believe that clothing will be cheaper and better methods of food packing and concentration will be available.

Sunday Dispatch 1933

NEGLECT OF CHILDREN.

Shocking Conditions in Shrewsbury Home.

Extraordinary descriptions of the conditions in which two children, aged six months and four years, lived, were given at the Shrewsbury Police Court on Tuesday, when Phoebe Horton, single woman. and her mother, Amelia Horton, stated to be 79 years of age, both of 41, Old Coleham, Shrewsbury, were summoned by the N.S.P.C.C. for the neglect of the two children.

Mr. C. N. H. Bowdler, who conducted the case for the Society, said the children were those of Phoebe Horton.

Dr. Urquhart said the baby, Cyril, was about half the weight of a normal child of his age. He was very wasted, improperly fed, and looked ill. There were marks on his skin of vermin bites, and there was some element of rickets. He was fairly well clothed.

The baby was very definitely suffering from want of fresh air and from improper nutrition. His skin was unclean. The elder child was pale, anaemic and undernourished. His skin was unwashed.

The house was full of all sorts of rubbish, and the atmosphere was foul. The windows had not been opened for a long time. and were thickly covered with cobwebs. The sleeping accommodation was very poor, and the bedding in a bad state.

Inspector F. Grinter,, of the N.S.P.C.C.. gave evidence as to the income of the house.

He said the living room was filthy, and the table littered with "dirty. filthy crocks."

Dr. A. D. Symons. medical officer of health for the borough. said the case had been one of peculiar difficulty to the health authorities.

"According to the law," he said. "anyone in this country can live like a pig in their own house if they want to, provided they don't make themselves a nuisance to other people."

When he visited the house there was a "smell of unwashed humanity and stale food."

Thomas Speake, chief sanitary inspector of the borough, gave similar evidence.

The defendants both said that much of the evidence was untrue. As soon as there was time the whole house would be altered.

The magistrates considered the case for a long time, and on returning said their difficulty had been to avoid sending the defendants to prison. Amelia Horton would be fined £2 and Phoebe Horton £3, with an alternative in each case of one month's imprisonment.

Shrewsbury Chronicle 1933

PEER'S SONS OPERATED ON,

The two sons of Lord Brabourne, the Hon. Norton Cecil Michael Knatchbull (aged 12) and the Hon. John Ulick Knatchbull (aged 9), underwent operations for appendicitis in a London nursing home yesterday. They were reported to-day to be going on well.

Birmingham Mail 1934

CHILDREN IN POOR LAW INSTITUTIONS

Suggesions at Tiverton Guardians Committee

PRIVATE HOMES

THE boarding out of suitable children in private homes by Guardians Committees throughout the county as a means of helping the Devon Public Assistance Committee in their campaign for reducing the number of children in their institutions, was suggested to members of Tiverton Guardians Committee at their meeting on Tuesday.

It was estimated that if every Guardians Committee in the county found homes for two or three children there would be no necessity to provide another home for forty children as was at first thought.

HOUSE COMMITTEE'S ANXIETY.

The Clerk (Mr. K. Bareham) read a letter stating that the Children's Home Committee of the Public Assistance Committee was very anxious to reduce the number of children at present in their institutions and to prevent any future children over three years of age remaining in Public Assistance institutions any longer than six weeks allowed by the Ministry of Health.

The Committee enlisted the co-operation of every Guardians Committee and hoped that the possibility of placing some of the children in private homes would be seriously considered by them with as least delay as possible.

The Master (Mr. H. D. Bowman) informed Mr. H. G. New that there were two children in the Tiverton Institution over three years of age, and they were to be removed to the care of an aunt at Newton Abbot.

BOARDING-OUT SUGGESTION.

Mrs. Candler suggested that homes might be advertised for, and the Clerk thought that some of the children at the Ayshford Homes, Uffculme, might be boarded out so as to make room for children under Poor Law supervision. The matter was referred to the Boarding-Out Committee.

Exeter Western Mail 1933

RAN A CINEMA AT 13.

BOY'S SHOW ATTENDED BY 70 CHILDREN.

ROOM DESCRIBED AS "A DEATH TRAP."

How a 13-year-old boy conducted an underground cinema at Ramsgate, for large audiences of children, was described in the local police court yesterday.

The boy's mother, Mrs. Lucy Elizabeth Oliver, tenant of the building, was fined 20s. for contravening the Public Health Acts, but the Mayor said the Bench admired the boy's spirit of enterprise.

It was alleged that the building, which is in Farley Place, Ramsgate, was not substantially constructed and supplied with ample, safe, and convenient entrances and exits, having regard to the use to which it was put.

Describing a visit to the underground cinema, Detective-Sergeant Petley said 70 children, ranging in age from 2 to 14 years, had paid a penny each for admission. After the performance balloons were given away, and there was great congestion.

"I have never seen anything like it in my life," he added, "and if I had not been there with the chief of the fire brigade there would probably have been a catastrophe."

Non-Inflammable Films.

Chief Officer West, head of the fire brigade, said the room where the films were shown was about 12ft. by 13ft., lined with match boarding, and approached through a scullery. The one window was covered with plywood, through an opening in which the films were projected.

The electric light cable was attached to the ceiling by a steel cable, and could easily have short circuited. He had seen children playing with an electric light flex through which a current of 240 volts was passing.

The only gangway was about 20in. across, and the only other exit was through a kitchen used for keeping grocery stores for a shop upstairs.

Mrs. Oliver said her son had been giving performances for three years. The police had visited the premises every week-end for the past 13 months to take cuttings of the films, which were all non-inflammable.

The Chief Constable, Mr. S. F. Butler, said he would not have prosecuted had not an entertainment been given after Mrs. Oliver had been warned that the premises were a death trap.

He had tried to secure control under the Cinematograph Act, but could not, because the films were not inflammable. He had communicated with the Home Office, and hoped legislation dealing with such cases would be introduced.

If anything had happened 20 or 30 children would probably have lost their lives, with a boy of 13 in charge of 70 children.

Mrs. Oliver gave an undertaking that the room should not be used again for the purpose.

Birmingham Mail 1934

BRINGING UP CHILDREN, BY A VICAR

"Sound Thrashing Better Than an Angry Slap"

DR. CORNELIUS' VIEW

A word of advice to parents on the training of their children is given by the Rev. Dr. Cornelius, vicar of All Saints', Peckham, in an article in his church magazine this month.

"The best leaders in Church and State," he says, "are those who have had the inestimable benefit of noble-minded parents and a home which has been used as a school for elementary training in character, conduct and learning.

"It is manifestly wrong to permit children to grow undisciplined and reckless and then to expect the schoolmaster to correct these errors and to turn out responsible and law-abiding citizens."

While admitting that there are difficulties in telling children about certain aspects of life, Dr. Cornelius says:—

"Convention has made things difficult but that is no reason why parents should not prepare for a healthy and happy future by telling their offspring what they will, without doubt, learn somehow.

"Bad manners and careless behaviour are very prevalent in this age of freedom and bring in their train much discomfort and unhappiness.

"What shall I say of punishment for breaches of home commandment? Briefly this, that a good sound thrashing as a matter of justice is much better than the angry slap and misdirected cuff."

South London Press 1933

Sir James Jeans has been delivering a series of Juvenile Lectures on the theme "Through Space and Time," at the Royal Institution. On December 30, he treated his hearers to a tour of the moon, exhibiting a wonderful talent for turning the cold facts of Science into an exciting adventure. He even envisaged a game of cricket on the moon, which proved, however, unconscionably "slow"!—on account of the smaller gravitational pull of our satellite.

Illustrated London News 1934

THE CAMERA AS RECORDER: NEWS OF THE WEEK BY PHOTOGRAPHY.

SIR JAMES JEANS' JUVENILE LECTURES AT THE ROYAL INSTITUTION: THE EMINENT SCIENTIST AND HIS AUDIENCE.

A TERRIFYING AWAKENING.

Milk Lorry Bursts Into Tennyson Street Bedroom.

A young Battersea couple—Mr. and Mrs. Harry Painter, of Tennyson-street—and their ten weeks old baby had a narrow escape early on Tuesday morning, when a heavy milk lorry burst through the front of the house and stopped with its huge wheels suspended in mid-air over the edge of the bed on which the couple were sleeping. The baby was in its pram at the side of the bed.

The affair happened a few minutes before four o'clock. The tank lorry, which belonged to a Wiltshire dairy farm organisation, was filled with milk. It came along Silverthorne-road from the direction of Wandsworth-road, and was about to pass the corner of Tennyson-street when another lorry emerged from Messrs. Nestlé's milk depot. The driver of the Wiltshire lorry swerved to avoid a collision.

His vehicle slithered across the road in a long skid and knocked down the railings in front of Mr. and Mrs. Painter's ground floor flat, which is at the junction of the roads. The front wheels of the lorry rose into the air, and the lorry smashed through the wall, scattering the window-panes in thousands of pieces. It stopped with the bonnet and wheels suspended above the edge of the bed. A dressing table near the window was broken almost to matchwood. Ornaments and treasured wedding presents were knocked flying in all directions.

MRS. PAINTER.

MOTHER SEIZES SLEEPING BABY.

Mr. and Mrs. Painter in great alarm, leapt out of bed. As quick as thought the young mother seized her sleeping baby, and she and her husband rushed from the room.

The crashing noise made by falling bricks and breaking glass awakened not only those in the rooms above but also neighbours on both sides of the street. In a few minutes many were running to the house in their night clothes, in order to offer speedy help. It was remarkable that no-one received serious injury. The baby was entirely unhurt and the parents escaped with slight bruises and shock. The lorry driver, although he was very shaken, received no hurt.

An unfortunate result of the accident is that many of Mr. and Mrs. Painter's most treasured wedding presents were broken.

Mrs. Painter was very white, obviously still suffering from shock, when one of our reporters spoke to her in the wrecked bedroom. Holding Kenneth, a bonny baby, in her arms, she looked sadly round the little room. Even then she did not seem to fully realise the narrow-ness of their escape.

South Western Star 1933

A TUNE AND A TIP
MOUTH-ORGAN WELCOME FOR THE PRINCE
From Our Own Correspondent

LIVERPOOL, Thursday.

During the Prince of Wales's visit to Liverpool to-day a 13-year-old boy provided "musical honours." As the Prince was entering one of the new flats at Dingle Mount, the boy, Stanley Dally, began to play softly on a mouth-organ "God bless the Prince of Wales."

"Play that again as the Prince comes out," said the Earl of Derby, as he, too, entered the building.

The boy needed no second invitation, and as his Royal Highness reappeared in the doorway, he struck up the tune once more—and louder.

The chorus was taken up lustily by the families who thronged the tenement balconies and the crowds in the street.

The Prince patted the young musician on the shoulder, and as the party moved away Lord Derby slipped a 10s note into the boy's hand. There was glad surprise and another tune.

A report of the Prince's visit to Liverpool appears on Page Fourteen.

Daily Telegraph 1933

DAUGHTER FOR WOMAN NOVELIST

The birth of a daughter in a London nursing home to Mrs. Josephine Bott, wife of Mr. Alan Bott, the author, is announced today.

Mrs. Bott is a daughter of Mr. and Mrs. R. D. Blumenfeld and is herself a novelist. Mr. Alan Bott is managing director of the Book Society. They have one son, born in 1931.

Dorset Daily Echo 1935

EVERY CHILD SHOULD LEARN TO SING

BY
EVA TURNER

ON hearing that I began to study singing when I was only eight years old, the average mother holds up her hands in horror. For nine parents out of ten are still influenced by that curious fallacy, that children should not be allowed to use their singing voices, except in class work, until they are well into their 'teens or twenties.

Why do we consider it essential to develop all a child's other muscles while we neglect the vocal ones and leave them to become atrophied for want of proper exercise? The vocal cords are the first muscles that a baby uses, as any mother or nurse will testify! Yet although we expend endless time and trouble upon teaching a child to crawl and walk, to dance and play games, to read and write, we remain content to leave the voice, one of the greatest human gifts, untaught and untrained.

The Music Lover 1934

UNCLE JOHN'S PARTY.

ANNUAL "WEEKLY POST" EVENT AT TOWN HALL.

The thirtieth annual poor children's party given by Uncle John, of the "Birmingham Weekly Post," and his young Busy Bees, took place at the Birmingham Town Hall on Saturday night, and was attended by 1,000 guests. The Lord Mayor attended and warmly commended the work of the charity.

After tea Mr. George Jackson presided at a capital entertainment to which contributions were made by members of the Alexandra Theatre pantomime company and other local entertainers. There was a distribution of presents by Father Christmas as the young people left the hall.

Uncle John's Charity was the first charity in this country organised by children in aid of children. It was started by the young readers of the Young Folk's Corner of the "Weekly Post" in 1904, under the leadership of Uncle John, and each year the funds raised by these Busy Bees suffice to give this party to poor children and to send some hundreds of sickly children to recuperate in country cottages. In addition, Uncle John's nephews and nieces have established a "Weekly Post" cot at the Children's Hospital and have endowed it. They have also endowed an "Uncle John" cot at the Convalescent Home of the Birmingham Royal Cripples Hospital.

Birmingham Mail 1934

SUNDAY-SCHOOLS IN DERRY PRESBYTERY.

Rev. J. Houston, B.A., presented his report on Sunday-schools during the past year to Tuesday's meeting of the Londonderry Presbytery.

He had to confess, he said, that they still had no Sunday-school Union of any kind in the Presbytery. Contact with others engaged in the same work and information about the best methods would seem an ideal way of keeping the school up to a higher standard. In school and Bible classes they had over three thousand of as fine boys and girls as any Presbytery could boast. On the whole, the atmosphere about them was pro-Church. Children were encouraged by their parents to align themselves with the Church, and they had not heard so much of the draught and drift of which they heard so much elsewhere. "Nowadays," Rev. Mr. Houston pointed out, "an increasing effort is being made to understand the children and to give them what suits and interests them. Is the Sunday-school to be the first place where they are bored and mismanaged? What notions are we unconsciously giving them about religion? I wonder if we ministers are fully alive, as we ought to be, to the unique field given us in the Sunday-schools."

The report was passed, on the motion of Rev. Joseph M'Corkell, seconded by Rev. J. Leslie Rankin.

Londonderry Sentinel 1935

Youthful Derry Gangs.

Becoming a Danger, Says District Inspector.

Seven Boys For Reformatory.

Judgment, which a fortnight ago had been deferred for full consideration, was given on Tuesday in cases in which nine boys appeared at Londonderry Children's Court on a series of theft charges.

Two of the boys figured in ten charges, another had four charges to answer, another four, and another three, while two had but a single charge against them, one receiving and the other larceny.

District Inspector Lynn prosecuted, and Mr. A. Robb appeared for one boy and Mr. P. Maxwell for another.

The charges ranged from breaking into the store of the Irish Agricultural Wholesale Society at Duke-street, where, in addition to stealing fruit, thirteen or fourteen bags of flour and meal had been slashed with a knife and damage done to the extent of £2, to the stealing of a pair of shoes out of a motor car parked at a Rugby football match. Other charges included the stealing of eleven shillings from a coat in a badminton hall at the Waterside and the theft of money and cigarettes from shops.

The magistrates present on Tuesday were—Mr. J. Anderson (presiding), Miss Osborne, and Mr. J. M. King.

The Chairman said the evidence in these cases formed a deplorable story, and they had reached their decisions after making private inquiries. The first boy would be sent to a reformatory until 23rd December, 1938, the father to pay 2s 6d per week towards his support; the second and third boys would go to a reformatory for five years, the father to pay 5s weekly for each; the fourth boy, against whom there were six cases, would go to a reformatory till 8th October, 1938, the father to pay 5s weekly; the fifth boy, against whom there were eleven cases, would go for five years, the father to contribute 3s weekly; the sixth boy would go until 13th March, 1939, the father to contribute 5s weekly; the seventh boy, against whom there were six cases, would go until 18th July, 1939, the father to pay 2s weekly.

Londonderry Sentinel 1935

NATIONAL BABY WEEK

This week the British Empire celebrates National Baby Week, which has become an annual stocktaking of all nationalities of babies. Britain is not the only country concerned; as far away as Lagos and Mombasa great enthusiasm is aroused this week for the welfare of the young. Last year the state of Mysore won the Imperial Baby Week Challenge, which is awarded to the best Baby Week celebration held in the British Empire. So far, Scotland does not hold a special Baby Week; its contribution to the scheme consists in taking part in the National Conference on Maternity and Child Welfare to be held in Birmingham, at which experts from all parts of the country discuss their experiences and work together for the betterment of babies all over the Empire. Children are, after all, apart from the joy of their

is a heavy tax on the parents' time and energy, to say nothing of the burden on the expenses of the household. The Infant Welfare Centres are striving to improve the conditions of the young, and their reward will be a strong and healthy nation.

Two Great Influences

The two great influences which are here brought into play are parentage and nurture. Good parentage, that is, "good" in the sense of "healthy," guarantees a much better chance of healthy children, and it is therefore incumbent on the parents to look after their own well-being. Nurture likewise depends on the sagacity of the parents, and the National Baby Week Council urges all mothers to take advantage of the pre-natal clinics which are at their disposal, not only for their own sakes but for the sakes of the children. Sunshine, fresh air, and good food are indispensable in building up sturdy bodies; good food

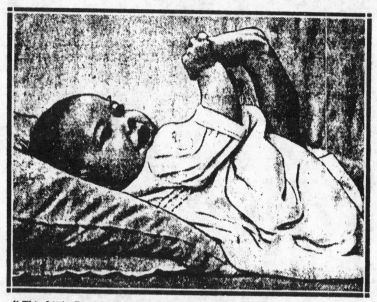

"This Little Pig Went to Market"—one of the delightful studies of babies on exhibition at the Iford Galleries, London.

parents, "the potential wealth of the nation and its hope for the future."

Importance of Babies

Babies are the most helpless of all living creatures, and, being helpless, depend, therefore, on their parents doing all they can to ensure bodily and mental health. The babies of this country, at present, in many cases, do not get fair play, and the high death-rate bears out this statement. Twenty years ago even less care was taken of young children, and according to statistics one out of every seven died before reaching the age of 12 months. To-day there is a great improvement, parents have been educated more thoroughly, and the importance of healthy child-life has been impressed on them, and has taken practical effect. Much has yet to be done, however, and the object of Baby Week is to prevent this terrible loss and damage to infant life, and to bring home the fact that scores of thousands of young lives are being sacrificed every year.

Meaning and Aim of Week

The first National Baby Week was held in 1917, and the best results of the work of the numerous Child Welfare Centres has been the improved health of the children entering the schools, their height and weight have increased, and they have, thereby, much more energy to devote to their studies. Although 90 per cent. of children are born healthy, bad housing conditions, neglect, and improper feeding render about 35 per cent. physically defective by the time school age is reached. A proverb which may well be practised by parents is that "prevention is better than cure." Illness

does not mean rich food but fresh vegetables, fruit, milk, butter, and eggs, and it is every parent's task to see that their children get as many as possible of these simple things.

Fathers' Councils

A mother's duties in the upbringing of her children, though numerous, do not complete the training which is to form the character of her family. The father must co-operate with her and he, himself, can do much to improve or mar the mother's work. Obviously, before he can start his part of the work he must know what he is doing, and for this purpose, in many districts, a Fathers' Council has been formed. This consists in meetings for fathers at the local Infant Welfare Centres, where either lectures are arranged or the fathers do some practical work to help the resources of the home. One can easily imagine what tremendous help the education of fathers in the care of children must be to women who have several young children to look after, besides the running of the home with no outside help. With the co-operation of the fathers their attitude towards the difficulties of their wives becomes one of sympathetic understanding, which he can show by practical assistance on the lines laid down by his Welfare Centre. While every opportunity is being given, therefore, to ensure safe motherhood and healthy childhood, advantage should be taken by all those who need advice and help of their local Infant Welfare Centres. Then the ambitious and comprehensive ideal of the National Baby Week that "an A1 nation is composed of A1 individuals" will be more than just an ideal—it will become a reality.

E. P. T.

Edinburgh Evening News 1934

CAUSE OF FEWER BIRTHS.

The declining birth-rate in Kensington is so marked that it is causing some concern. In the south part of the borough it has never been high, but the number of births in North Kensington is now amazingly low. However, having regard to the housing conditions in the north and the overcrowding, the authorities would prefer to see a higher birth-rate in the south. Few councils have been more alive to the necessity of slum clearances as the Kensington Council, and the northern division of late has been considerably improved. Nevertheless, there is still much overcrowding. My opinion is that the population has decreased through families having gone further afield.

West London and
Chelsea Gazette 1934

Jubilee Babies.

Mr. Alec Clarke was to have driven one of the Councillor's horses, but he was called away by the news that his wife had presented him with a daughter. He was understudied with complete success by one of the Councillor's sons.

Which Baby.?

With his usual enthusiasm, Councillor Chapman at once made a shilling collection for the Jubilee Baby, hoping it would be for his driver. But this little present will probably go to Mr. and Mrs. Rowlands, of 319, Lansdowne Road whose baby came immediately after midnight was struck on Sunday.

Cardiff and Suburban News
1935

"I think babies should wear veils . . . That vacant grin! That awful feeling that it is a sort of human bomb . . ."

Good Housekeeping 1934

"Why do you keep scratching your arm?"
"Because I'm the only one that knows where it itches."

Chuckler 1935

THE STRAIN ON CHILD PERFORMERS.

(To the Editor of the Dover Express.)

Sir,—As a parent, may I appeal through you to all teachers and parents not to encourage young children under the age of nine to take part in our public performances arranged in aid of charities. This form of self-expression may be good for older children, but the strain of rehearsals on little people, culminating in the unhealthy excitement of a late performance, must be injurious. Our children are given to us, not to be used as toys for our amusement, but to be built up into healthy citizens with a hard task before them. Our charities deserve every support, but surely we can find some means of helping without mortgaging on the future. I enclose a small cheque, which kindly pass on to the Mayor's Charity Fund.

RONALD H. BRADLEY.

13, Leyburne Road, Dover,
November 30th, 1935.

[The cheque has been forwarded to the Mayor.—Ed. D.E.]

Dover Express 1935

SMILE AT THESE

Mother: "Where have you been?"
Son: "Listening to an organ."
Mother: "What organ?"
Son: "My mouth organ!"

———

Father: "Take your cap off while you are at the table."
Jack: "I have not got my cap on."
Father: "You have."
Jack: "I have not. It's Tommy's."

———

Policeman: "If you move you are a dead man."
Burglar: "If I move it shows that I am alive."

Target 1936

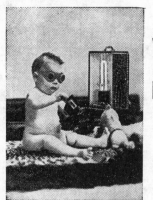

In Sunless Winter

USE A

VI-TAN

HOME UNIT

When summer sunshine wanes *Vitality* is lowered and healthy *Tan* fades. These deficiencies can now be remedied. Simply plug in the *Vi-tan* Unit to any standard plug or socket and switch on. Health-giving Ultra-Violet Light is available immediately. Robust, self-contained and portable, the unit can be used in any position and is economical to run, 20 hours for 1 unit of electricity.

FOR ALTERNATING CURRENT ONLY

THE
THERMAL SYNDICATE Ltd.
Makers to the trade for over 25 years
Vitreosil works:
WALLSEND-ON-TYNE
London Depot: Thermal House
Old Pye Street, S.W.1

Home and Country 1936

The Welsh Children's Peace Message to the World.

Viscount Snowden writes on May 20th, 1935: "Europe is drifting into War. In the name of Peace the nations are preparing for War. Armaments are being increased beyond all precedent."

Lord Hewart, the Lord Chief Justice, a few days afterwards, said: "We have the astonishing spectacle of statesmen at conferences for peace, spending their time discussing the armaments to be used in the war they were going to prevent."

Then Mr. Stanley Baldwin made the following sensational statement in the House of Commons—words that should be printed in letters of gold and placed in every home in the land:—

"I have occupied myself studying questions of air-raid precautions, and I tell the House that I have been made almost physically sick to think that I and my friends, and the statesmen of every country in Europe, 2,000 years after our Lord was crucified, should be spending our time seeing how we can take mangled bodies of children to hospital and prevent poison gas from going down the throats of the people. It is time that all Europe recognised that."

And in the midst of all this peril, this misunderstanding, and these contradictory effusions comes the Welsh children's beautiful message of peace to the world. "Cast thy bread upon the waters and thou shalt find it after many days"!

• • • •

*Cardiff and
Suburban News
1935*

COW RUNS AMOK

FOUR SCHOOLCHILDREN INJURED

Haverfordwest Street Terror

An infuriated cow ran amok in Barn Street, Haverfordwest, on Tuesday, and injured four young scholars of the Barn Street N.P. Girls' School.

One of the little girls, Iris John, aged 8 of 15, Barn Street, was so seriously hurt that she had to be removed to the County Hospital, where she has since undergone an operation.

The cow, which had a calf at heel, belonged to Mr. John Davies, Neeston Hall, Herbrandston, and was being driven to the Swan Square mart by one of his workmen.

The cow turned off the road half-way down the hill and made its way back up the 'bank' past St. Martin's Vicarage. It was noon, and laughing and chattering children were pouring out of the National School.

Seeing them, the cow made a sudden dash and the children scattered in all directions, screaming. Many escaped, but others were not so fortunate.

The maddened beast pursued the little girl John across the roadway and after knocking her down tossed her into the air. One of its horns penetrated the child's neck and the other caused a wound in her leg.

By this time the children had become terrified and those who could not find shelter were running in all directions. Several were knocked down, and when little Bronwen George, Pembroke Road, tried to regain the school bank, she was violently thrown to the ground and the cow commenced to gore her. Luckily her plight was noticed by Miss John, one of the teaching staff, who courageously went to her assistance and saved her at the expense of a damaged ankle. Bronwen suffered considerably from shock and had to be medically attended. Her clothes were also ripped off.

Little Miss Joan Vaughan, Portfield, also sustained a nasty injury.

A terrifying experience also befel Mrs. Morgan, Fountain Row, who was confronted by the maddened beast when making her way home from Barn Street. The cow had been headed away from the school precincts and was being driven up Barn Street, when Mrs. Morgan heard it's snorting behind her. She turned into Fountain Row and had just enough time to reach the safety of the Roman Catholic priest's residence (Dr. Mostyn).

Unknown to her, her eighteen months old son, Gerald, came toddling up the street towards the cow. The little chap was knocked over and the cow's foot actually brushed his face. Fortunately a number of men were at hand and the animal was driven off.

Not until the cow had reached the Pig Bank in Dew Street was it finally got under control.

West Wales Guardian 1936

ALL those little girl readers who have dolls' houses will be ever so pleased to see this sweet little feather broom ! It was sent to me by Jean Mills, of Manchester, and I am awarding her a prize for it.

To make it, you must collect together a few of those tiny feathers that sometimes work their way out of cushions, and bind them to the end of a matchstick. Isn't it easy ? But it is just the very thing you need to dust your dolly's furniture now that the 'spring cleaning' season has come round again !

Rainbow 1936

DRINK MORE MILK.

DEAR EDITOR, I was interested in the letter on this subject in November "HOME AND COUNTRY." We have five children under nine years and for most of their lives we have lived in the east of London, where the children grew up fine and bonny in spite of overcrowding and lack of play space. We all had pasteurized milk. We always wished for a country life and so were pleased when an opportunity to live in the country came in the spring of this year. I knew the milk question in the country would arise and I made careful enquiries before choosing a milkman. After a week or two the children started having feverish attacks which ceased when they were taken off milk. I changed the milkman to one who supplies the Welfare Centre. All my children have been ill since. Two of them are very ill. All have developed gland trouble. One boy has had to have his neck opened, another has a T.B. gland in the stomach, another large swollen glands in the neck. The children were never ill before. We have no history of T.B. in the family. It must be the milk. My baby is now due for weaning and I dread giving him the cows' milk available. What shall I do ?

Yours faithfully, EVELYN MORGAN.

Home and Country 1936

ORDER AGAINST A MAN.

At the Dover Police Court on Friday, before Mr. W. B. Brett, Mr. T. Francis and Mrs. Binge.

William Murton appeared on an affiliation summons as to twins, issued by Nora Ellen Biggs, a married woman living apart from her husband.

The Magistrates' Clerk: Do you admit you are the father?

Defendant said that he had married the woman.

Applicant said she had been living with the defendant for nearly four years, and had twins by him in August, 1932. He had been very cruel to her at times, and she left him when he failed to support her and the children.

The Bench made an order of 15s. a week, and remitted the costs.

Dover Express 1935

CRUELTY TO CHILDREN

ENGLAND'S "VILE RECORD"

Kinder to Animals

England's "vile record" in the treatment of children during the last century was advanced by Canon F. W. Green, of Norwich, as evidence of the fact that English people do not naturally love children. He was speaking at a meeting in connection with the National Society for the Prevention of Cruelty to Children at Norwich.

"Historically I can find no records in other countries to equal ours in the public and declared treatment of children from the beginning of the industrial revolution to the end of the Factory and Education Acts," declared Canon Green.

Seventeen Hours a Day

"When Lord Melbourne was premier at the beginning of Queen Victoria's reign children were working in his coal mines up to seventeen hours a day and scarcely ever seeing the light of day.

"*There is no form of cruelty, whether in the schools, factories, or in agriculture, that we did not perpetrate on the children of this country for at least fifty years. And we have not seen the end of it yet.*

"I am afraid it means that English people don't naturally love children. There are individual exceptions, but as a race we have not the same love of children that the French or the Italians have, or even the Germans. In some ways we gain because the children of the Latin races are very largely spoilt.

Making Cruelty Impossible

"Because we have such a frightful history and because we are the kind of people who have to be careful about our treatment of children, it is our extraordinarily plain duty to see that we organise our work to make cruelty impossible.

"*I know the sort of dangers children are exposed to. You won't find them so much in the great centres of poverty. Very often there you find the kindest* hearts and people are extraordinarily good to each other.

"It is in the outer suburbs and the waste spaces where people are not in touch with each other to the same extent that you find unspeakable cruelties still.

"*We have made greater progress in our work for animals than for children—that again is like us. We have always been kind to animals, not always to children.*"

A Christian Characteristic

Canon Green went on to say that kindness to children had always been one of the outstanding characteristics of Christianity, and it was one thing which the pagan world noted about the early Christians.

Miss Hilary, of the headquarters organising staff, spoke on the condition of children in England to-day, and the need for the work that the N.S.P.C.C. is doing.

Although it was fifty-one years since the society was founded, last year there were over 106,000 little children on whose behalf the society had to step in to see that they were given a fair chance.

They were by no means all orphans. All over the country there were cases where children were being brutally treated, neglected, or starved.

A Terrifying Thing

Miss Hilary emphasised that the N.S.P.C.C. was not a prosecuting society, and she said that whenever possible their work was done quietly behind the scenes and with the future welfare of the child in view.

"One thing which we are fighting at the present time," went on Miss Hilary, "is the leaving of children at home alone at night while the parents go to the pictures or to dances.

"It is a terrifying thing for a child to be left, and there is not only the physical danger but the serious hurt to the nerves."

The speaker went on to say that cases were not confined to poor homes. In lots of their cases there was no lack of money.

Catholic Herald 1936

Dying Boy Pleads: B.B.C. Stands Firm

B.B.C. regulations forbid radio stars to give their autographs to listeners who ask for them.

In Blackpool last week a little boy was dying. He had one wish—to see the signatures of the men and women whose voices he heard on the radio. His father wrote to Broadcasting House. The request was refused.

One official, human feelings outraged, defied authority, spent hours of his spare time collecting signatures. He sent fifty of them to Blackpool. And the dying boy smiled.

Sunday Referee 1936

THE SUNBEAM GUILD.

THE SUNBEAMS OF ST. CHAD'S.

My dear Sunbeams,

Here is a piece of news that will please all our members who are keen in supporting our Cot at Peshawar. Our Sunbeams of St. Chad's have again sent £1 for their quarterly subscription. I do thank them all very, very much for this great help, as it means real self-denial. Also, I wish to thank our kind friends who interest these children so much in missionary work and who arranged a special service so as to complete this subscription of £1. I heard a little about this service. The children repeated their anniversary music hymns. They are a choir of about eighty girls, all dressed in white, with fine linen veils on their heads. Two of the bigger girls, aged twelve, sang a solo each in two hymns, and two tinies each sang a verse in their hymn, "Lambs of the Good Shepherd's Fold." Don't you wish that you and I could have been present at that service? We all would enjoy hearing the children sing their hymns.

I am sure that your hearts will go out in loving sympathy to one of these St. Chad's Sunbeams who has had a very sad loss. I knew that her father was very ill, but hoped he might recover; now I have heard that he has passed away. I also want you to think of two more Sunbeams—a brother and sister—whose father died a short time ago. Will you think of them, too, with loving sympathy? Both the brother and sister have been such keen Sunbeams, interested in all our doings. I enjoy having their letters and competitions, and they have been splendid little contributors, too. Though they may not be able to do much now, they are going to help as much as they can. Knowing that these three children are Sunbeams, I feel that they will try harder than ever to scatter smiles and sunshine and so bring comfort and cheer into their homes.

To-morrow is the first day of August, the month which means holidays and a rest from lessons. May you all have the very happiest of holidays, and may you, each one, try to bring happiness to others.

Yours affectionately,

"AUNTIE MAY."

Church of England Newspaper 1936

Children: Their Bringing-up and Conversations

Although it is never explicitly stated by the authors of the two volumes under review, the object their work is probably intended to serve is to spare the world of the future the terrible scourge of odd people which recent generations have suffered. In fact, this seems to be the object of all literature of the kind, and the vast number of books now being produced about the child, its education and early training, might stand as an indication of the dread of adult oddness which recent experience has inflicted upon civilized mankind.

Given the belief that the origin of unsatisfactory behaviour is due to some fault in upbringing, or some unwise feature in the early environment of human beings, the present anxious concern about children, their thoughts, reactions and outlook, seems logical enough. The only trouble about it is—and this applies to a very large number of new psychological interests and methods—that the present spate of contributions to the science of child-psychology and child-training happens to occur at a moment when so much is hopelessly wrong with human life that the thoughtful layman cannot help asking himself whether the psychological aids and corrections offered are competent to do all that is necessary. How were former generations able to produce the harmony and order they undoubtedly must have produced, seeing that they had never heard of psycho-analysis, or of the psychological fundamentals of infancy?

New English Weekly **1936**

LOOK AT HIS QUILLS!

HERBERT HEDGEHOG: "I say, Mr. Chemist, this embrocation is no use. I cannot get anyone to rub it on my back!"

Rainbow **1936**

Parson Headmasters Becoming Scarce.

WITH the appointment of Mr. J. T. Christie to be headmaster of Westminster School the number of parson schoolmasters has been still further reduced, as he succeeds the Rev. H. Costley White. At one time most of the Public Schools were dominated by parsons who regarded the post as a stepping-stone to the episcopal bench. Nowadays, however, young laymen are preferred, as we see at Eton, Harrow, Winchester, Rugby, Uppingham, Shrewsbury, Charterhouse, Rossall and Repton. A silent revolution has gone on since the War.

Church of England Newspaper **1936**

Beano **1937**

FREE FISH!—Whiting have been so plentiful at New-haven recently that disposal of the fish has presented a problem. Here local fishermen are seen giving some of their catch away to children.

**Christian Herald and
Signs of Our Times 1937**

Banffshire Journal 1936

Caithness War Preparations

The gravity of the European situation is causing a good deal of concern in Caithness, and the lack of protection in the event of war breaking out. Gas masks have not yet arrived in the county although outlandish places little likely to be attacked have received their supplies many months ago. People travelling from the south carry their gas masks and they think it incredible that no supplies have been received in Caithness. — At the meeting of Wick School Management Committee on Monday, Provost T. W. Anderson, chairman, brought the matter before the notice of the meeting. He stated that the supply was expected at an early date. The meeting decided to approach the responsible authorities with a view to steps being taken with regard to the protection of school children.

It is understood the idea prevails that Caithness is not likely to suffer from a gas or air attack, but the point is that the masks ought to have been in the hands of the inhabitants. Measurements were taken for the gas masks many weeks ago but there have been no further developments. However, there is no reason for alarm as the gas masks will be distributed shortly.

Caithness Courier 1939

Vienna Boys' Choir: (a) **Sandmännchen** (Brahms), (b) **Kein Hälmlein wächst auf Erden** (F. Bach), and (c) **Rosestock, Holderblüt** (Folk-song); sung in German. Parlophone-Odeon, RO20428 (10 in., 4s.).

Like a number of others, this is a famous choir. Its history and triumphs are related in an article in THE GRAMOPHONE for December, 1937; the choir-boys' home and training are also described. It is clear from these recordings that the lads sing as a well-trained band. How far their work is found pleasing will depend mainly, I fancy, on how far their tone is regarded as agreeable. Personally, I find the sound of their united voices unpleasant; but quite likely my reaction is shared by only a small minority. Interested readers should certainly hear the record.

Gramophone 1939

ALLENDALE BOY'S SUCCESS

Boys, usually shy of speaking in public, outnumbered the girls in the Richard Thompson bequest oratory competition in the Northumberland Road Council school, Newcastle. The girl, Miss Ethel G. Henderson (Newcastle Church High school) shared first place with Arthur E. Charlton (Municipal College of Commerce) Wm. Arnold Philipson (Municipal College of Commerce) and Allendale boy, was third. The subject was "The Use of Leisure," and each competitor had to speak for 15 minutes.

Hexham Courant 1938

"Stink Bombs"

So many readers write to us to know how to make these bombs that we had better say here that it is difficult to make bombs which "explode" in their small way, as these bombs, which you buy from novelty stores, are made by craftsmen and usually take the form of small glass bulbs each containing a little hydrogen sulphide.

It is the sealing of these bulbs which causes wrinkles to appear on the foreheads of amateur experimenters! It is really up to each reader to

TOP CRUST WITH A SMALL HOLE PIERCED EACH SIDE

MOLTEN SULPHUR

Producing Crystals of prismatic sulphur   *Group of prismatic crystals of sulphur much magnified*

use his ingenuity in evolving some form of container for the sulphide. We are not keen on recommending the use of stink bombs, as it is not a particularly pleasing or dignified pastime, but since so many boys seem attracted by them, well, there you are!

Hydrogen Sulphide

We can certainly tell you how to produce the hydrogen sulphide, by placing some fragments of ferrous sulphide in a two-necked bottle and pouring upon it some dilute hydrochloric or sulphuric acid. The gas is given off and can be collected over warm water, or if you prefer to have it in solution, use cold water as this will dissolve about three times its own volume of the gas.

Hobbies Weekly **1937**

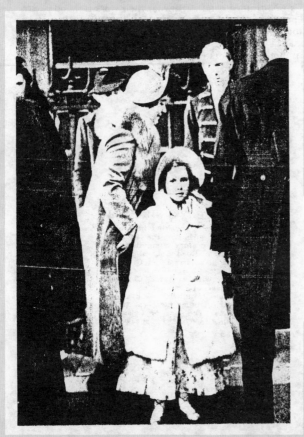

Left : When Princess Margaret Rose went to Lady Astor's children's party last month she was, as can be seen, charmingly attired in fancy dress, and wore a picturesque poke bonnet.

Children's Outfitter **1938**

To the Editor.

QUEEN CHARLOTTE'S MATERNITY HOSPITAL.

DEAR SIR,—Would you be kind enough to allow me a little of your space to give the Trade some information concerning the bed in the Queen Charlotte's Maternity Hospital, which has been endowed in the name of the Society as a result of proceeds from the sale of rare Wines and Spirits in April last year.

Mr. E. Lonsdale Deighton, the organising and appeal secretary, has written us as follows:—

"The Wine and Spirit Trade Bed is nominated and a plaque with the full name will go up over a bed in the new hospital, part of which is just completed but is not being furnished till the adjoining section is completed next year.

"But benefits began a few days after the sale last April, when an application was made if I remember rightly. We are very pleased to receive applications through you at any time.

"There is one point to remember, peculiar to *maternity* hospitals—for medical reasons, the expectant mothers, in their own interest, must 'book' with us or be seen by our pre-natal clinic some months before the event is due. On account of these bookings, all maternity hospitals are full up for months ahead with normal cases. Therefore we would prefer to be told well in advance. It is better to write to me at 29, Dorset Square, London, N.W.1, or to Mr. Stokes (our Secretary-Superintendent) at the hospital, mentioning the Wine Bed. If it is a destitute case, she would of course be treated free, but the patients usually like to give us at least their insurance benefit if they are insured under National Health Insurance."
—I am, your faithfully,

E. W. C. BODLE,
Chairman of Committee.

The Wine and Spirit Trades' Benevolent Society,
10, Byward Street, Mark Lane,
London, E.C.3.

2nd June, 1938.

Wine and Spirit
Trade Record **1938**

Adolescent Love

By Theodore Faithfull

In recent years the opinion has apparently been widely held that adolescence is a period of repressed desire for coitus, and that given " freedom " children between the ages of 14 and 19 would cohabit on an extensive scale. Many co-educational schools have, however, come into existence, for the most part since 1918, founded by those who held the opposite view, that human coitus is a mode of expression belonging to physical maturity, which in the Northern races is reached in the girl at approximately 19, and in the boy approximately two years later; and that for healthy growth during adolescence both boys and girls need the comradeship of the opposite sex.

The book under review* is a welcome addition to the growing mass of psychological literature dealing with child development. It consists largely of the diary and letters of one boy from the commencement of male puberty until the approach of physical maturity. N. M. Iovetz-Tereshchenko has attempted a scientific presentation of this diary and has been at great pains to date to the nearest half month the various events in the life of the writer of the diary, and to relate them to incidents recorded by the boy's intimate friends, or to similar material available from other children of approximately the same age. The value of this emphasis on the time factor is, in my opinion, minimised by the absence of other important data about the boy's early life and his environment.

In his diary " John " makes no mention of his father; the mother is apparently the dominating personality in his life. She is, one gathers, a wise woman, but she remains the authority in his life. The absence of any interest in games suggests that " John " has failed to pass from the narcissistic self-completeness of the pre-pubertal period into the group life and group love belonging to those years when a boy is passing through his female puberty, concerning which valuable work has been contributed by Marañon, the Spanish sexologist. These signs suggest inhibited growth which must indubitably have operated to modify the normality of the recorded experiences, especially in relation to the time factor.

* *Friendship-Love in Adolescence.* By N. M. Iovetz-Tereshchenko, D.Litt., Oxon., Ph.D. (Lond.). Allen and Unwin, 16s.

An Esperanto Broadcast

On May 18th, the Welsh Regional Station will once again broadcast a message of peace and goodwill from the children of Wales to the children of the whole world. This message is broadcast annually in the principal languages, including Esperanto.

Cab Trade News 1939

At any period of re-birth, or development into a new phase of life, we tend to revert to more primitive satisfactions. " John " is no exception, and his interest in the mature female form, satisfied by visits to bathing beaches, shews the revival of the emotional interest of the infant in the breasts and bodily structure of the mother who had provided warmth and nourishment. After two summers this satisfaction is discarded, and is replaced by increasing pleasure in psychic association with girls of approximately his own age. It is legitimate to question if this inspectionist satisfaction would have been so conspicuous if it had been adequately satisfied at, say, 7 or 8 years old.

The diary records the progressive escape of "John" from the narcissistic and pre-narcissistic mother-attached states into one of projection of part of his personality upon his boy and girl friends, a state of affairs which he finds is conducive to a previously unexperienced " joie de vivre." The state of " love " thus experienced is not correlated in the boy's consciousness, or his unconsciousness, with his periodical seminal discharges, which are definitely linked to the infantile love of the mother and his inspectionist experiences above referred to. It is important to realise that a large percentage of boys are psychically more female than male until the end of adolescence, and that it may be late in life before the activity of his reproductive organs becomes associated with the positive dominating male side of himself. This is most certainly the case with " John,," whose love reactions shew no sign of a dominating forcefulness. It is probable that in the friendship-loves recorded in the diary " John " was playing the female role. Dr. Iovetz-Tereshchenko does not apparently appreciate the fact that " sex " enters into all love relationships, but that in emotional and intuitional love expressions the " cutting " or " dividing," which is the root meaning of " sexual," does not necessarily follow the physical differentiation evolved for the purpose of reproduction of the race. " John's " friends may all have been playing the psychic male role.

Slowly as he grows towards maturity " John " becomes more positive. He wishes to learn to dance, and eventually he definitely and consciously discards the mother image as an emotional stimulant to seminal discharge, and substitutes at the age of 18 years 3 months that of his adolescent girl friend.

A carefully edited piece of work, this will most certainly help to establish the fact that the normal love relationship of adolescents is intuitional, that adolescence is the age for poetic fantasy, symbolism and " religion," and that in civilised races the correlation of this love to its physical expression in the act of coitus is not normally achieved until the end of adolescence. When we have available diaries of children who have been reared in an atmosphere free from Mrs. Grundy, and provided before puberty with adequate biological knowledge, which " John " was not, it will be possible to prepare, within limits, a time sheet of normal development.

The Teaching of ENGLISH to Young Children 6. Poetry

By Barbara Priestman

A CLASS OF SEVEN-YEAR-OLD children had begun their morning by learning the lyric from "PIPPA PASSES." About noon a much-loved grown-up friend entered the classroom to bring them a great armful of flowers from her country garden. These were received with acclamation, but one little girl with entire naturalness and conviction quoted :

> " God's in his heaven
> All's right with the world."

It seems to me that this is an example of the best sort of " expression work " after a poetry lesson. Something occurred which gave to one child at least, understanding of the emotion which lay behind the poem.

The " Poetry Period "

How often " Poetry " appears on the time table, and we wonder what to do with this period. " Shall the children learn by heart ? Shall we read to them and let them dramatise ? Shall they illustrate the poem they like best of those we have read ? " And all the time we are thinking—briskly or gloomily according to our mood—of a half hour which is to be filled—filled with what ? with something the children can do ? or learn ? or be filled with poetry ?

The trouble with poetry is that it is so personal a subject, so sensitive. We do not always feel in the mood. It seems impossible to fill a whole period with poetry and so we think of other ways of using up the time : recitation, dramatisation, illustration. Sometimes, quite magically, the poetry comes to life and fills the classroom, but often we suddenly realise that the poetry has fled and we are left with a noisy repetition, a clamorous and possibly exciting drama, or a busy but thoughtless chalking.

Child Education 1938

CAKES WERE SALTED
INSTEAD OF SUGARED !

Princess Elizabeth will probably take this opportunity to tell her mother of the progress she has been making in her own cookery lessons, for in the past few weeks she has been receiving instruction from the royal chef, M. Bouflin, in simple cookery.

She has been learning how to manipulate a gas oven, and has made cakes and scones.

Some of them were served recently at one of the Princesses' own tea parties, and thereby hangs a tale.

One of the young guests asked if she might have one of a plate of little cakes.

"Well, I don't think I should f I were you," said Princess Elizabeth with youthful frankness. "You see, I made those myself. And I put salt in them instead of sugar . . ."

After tea the King will probably set up his home cinema apparatus and give his children a private film show.

But first in the little programme will come the films that Princess Elizabeth has taken of the adventures of her and her sister with her own cine-camera.

Like her father, she is a camera enthusiast. She has taken scores of snaps apart from the films.

The King will run through those of his own films of the tour that have been developed. That way he will be able to tell his children of what happened to the first English King and Queen to set foot on North American soil.

Canada and the United States, merely names to the two Princesses, will live in pictures for them.

Sunday Pictorial 1939

Above : Miss Diana Chieseman and Master John Percival leaving for the wedding of Miss Una Swan and Mr. Charles Terry, held at St. James' Church, Spanish Place. The brides-maid is wearing a simple dress of taffeta with an inset of net at the neck gathered into a bow. The puff sleeves are also banded with net.

Children's Outfitter **1938**

There is much to tell about the mothers and children who have been evacuated from the big cities. One hears varying reports from different parts of the country ; in some places things have settled down excellently, in others, where roughly brought-up children from the East End have come into quiet villages, there has been a good deal of friction. I hear of children with dirty habits scandalising their cottage hosts. Sometimes financial difficulties arise—when, for instance, the children's clothing has to be burnt or the town parents are too poor to provide money for boot repairs or a change of underclothes, and the cottagers find themselves forced by their own sense of decency and humanity to provide for their foster children. Two children I heard of, who had come from a large family in the East End, went on hunger strike apparently because it was dull in a small family in the country. The labourer, who was looking after them, killed a chicken for dinner, but they refused to eat it, announcing that they "wanted brawn."

One true story out of many. A mother with a baby in a big house is forbidden by a patronising hostess to go into the kitchen. " But I have to get my baby's food at the proper times." Hostess : " *I* will see to it that the child is fed when it is hungry." After much to the same effect the mother borrows an ancient perambulator, long stored away, and is enjoined to be very careful of it, etc. The mother goes out with the child and sees a passing London bus. She stops it and asks the driver if he can get her to London ; she has not quite enough money, but he offers to make up the odd coppers. " But what about the perambulator ? " " Oh, we'll leave the damned perambulator in the bleeding ditch." And they did.

New Statesman **1939**

Beano **1939**

Thurso District School Management Committee

AIR RAID PRECAUTIONS

No Evening Classes this Winter

The monthly meeting of Thurso District School Management Committee was held in the Library, Miller Academy on Tuesday afternoon—Provost W. M. Brims, chairman, presiding. Also present — Messrs John Bruce, Jas. B. Docherty, G. T. Ironside, M.A., J. W. Wilson, M.A., Thurso ; J. Abrach Mackay, Castletown ; D. Sinclair, Halkirk ; A. H. Mackenzie, Westfield ; Wm. Oag, Clatequoy, and Mr J. W. Galloway, clerk.

An application for exemption was granted and one deferred.

School Cleaner

The resignation of Mrs Swanson, Barrock Street, as school cleaner, was intimated as from 15th September, 1939.

The meeting agreed that in the event of Mrs Swanson failing to reconsider her decision, the appointment be offered to Mrs Walter Swanson, Holborn Avenue.

Continuation Classes Discontinued

The Chairman said he had several reasons for recommending that the Evening Continuation Classes be discontinued this winter. First, there was the difficulty of lighting ; second, the darkness of the streets owing to the lighting restrictions ; third, a probable curfew for children in the streets ; fourth, the difficulty of the staff. After consultation with the Director of Education he was of opinion that the evening classes should be discontinued this winter.

Mr J. Abrach Mackay—That is a matter for the Education Committee.

The Chairman—This committee has to decide. What have you to say Mr Rector ?

Mr Ironside—That is a matter for the headmaster, Mr Meiklejohn, and it was his opinion that there should be no classes this winter.

The Chairman—Frankly, there is no one more disappointed than myself, as I am deeply interested in the work of the evening classes, but we cannot do otherwise.

The Chairman stated that this was appointed as a shelter for people caught in an air raid while shopping.

The Rector pointed out that the room allocated was not suitable as it would interfere with the work of the school. This room was really a double room used for Commercial Work where one teacher could supervise two subjects. He suggested that the room on the opposite front of the school be used. How is it they have taken the two best rooms ?

The Chairman—I can only refer you to the authority responsible.

Mr Abrach Mackay—You cannot make any provision for citizens in a school until protection is provided for the children. (Hear, hear).

Mr Wilson—Where are we to put the country pupils ?

Mr Abrach Mackay—Supposing a bomb fell on the school ? We must see that protection is provided for the children. The authority is wrong in providing protection for the shoppers in the school.

The Rector—The school is getting the southerly room and the shoppers the other side.

Mr Mackenzie—Supposing a raid takes place will the children be sent to their homes ?

The Rector to the Chairman—I want you to put the matter before the Education Committee at their meeting on Friday. I want definite orders.

The Chairman—The matter is in the hands of the A.R.P. Controller.

Mr Abrach Mackay — What definite instructions have been conveyed and whom are they from ?

The Chairman—It is not done by the Education Committee.

The Chairman to Rector—You ought to have expressed your views to the Authority responsible at the time.

The Rector—I want the committee to object.

Mr Abrach Mackay—So long as the power lies with the headmasters, they must to the best of their ability protect the children.

The Chairman—So long as it is in compliance with the Authority.

The Rector—Yes, but I must use my own judgment.

Mr Wilson—What about the country pupils ? Town pupils are safe enough.

The Chairman—The discussion is now closed.

It was unanimously agreed not to hold the evening continuation classes this winter.

Lighting Restriction

The Rector—With regard to the objection as regards lighting, the schools will still require to be lit for cleaning, etc.

Mr Wilson suggested that the school be closed a little earlier, say at 4 p.m. instead of 4.15 as at present.

The Chairman—That is a matter which rests with the Rector and staff.

The Rector—Oh, no. The difficulty might be got over by closing an hour before sunset and giving an opportunity to the cleaners to clean the school.

The Chairman—How about the country pupils ?

Mr Wilson—The country pupils would get the 4.30 bus.

Mr Abrach Mackay—The Castletown pupils wont get a bus till 5 p.m. It would mean they would be an hour in the dark streets.

The Rector—That is a serious objection.

Mr Oag—An arrangement might be made with the Highland Transport Coy.

The Chairman—The buses are being commandeered by the naval authorities. It may be difficult to get buses.

The Rector—Better leave the matter over for enquiry.

Mr Wilson—I think 4.15 too late with lighting restrictions.

It was agreed to defer the matter for consideration.

Blinds for School

The Rector—Are we not going to put blinds on the schools' windows ? Is the authority to put blinds on the schools' windows so that cleaners can do their work ?

The Chairman—Appoint a committee.

It was agreed to remit the provision of blinds to the following committee, with powers :—The Chairman, Messrs Ironside, Docherty, Bruce and Wilson, along with the clerk.

Re-opening of Schools

The Chairman said the schools were understood to be re-opened on Tuesday first. Personally, he didn't want to close the country schools longer than this week.

Protection for Children

The Rector drew attention to the two windows in the Miller Academy, facing Sinclair Street, which had been protected by sandbags.

Caithness Courier 1939

1940
1949

Solving the Nursery Black-out Problem

CURTAINS of printed cotton or linen with Beatrix Potter or Walt Disney designs, or flowered Cubaleen—a satiny fabric which can be laundered more easily than glazed chintz—are a pretty finish to the nursery scheme. Make the curtains with a dainty frilled valance or, for the sake of hygiene, a painted wood pelmet, which can be cleaned so easily.

The question of black-out presents a real problem in the nursery. Fresh air at night is all-important, and yet it is not safe to take down the black-out curtains after baby is asleep, in case he needs attention quickly during the night. We suggest, therefore, that you line the curtains with a closely woven coloured casement or sheeting (no black for this room), and see that they are amply full, so as to leave no gaps in the centre or at the sides. Then fix to the window a ventilating device (costing less than £1), which enables the curtains to be drawn, yet gives free access of air to the room. A specially designed ventilating pelmet is also available, but this is a rather more expensive fitting.

Good Housekeeping 1940

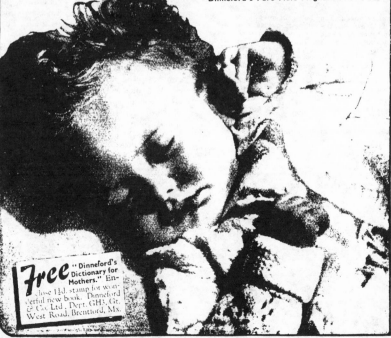

She used to wake up and cry

five or six times a night until they gave her **Dinneford's**

Night-crying—what can be done to stop it and bring comfort to all concerned? This letter will help many parents: "My daughter has a little girl and she has had a lot of trouble with her waking up at night and crying. I got some Dinneford's and since baby has had this she has not had a bad night's sleep. My daughter's husband says Dinneford's has done the trick." A teaspoonful or so of **Dinneford's Pure Fluid Magnesia** will settle a child's stomach and prevent food turning sour before it has time to digest. Dinneford's added to each feed will bring peaceful nights—and the child will thrive. Your chemist has Dinneford's at 1 3 and 2 6 a bottle. It is worth while to insist on **Dinneford's Pure Fluid Magnesia**.

Free "Dinneford's Dictionary for Mothers." Enclose 1½d. stamp for wonderful new book. Dinneford & Co. Ltd., Dept. GH3, Gt. West Road, Brentford, Mx.

Good Housekeeping 1940

At the sound of the Siren . . . .

a suit to keep the children warm and cosy in an emergency

Girls' Shop:
Fourth Floor.

The "On Guard" Siren Suit.

This practical hooded Siren Suit is of unequalled value. It is in a warm woolly material, cleverly designed to meet the emergency need of children roused suddenly from sleep. They can draw it on quickly themselves, and are immediately warm and snug, and protected against chilly nights. It has a drop back, and elastic at wrists and ankles. In navy only, with contrasting check hood lining of blue, red or green. This suit can be worn by boys or girls.
Sizes to fit ages 6 to 9 years. **15′11**

To fit ages 10 to 13 years. **18′11**
Post Free.

Order it by post:

Quantity..................................

Age........Colour (hood lining)..............

(Give second choice)..............

Name ....

Address ....

....

Swan & Edgar
Piccadilly Circus, W.1
Swan and Edgar, Ltd., Piccadilly Circus, W.1.

Good Housekeeping 1940

HAPPY CHILDREN.

VARIED LIFE IN AUSTRALIA.

(From an Australian Correspondent.)

Those British children who are transferred to Australia under the evacuation plan will go to a country so vast that Great Britain and Ireland could be fitted 25 times in it.

There is a wide difference in climate and the temperature of the north varies greatly from that of the south. Tasmania is in these respects rather like the South Coast but Darwin's temperature in the North has been likened to that of Aden.

British parents will be interested in Australian schools and pleased, too, to know that in the Commonwealth the poorest boy with the right degree of perseverance and ability can rise to occupy high positions.

Education up to the age of 14 is free and secular, although in some States Scripture lessons are given. But outside the national system there are many Church schools, some of them so finely developed that they are a counterpart to the famous British public schools.

In Australia education searches out all children and goes into the outback districts where the little rural schools are as efficiently managed as the larger institutions.

The children walk to them over long distances or ride in buggies or on horse-back. Bush fires do not stop them in summer or floods in winter.

Scholarships and bursaries are awarded freely to pupils of merit. Technical schools teach boys trades and professions and girls are helped to become doctors, teachers, to go in business life or to be artists.

Higher elementary and central schools are for pupils who can stay till they are 15 ; high schools take them to the age of 18 and from these pupils go into the banks, farms, commercial houses or to the universities, which also receive students from the fine technical schools.

But all is not work for children in Australia. Cricket, as everyone knows, is the national game. Lawn tennis is becoming more popular every year. Football in both codes has many adherents and the "Australian game" for those who like excitement.

Good horsemanship is a commonplace among Australian children, and if you are lucky enough to live near the beach then there are swimming, surfing, yachting and rowing in the clear blue sea.

Australia is an open-air country and that is why children have such a good time there.

York Star 1940

Borstal Boys Escape in Governor's Car

Two Borstal boys who escaped from the Portland institution yesterday, and got away in the Governor's car, were still at large last night.

Five boys tried to escape, but three were caught.

News Chronicle 1941

RHONDDA RECEIVES 393 CHILDREN FROM LONDON

THREE- hundred - and-ninety three evacuee children from the London area arrived in the Rhondda Fach on Saturday afternoon.

Of these 270 were taken to homes in the Tylorstown areas and the remainder to Mardy.

The children came from those districts of London which have suffered most from Nazi frightfulness.

Among the party were four little sisters, the Robinsons, whose ages ranged from nine to four. Their home had been ruined by Nazi bombs, and since then they had lived in a school—during the hours they were not in shelters. Frances, the eldest, was a true little mother and kept a watchful eye on her young sisters.

"Mam was worried when we said 'Good-bye' to her," said this plucky youngster, "but I promised to look after them."

"A NIGHT'S SLEEP"

An evacuee teacher told a *Western Mail* reporter, "All they have left is the few clothes that they have brought with them."

Several members of the party had had little rest for days. "Thank heavens we shall get a night's sleep now," said one.

Among those who welcomed the children were Mr. D. J. Jones (clerk to the Rhondda Council), Mr. E. D. Wilde (deputy-clerk), and the local councillors; Mr. S. Royall and Mr. Theo Evans (education department), Superintendents William Davies (Ton Pentre) and William Macdonald (Pontypridd), and Inspector W. H. A. Davies, of the N.S.P.C.C.

Evacuee children who have already spent some time in the Rhondda were also among those who waited to welcome the newcomers.

One of these children observed: "If any of my old pals arrive to-day I want to tell them what good times we are having here."

HOSPITABLE PEOPLE

On their arrival the children were taken to local schools for medical inspection and afterwards carried in a fleet of cars to their billets.

One of the evacuee teachers observed: "I think Rhondda people are most hospitable. We have had a Royal welcome."

Western Mail 1940

Who'll help Mrs. Harrison?

Mrs. Harrison has had Molly with her for six months now. Molly arrived in those troubled September days, and she came pinched and peeked and feeling very strange. Molly doesn't feel strange any more. Neither is she pinched or peeked. It's been hard work for Mrs. Harrison; but she hasn't grudged it. First she did it for her country's sake; and now she'd like to do it for the girl's as well.

But the trouble is this. Mrs. Harrison cannot keep her forever. A child is a tie and Mrs. Harrison feels it is a tie that should be shared. Will you be neighbourly and take Molly for a while?

All you need do is enrol your name with your local Authority. You may be asked to take a child now, or your name may be kept against the time when raids make a second evacuation necessary. When you enrol, you will be doing a splendid service for the nation. You may be saving a child's life. The child, the parents and the Government will be grateful to you. And if you take a child now, one of the 300,000 Mrs. Harrisons will be grateful to you too.

The Minister of Health, who has been entrusted by the Government with the conduct of evacuation, asks you urgently to join the Roll of those who are willing to receive children. Please apply to your Local Council.

Stratford upon Avon Herald 1940

Died At 100, Never Went To School

Mrs. Mary Ann Jenner, of Wallington, Surrey, who has died in her 101st year, never went to school and could neither read nor write.

She attributed her old age to hard work, wholesome food and a glass of ale for supper.

News Chronicle 1941

A claim that aeroplane flights will cure whooping cough is being tested in Switzerland, where children suffering from the complaint are said to have benefited from air trips.

Salisbury and Winchester Journal 1940

Salisbury and Winchester Journal 1940

Her broadcast voice is like the Queen's

AS Princess Elizabeth finished her five-minute broadcast in the Children's Hour last night she turned to her sister standing behind her and said: "Come on, Margaret."

And Princess Margaret leaned over the microphone and said, in a clear, delighted treble: "Good night, children."

Princess Elizabeth is the most outstanding child radio personality I've yet heard, writes Jonah Barrington.

She radiates friendliness, sympathy and a kind of sunny graciousness. Her voice is musical, precise and fresh—a lighter, higher edition of the Queen's. And she says "Australia" just as the King says it.

NEVER PAUSED

She had a script, typed on notepaper, on a table before her, but she was not reading from it. This heartfelt little talk had been thoroughly learned in advance: the Princess spoke it without once pausing or hesitating for a word.

Princess Elizabeth was speaking from an underground room (not in the B.B.C.). I am particular, asked not to say where it was. It is hoped she will broadcast again.

After sending "love and best wishes" to the boys and girls who have gone overseas, she said: "I can truthfully say to you all that we children at home are full of cheerfulness and courage.

"We know that in the end all will be well; for God will care for us and give us victory and peace. And when peace comes, remember it will be for us, the children of today, to make the world of tomorrow a better and happier place."

PRINCESS ELIZABETH
"Come on, Margaret," she said.

Daily Express 1940

HARK AT US!

We're Two Wise-Crackerjacks!

"WHAT-HO, Harold, my fruity old filbert! How's business with you now?"

"Oh, very over-ripe, Gus! The shortage of bricklayers is holding up all my new houses!"

"Just fancy that now! I always thought you relied on the wallpaper to hold your houses up!"

"Ah, but that was ages ago!"

"Before the paper shortage, I suppose?"

"You've said it! I'm having a big buttress on all the walls now."

"What ever for?"

"Why, to support them, of course!"

"But you'll never get the poor animals to stand still long enough!"

"Eh? What animals?"

"The female goats. They're buttresses, aren't they?"

"Ah! That reminds me of a fellow I know. He's going down in the world a lot these days."

"Hard luck, old scout!"

"But he still manages to pick up quite a decent living!"

"Oh, ho! And what might he be?"

"A coal miner!"

"Wow! Get off! You're standing on my foot!"

"Sorry, old sock!"

"You clumsy great lump! Surely my feet are big enough to be seen!"

"Of course they are, old dear; but I can't see them!"

"What? You've got eyes in your head to see with, haven't you?"

"Quite so! But how do you expect me to see your feet with your shoes on?"

"Oh! But say, are you going to a fancy-dress ball?"

"Why, no. This is my shooting suit."

"H'm! It looks as if it's had some bullseyes scored on it, too!"

"Well, it suits me, and my pocket! And now I must pop off, old sport. Cheerio!"

"Toodle-oo! I'll see you again next week!"

Comic Cuts 1941

Many children in the poorer districts of London who lost their toys when their homes were bombed have received new toys sent here by the Junior American Red Cross Society.

Salisbury and Winchester Journal 1940

Mothers and Children First

Two recent London Conferences have given a picture of wartime problems of working mothers and small children, of the solutions reached and the needs still unsatisfied—the Annual Meeting of the National Baby Welfare Council (addressed by the Minister of Food), and the Conference of the National Association of Maternity and Child Welfare Centres (addressed by the Minister of Health).

The malnutrition of the last war has not been forgotten and the food situation today of mothers and small children leaves little to be desired. There is sufficient orange juice for the under-twos and blackcurrant juice for the under-fives for next winter, milk schemes are working smoothly (largely because of generous supplies of milk from America which released our own fresh milk for children), and school meals and canteens for working mothers are becoming universal. It is hoped that we may build up stocks of food and an organization to distribute it to the children of Europe when we are able to invade the continent.

Tuberculosis is the one disease which has increased since the war and the need for compulsory pasteurization of milk for mothers and infants and careful medical examination of children and personnel in nurseries and mothers in factories was urged.

There are 644 war nurseries set up and 750 planned, 230 new nursery classes in factory areas, 1,300 approved " minders ", 376 nurseries for evacuated children, 60 hostels for ante- and post-natal care for evacuated mothers. But still provision for working women with families is inadequate. Still too many women have two full time jobs of work and home. Minor ailments are increased by strain and irritability and by the disinclination to confide in the factory doctor.

Social legislation affecting the mothers during pregnancy and after childbirth needs to be overhauled. There is a small lump sum payment at birth but no insurance to draw on. Russia is the only country in the world which has a system of adequate rest and pay after childbirth.

As with all social reform the problem of parental education as well as physical provision goes along with it, and this is perhaps the greatest problem of all.

Home and Country **1942**

Revenge bombs on children's hospital

Daily Express Raid Reporters

SEEKING revenge for the R.A.F.'s heavy blows at Munich and the Krupp works, large numbers of German bombers attacked London last night in the fiercest blitz for weeks.

More raiders were over London together than for a long time. Heavy anti-aircraft fire began before the alert, and the shelling became terrific.

A bomb burst in front of a children's hospital. A maid sheltering in a strengthened basement was buried under debris and killed, and nine people were injured—among them the matron and a doctor.

Both ignored their own injuries, and gave first aid to others.

None of the children or nurses was hurt. An official said: " All the children are safe in their ward, which is untouched.

" Fortunately the bomb missed the main building by a few feet.

" It exploded near our dispensary, which was badly damaged, and the kitchens were partly wrecked."

Daily Express **1940**

Mask Law For Schools

ALL children must take their gas masks to school, no matter where they live.

Practice in wearing masks for five minutes and extending to 15 minutes will be given once a week.

This is the latest instruction by the Board of Education.

Masks are to be examined by experts at the beginning of each school term and at not less than monthly intervals.

Children attending State-aided schools will have their gas masks reserviced or replaced free where necessary.

But the local authority must satisfy themselves that the damage is due to fair wear and tear or that a satisfactory explanation is given to them.

Daily Herald **1941**

BRITISH CHILDREN WELCOMED

A friend from Texas, who, by the way was born in Germany, sent me a clipping from her home town paper telling of the arrival of two English children. They were met at the station by a friendly reporter, among others, and he " wanted to make them feel at home," so gave the boy a cowboy suit and the girl a Scarlet O'Hara doll. (Scarlet being the heroine in " Gone with the Wind " in case you have not seen the film.)

Another friend who is a Roman Catholic spent the day driving around to different convents and got two little girls who were of that faith taken in as boarders free for the duration. The mother and three other children will live nearby. There were plenty of homes that would have taken these children, but no one wanted to break up the family, and as the children had been to boarding schools before, this seemed a way to take some of the load off the mother's shoulders.

Salisbury and Winchester Journal **1940**

THE SKIPPER'S BEST LIMERICKS

There was a young man of Devizes,
Whose feet were of different sizes.
    With his brawny right foot
    Many goals did he shoot,
And with his left won dancing prizes.

———*———

There was an old glutton of Duns
Who said, " I'll eat ninety-three buns."
    At the seventy-first
    He unluckily burst,
So the rest were consumed by his sons.

———*———

There was a young man of Key West
Who measured ten feet round the chest.
    Said he, " It gives vigour
    And strength to my figure,
But it costs a darned lot for a vest !"

———*———

" Bring a light !" cried a fool in Madras,
" I will look for that leakage of gas."
    His funeral procession
    Made quite an impression;
It took twenty minutes to pass.

———*———

There was an old man of the Rhone
Who went to his new telephone.
    When they said " Number, please ?"
    He gave a loud sneeze,
'And said, " I'm just testing the tone."

———*———

There was an old man of Black Rock,
Who never wore more than one sock.
    If you say this is quaint
    I deny it, it ain't,
For he was a one-legged crock.

———*———

There was a young fellow of Graney,
Incredibly clever and brainy;
    When he put up his gamp
    If he found it was damp
He could tell that the weather was rainy.

———*———

There was a young man of Great Sankey,
Who was so exceedingly lanky,
    He'd stand on a chair
    When brushing his hair,
'And tip-toe to reach for his " hankey."

Skipper 1941

PRICES OF SWEETS FIXED

1/4 TO 5/- PER LB.

The Ministry of Food has made orders under which, from a date to be fixed, the prices of chocolates and sugar confectionery will be controlled.

Maximum prices, ranging from 1s. 4d. to 4s. per lb in the case of sugar confectionery, and from 1s. 8d. to 5s. per lb. in the case of chocolate, will be fixed for various product groups. There is, however, under each order a basic price of 1s. 8d. per lb. for un-classified products.

It will be an offence for any retailer to sell any chocolate or sugar confectionery at a figure in excess of these basic prices of 1s. 8d. per lb. unless he can show (1) That the article in question has been classified in a higher products group, and (2) That he has displayed to the consumer an authorised price ticket showing the name of the product, the number of the approved product group, and the price.

Allocation of sugar for chocolate and confectionery making has been increased by the Ministry of Food. The Ministry are doing their best to obtain a maximum production of the cheaper lines.

MILK

If present satisfactory production continues, it may not be necessary to introduce the milk scheme on October 1st.

An official of the Ministry said that manufacturers of chocolate and confectionery had exercised a large measure of control and, generally speaking, the distributors had co-operated with them. Nevertheless a certain amount of chocolate and confectionery was being sold to the public at unjustifiably high prices. The orders would be brought into operation "very shortly," when manufacturers had had an opportunity of having their products classified and the necessary tickets and labels had been printed and distributed.

The public could rest assured that in paying a higher price than the minimum they were getting a type of sweet or chocolate which was definitely better than the cheaper-priced article. There would be no limitation on sales by the Ministry.

East Anglian Daily Times 1941

CHOIRBOYS AS RECRUITS.
To the Editor.

Dear Sir,—If you don't mind my writing again so soon I should like to add a little to my last week's letter.

I disagree with Mr. F. E. Pitman. It is quite true that the problem of what to do to keep choirboys when their voices break is a real and important one, but it has nothing to do with us as ringers, and we do not want the belfry used as an experiment and a dumping ground for used up choirboys. Now and again a good recruit may be had from the choirboys, but they are just as rare as anywhere else and want just as much finding. I would welcome any choirboy who wished on his own accord to become a ringer, but I would not do any pressing. They are too young to be much permanent good. They might come out of curiosity; and perhaps stay for a while, long enough to give a lot of trouble in teaching, and then as other interests come along they fade away and are seen no more.

I would try and interest the young men in the choir. If one of them was induced to learn ringing and had any aptitude for the art there would be a good chance of keeping him.   A CHURCHMAN.

Ringing World 1942

These Pupils Do Not Want To Grow Up

From Our Special Correspondent

YORK, Tuesday.

Youngest delegate to the National Union of Women Teachers conference, Miss Gwen Joynes, won applause from her colleagues here today when she gave a first-hand account of village school difficulties in Derbyshire.

Miss Joynes has' not been through her college training course yet, but she is in charge of nearly 40 children at a village school near Chesterfield.

"There are just the head-mistress and I," she said. "She takes the scholarship class. I have 38 children from five to ten years old. I don't mind that because I love them, but it is so hard on the children."

PREFERRED BABY GAMES

Miss Joynes added that one result of the inability to get another assistant teacher—the authorities said they had been searching in vain for six years—was that boys and girls of 11 did not want to grow up. They still preferred to play baby games.

After Miss Wainwright, of Manchester, had complained of mass production in schools leading to lack of real intelligent thinking, the conference passed resolutions protesting against the combination of junior and infant departments and demanding that the maximum number of scholars in a class should not exceed 30.

They also asked for better air-raid shelters and the granting of equal pay to men and women in the profession.

News Chronicle
1941

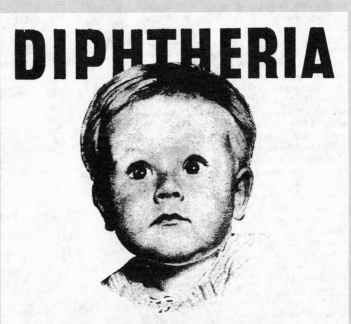

DIPHTHERIA

IS DEADLY-

Give your child the protection medical science now offers. Read the facts below and apply at once to your Council Offices or Welfare Centre—treatment is free.

IMMUNISATION IS THE SAFEGUARD

FACTS ABOUT DIPHTHERIA

Over 50,000 cases occur yearly in Great Britain. Between 2,000 and 3,000 of these die.

Even the best-cared-for child can get Diphtheria—it is not due to dirt or drains—and there are no "safe" areas.

Diphtheria is one of the worst dangers to children. It is particularly deadly to children under six years of age.

Even when not fatal, it may leave ill effects which last a lifetime.

FACTS ABOUT IMMUNISATION

There is nothing to be feared from immunisation. It is SAFE and simple. Merely a "pin prick" which is over and forgotten in a moment. If an immunised child gets Diphtheria it is usually in a mild form. Immunisation gives almost certain protection against death from Diphtheria. Only two treatments are necessary. The best time is soon after the first birthday. Protection takes three months to develop so get your child treated NOW—it is dangerous to delay.

Issued by the Ministry of Health & the Central Council for Health Education

D7a/1

Less Soap

"What do you think of the soap ration?" we asked a small boy of our acquaintance. "It hasn't come a day too soon," he said—rather enthusiastically, we thought. "It has been a perfect scandal the way people have been using soap up to now. Some of us have done our best to cut down our consumption, but it has made us very angry to see the shameless way people have been indulging in this luxury. It will do the country a lot of good to use less of it. Personally, I don't see why it shouldn't be cut out altogether." "I say," he added anxiously, "there won't be any extra rations of soap for children, will there? I mean like oranges and milk?"

The Scotsman 1942

Good Housekeeping 1943

GAMBLING AMONG BOYS

CARDIGAN POLICE INSPECTOR SAYS THERE ARE MANY COMPLAINTS.

Cardigan Sessions were held on Monday before the Mayor (Mr. W. J. Morgan, presiding). Messrs. Jenkin Richards, Arthur Thomas. and J. E. Jones.

Ronald Starkey, Llysmyrdin, Priory St., Cardigan, Harold Davies, 10, Greenfield Row, Cardigan, and Wynne Richards, 23, St. Mary Stret, Cardigan, were summoned for gaming in a public place near the Drawbridge, Cardigan on February 21st.

The three defendants pleaded "not guilty."

Woman Police Evans Davies stated that at 2.40 p.m. on Sunday, February 21st, she was proceeding towards the Gasworks from the direction of the cemetery when she heard voices and the tinkling of money. Witness approached quietly and on the wall she saw the three defendants playing cards. Witness noticed Davies pick up some coins from the wall and she heard Richards remarking, "That will be another penny I'll owe you." Davies saw witness coming down the road and he hastily put the cards into his pocket. Witness asked the boys what they were doing there. They replied, "We were only playing cards." When accused of gaming, Richards said. "I have no money on me to play." Witness told Richards she had heard him say, "That will be another penny I'll owe you." He made no reply. War Reserve W. Jones came on the scene and witness told him in the boys' presence what had transpired. The boys were asked how much money they had. Davies produced a handful of coppers which he said he had for selling Sunday papers. Starkey also produced some coppers but Richards did not have any. The cards were taken from the boys.

War Reserve W. Jones gave corroborative evidence.

Inspector E. O. Williams stated that they had had no end of complaints of gambling on a Sunday in the vicinity. Police were detailed to visit certain places but when they arrived the boys had usually gone. He thought it was time this kind of thing stopped.

Defendants denied that they had played cards for money.

MAYOR'S WARNING.

Imposing a fine of 5s. each, the Mayor said. "We were very hesitant about the fine. We should have imposed far more, but if you appear before us again you will be heavily fined. This kind of thing is on the increase in Cardigan and it is high time it was checked. It is very disturbing that young boys like you take up this habit. I would like to compliment the Woman Police on her smartness in catching the boys."

Cardigan and
Tivy-side
Advertiser
1943

ANTHONY
(Born during my leave)

When my son smiles, in trust content,
  His eyes like starry midnights shine;
Fists fast about my finger bent
  Claim me his own, as he is mine.

As on his mother's breast he lies,
  My arms enfolding both, I see
In each my present paradise,
  In him my immortality.

Grey ships unshackle from the buoy,
  The convoy weighs, and leave is done,
But grief can never quench my joy,
  For I have lived to see my son.

Personal, deadlier, bolder now
  Each blow I strike, so Anthony,
His harvest sure, in peace may plough
  My wilderness of victory.

D. C. BRAY.

Good Housekeeping 1943

Sister On Air Revived His Memory

New York, Saturday.

SINGING "I'm Dreaming of a White Christmas" in a B.B.C. studio, eight-year-old Sylvia Thornton, of Hull, has revived the memory of her brother, seventeen - year - old Maurice Thornton, a torpedoed merchant seaman, and perhaps saved his life, 3,000 miles away in a New York hospital.

When he heard his sister's voice, Maurice lifted his head and smiled. "That's Sylvia. She's got more grit than I have," he said.—B.U.P.

People 1943

Child Wear Increase

FURTHER action to increase the supply of children's clothing has been taken by the Board of Trade.

To enable manufacturers and wholesalers to release supplies immediately the Board are allowing them to supply this month one and a half times the value or quantity they would ordinarily have been allowed to release under the existing quotas.

This concession applies to children's clothing, which is exempt from purchase tax. For children up to the age of four clothing is not restricted.

The position will be reviewed by the Board at the end of May, when the current restriction period under the Limitation of Supplies Order comes to an end.

In the meantime, manufacturers are asked to do everything possible to increase the production of children's clothing.

Hosiery circles stated yesterday that the production of underwear is likely to be further restricted.

Daily Mirror 1941

More Dried Bananas

Mr. Mabane, Parliamentary Secretary to the Ministry of Food, announced yesterday that arrangements are being made to import enough bananas in dried form to provide all approved cases of children with coeliac disease with the supplies they need.

Daily Mail 1944

CINEMA CHILDREN PROMISE TO OBEY

By ERNEST BETTS

"I PROMISE to tell the truth, to help others, and to obey my parents." This promise, uttered standing by 2,000 children at the Odeon Cinema, Morden, yesterday, launched a new "Young Citizen" movement in the cinema which has no parallel since "the pictures" began in this country.

After the promise was spoken by Mr. Arthur Rank, chairman of Odeon Cinemas, on the stage, Arthur Askey told the children, with a song, a film, and in "gags" which brought yells of delight, that they must clean their teeth, behave with kindness, and look after their personal appearance.

Yesterday morning the same ceremony was being attended by 150,000 children at cinemas in London and throughout the country.

It was the official launching of an Odeon National Cinema Club, designed to build up ideas of citizenship and patriotism in the future generation.

Moulding character

The children pay sixpence and ninepence every Saturday morning for these shows, which are given in areas governed by police regulations.

They see cartoons and slides dealing with health and road safety, and rhymes dealing with "less bread and more potatoes."

A statement issued by Odeon Theatres yesterday declares: "Entertainment is not enough. A tremendous responsibility rests on any organisation which shows films to thousands of children. We attempt to discharge some portion of this responsibility by helping to mould the characters of the children so that they may become better members of the community."

Sunday Express 1943

YOUTHS SHUN INTERVIEWS

The majority of the youths who register in Birmingham refuse to go for interviews.

Of 7,028 aged 16½ who registered in March, 3,639 were boys and 3,389 girls. But one-fifth of the boys and one-third of the girls refused to go for an interview.

Sunday Express 1943

2 Children 'Are Not Enough'

Says Mother of 16

By Daily Mail Reporter

IF the Royal Commission on Population need first-hand evidence on how to bring up 16 children in an eight-roomed country cottage, Mrs. Mildred Booth is their witness.

Most of her children were born and brought up in the Booths' present home, Lilac Cottage, in the Derbyshire border village of Stanton (population 284).

"I think I know as much about rearing a big family as anyone," said Mrs. Booth—dark-haired, though in her early fifties—yesterday. "I'm not saying people should have families as big as mine, but I believe wives should have more than one or two children if they can afford them."

Independence

This is how she sums up the joys and problems of bringing up an outsize family in a home too small for them:

Advantages: "With 16 children you haven't a lot of time to worry about things that do not really matter.

"All my children have been taught to be independent. The older ones have taught the younger ones how to help themselves."

Disadvantages: "Money has never been very plentiful. My husband and I started our married life on £2 a week.

"No water is laid on, so for 24 years I've had to carry buckets 100 yards from the village pump. The children help, of course."

Washday Troubles

"Washday is my big trouble because, with no boiler or copper, I have to wash and boil the clothes over the fire."

Mrs. Booth's 63-years-old husband, Frank Booth, has been unable to work for two years because of ill-health, but she still finds time to be a Red Cross leader.

Three of the children have married and have homes of their own. One of the unmarried sons has left home to join the Navy, two others are dead, but ten are still living at Lilac Cottage—as well as a grandchild Hilary, who is four years older than Mrs. Booth's youngest child, Hilary's "Uncle" Roderick, aged five.

Footnote: Mrs. Booth was an only child.

Daily Mail 1944

They had never seen bananas

A sailor's bounty

A SHIP'S engineer, Gerald Ross, of Coolhurst-avenue, Hornsey, gave six dozen bananas away to Hornsey children in the streets last week.

"They did not seem to know what the heck to do with them," he said. "Some of the kiddies had never seen any before."

He brought them from the Azores, and on the way back was torpedoed 250 miles from land, but the crew managed to beach the ship on the island of Flores. After making repairs they reached Britain safely, and the ship, claimed by the Germans as a total wreck, is now as good as new, and all the cargo, including the bananas, was saved.

Sunday Express 1943

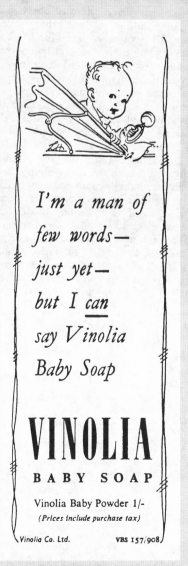

Good Housekeeping 1944

TRAINING BOYS IN HOME-MAKING

BY MARGERY CALLIS

Organiser of Domestic Subjects Instruction, Manchester

Many good things have come out of this war. Amongst them may be included an improved and more intelligent standard of nutrition; the disclosure, through the evacuation scheme, of the shocking living-conditions of sections of the community; and I would add to these the need for changes and experimentation in the curricula of boys' schools brought about by the difficulties of finding equipment and materials suitable for the usual boys' activities, and by the call-up of men teachers. The development of cookery and other domestic subjects classes for boys is one of the beneficial results of this, and has proved an immense success.

Domestic Subjects for Boys

It is interesting to note that there has never been the slightest suggestion on the boys' part that domestic subjects are " girlish " or beneath their dignity. Many of them have home duties in these days, as well as the girls. It has not been found necessary either, to win them over to a liking of cookery or laundry-work by appealing to their essentially boyish interests such as camping and scouting. Nor is the vocational aspect over-stressed; though both these elements naturally play a prominent part in the planning of a suitable and interesting syllabus. I consider that the following topics at least should be covered in a good scheme : the correct setting of a tray and a meal-table and the preparing of sandwiches and beverages; simple breakfast and dinner dishes; camp cookery and packed meals for hiking and cycling; a working knowledge of ventilation, water heating systems, electric installations, cookers of all kinds; washing and pressing of suits, shirts and collars, sewing on of buttons; darning; sponging and pressing ties; repairing and fixing tap washers; buying of foodstuffs; a knowledge of cleaning materials.

Mother and Child **1944**

Vetches Damaged By Children

Six children were at Fareham Juvenile Court on Friday each ordered to pay costs and damages amounting to 10s. for doing damage valued at £4 to vetches growing in a field belonging to Mr. A. Gammon, off Withy Bed Lane, Titchfield.

Evidence was that some of the vetches in an area of 150 square yards had been pulled up and others had been trampled down.

Gladys M. Tolfrey, a member of the Women's Land Army, said she saw the children playing in the field. Since then she had had to put up with bad language and abuse from the children, who were encouraged by their mothers.

Hampshire Telegraph and Post **1944**

'I MUST NOT CRY' SAID GUIDE AS SHE LOST ARM

BADLY injured in a road accident, ten-year-old Barbara Danree, of Middleton-on-Sea, Sussex, told the nurse at her side, "I must not cry, as I am a Girl Guide."

For her courage and fortitude during three months of operations following the accident, she has been awarded the Girl Guides' Certificate of Merit.

In the West Sussex Hospital, Chichester, to which she was taken after the accident, Barbara remembered her Guide Law No. 8—"A Guide smiles and sings under all difficulties" —and applied it so successfully that she was the inspiration of her ward.

Her head injuries were so serious that only a local anæsthetic was possible while her right arm was being amputated, so Barbara clenched her teeth and looked the other way.

Daily Sketch **1946**

SOS Oranges Help To Save Boy

ORANGES and lemons, sent to the hospital after an appeal had been made, have helped to save the life of a three-years-old child.

Raschid Mufti, of Putney-hill, S.W., was knocked down by a motor-cycle and received severe head injuries, necessitating a two-hours operation.

Raschid is now progressing.

Sunday Dispatch **1944**

AUNTIE POPPY'S MAIL BAG

Patricia M. Johnson. Your letter was most welcome, Patricia, and thank you very much for the Red Cross donation, I hope your baby brothers are quite well again. I see you have passed your music exam. Well done! Do practise, then one day you'll give such a lot of pleasure.

HOW THE COLLECTION GROWS

Auntie Poppy sends thanks this week for bottle tops from Patricia, Joan, Colin and Marjorie Ruddock, and from Carol and Anthony Richardson.

THE JUNIOR RED CROSS FUND

Auntie Poppy says thank you this week for a donation from Patricia Johnson.

Ripon Gazette **1945**

Children Like "Little Old Men"

There are thousands of Polish mothers to-day whose one prayer is that their children should die."

So said Mrs. Barbara Ayrton Gould during an appeal for the Polish Children's Fund, at a meeting organised by the London Labour Party in the Conway Hall yesterday.

"These children have been carted away in hordes to somewhere in Germany," she added.

"Many thousands have escaped, but they are suffering terribly. I have seen some who have got to Britain. They do not look any longer like children—they have been through so much that they have the faces of little old men and women."

Daily Herald 1944

Child Dies After Eating Four Bananas

Dorothy Kathleen Shippey, two-year-old daughter of Mr. and Mrs. Joseph Shippey, of Sewerby-avenue, Bridlington, Yorks, was found dead in bed after eating four bananas in an afternoon.

It is understood that other children at Bridlington have complained of stomach pains after eating bananas.

Daily Sketch 1946

Chorus of "come home to us" offers greet refugees

By Your Special Correspondent

QUEUES of men and women stood round the railway station barriers in Coventry yesterday eagerly volunteering to take into their homes the Dutch refugee children who arrived in the city.

But the 440 pathetic young victims of Hitler's Europe are in such a condition that they will have to go to a hostel for at least two months' intensive feeding and medical care.

After that they can join their foster-parents.

When the refugee train arrived, the children leaned out of the carriage windows and waved flags and a few began to sing.

One good meal on the way of stew and chocolate on the journey from the port of arrival had begun to revive their spirits, but other children were not strong enough to walk, and several had to be carried off the platform.

One was brought off on a stretcher and went straight to hospital suffering from acute malnutrition.

Among the generous people of Coventry who waited for hours in the hope that they could take home one of these little Dutch arrivals was Mr. Bernard Barker, a millwright, of Steppingstone-lane.

He had his own two children along with him—as eager as he, was himself to help these tragic youngsters.

Then there were Tiny and Betty Wainwright, who stood clutching a large box which held their sweet rations for six weeks.

Daily Mirror 1945

SOME THOUGHTS ON SCHOOL MEALS

BY EDDIE WILLIAMS, B.SC., M.R.S.T.,
Chairman, Children's Nutrition Council, Wales

The School Dinner

The school dinner, when properly prepared and presented, is the finest social and educational project ever introduced into the council schools. It should be done on public school lines and many elementary schools must be congratulated on their near approach to this standard.

I was deeply touched recently by a letter from a rural headmistress of a primary school published in the *Teachers' World*. Here it is : " We serve a midday meal for which my class lays the table. For the meal I have insisted on both spoons and forks for sweets (would you dine out twice where you were given a spoon only for the sweet course?). We have beakers for water, and while the six and seven year olds have flowers for table decorations, the three to five year olds have a toy animal, because it doesn't upset. We hold our spoons and forks correctly, even the three year olds, and when we have finished we put our spoons and forks together in the accepted style."

At a central school the other day I found the headmaster and his staff dined at a top table and six boys in rota joined them each day. At several schools a teacher or prefect acts as head of a table and does the serving. But these school dinners do make a tremendous difference to the children. Some evacuees we found hardly knew what cooked dinners were nor how appetising they could be. They now learn there are meals just as nice or nicer than fish and chips, and in them is created the liking for green vegetables and raw salads to be passed on from generation to generation. There is Grace before meat. Table manners are taught and caught. Cleanliness is certainly copied. The whole project breathes health, harmony and happiness. That is the way to fight anæmia and tuberculosis; that is the way to lay the foundations for a better British race. What an investment !

Mother and Child 1944

LEEDS BABY RESTORED UNHARMED

Taken by Girl Who Loved Dolls

It was a ten-year-old girl with a love for dolls who took away the curly-haired 18-month-old baby who disappeared from her pram in the busy shopping district of Briggate.

The baby, Mary Josephine Gallagher, an only child, was restored unharmed early yesterday to the mother, Mrs. Mary Gallagher, of Blackman-lane, Leeds. Police found Mary at an address in the centre of the city. There will be no court proceedings.

Mary's father works at Darlington.

Northern Echo 1945

All Star Comic 1945

Tʜᴀᴛ children have their rights may be a new angle to some parents. Not only their legal rights, nor even their moral rights, but childhood's own rights. These include the right to shout in the joy of being alive, to jump and skip and rush about the house, and generally make a noise. This, in reason, is just as essential to them as the food they eat or the sleep which transports them to dreamland every night.

The old adage, "Children should be seen and not heard," is responsible for many a repressed childhood and natures thrown back upon themselves in an unnatural quietude. It is an untruth, and quite a wicked one. Children SHOULD be heard laughing and singing, expanding their lungs, and exercising their limbs in running and romping. That is a fundamental law.

But, of course, grown-ups have their rights, too. In a small house where people of all ages live together, it must be understood that, for some part of the day and in some places, the children must give up their right of being noisy to the grown-ups' right to peace and quiet in which to read, or write, or merely think, without the disturbance of small voices and running feet. Surely, this is a good beginning for a later understanding of the conflicting rights of those in the wide world beyond the limits of home; and will make the children realise, while they are still children, the great law of give-and-take which must govern all human relationships, if they are to be happy.

Schoolmaster **1948**

THIS WAY, PLEASE!

Tᴀᴄᴛғᴜʟ. but firm supervision is necessary if children are to learn to write 'Thank you' letters promptly. A good approach is for Mother to say, "I'm writing to Granny; sit here beside me and write your 'Thank you' now for the present she sent you."

NOT
THIS WAY

Dᴏɴ'ᴛ encourage laziness in the little but important politenesses by saying, if he protests: "Oh, well, you hate writing letters as much as I do. But don't forget to do it to-morrow." That is to encourage the wrong attitude of mind.

THE RIGHT AGE FOR RUSKS

I am a little uncertain about how soon it would be safe to let Baby have a crust or rusk. What is the right age?

Iᴛ wouldn't be wise to let Baby have crusts or rusks before four and a half months. After that, if he puts everything in his mouth and knows how to hold the rusk when you give it to him, he is ready for it. You will find he will hold it in both hands and suck it. Offer it to him about ten minutes before a feed.

My Home **1945**

FILMS FOR CHILDREN

The recent controversy on the film, "The Birth of a Baby," makes one ponder over films in general and their effect on the impressionable minds of our children. Too many children to-day observe films which are really only entertainment for adults.

I wonder if it would be possible to acquire at least one picture house which would exhibit films for children only? These films could consist of educational subjects such as studies in bird, animal, or plant life; ship construction, agricultural work, deep-sea fishing, and coal mining. Also visits to foreign lands, with, of course, our ever-popular Walt Disney cartoons as an extra.

Naturally, it is not a very attractive idea from a financial viewpoint. But, on the other hand, there would, undoubtedly be an advance in the education of our children. What do other readers think? D. E.

Edinburgh Evening News **1947**

Stamps Versus Coins

Tʜᴇʀᴇ are two simple reasons why it is easier and more popular to collect stamps than coins.

A boy can get the first thousand stamps almost for nothing, and if he has friends with correspondents abroad he will go on getting comparatively rare stamps as gifts.

Quite common coins cost something, if only a penny each. Then there is the question of weight and space.

A valuable collection of stamps can be carried under the arm and kept in a small drawer. A collection of coins may soon weigh as much as a man and needs much more space.—W. OWSTON SMITH, Tunbridge Wells.

Daily Sketch **1946**

Good English

Pʟᴇᴀsᴜʀᴇ ɪs ɪɴᴠᴀʀɪᴀʙʟʏ ᴀᴅᴅᴇᴅ to the clarity of commercial correspondence if the letters are written in good English. However, notwithstanding the advice given from various quarters during the past year there are still many firms whose business communications leave much to be desired; what is more regrettable, there seems to be a deplorable lack of good English usage among some of the younger generation who are aspiring to business careers. The Chartered Institute of Secretaries, by virtue of its professional capacity, has a particular interest in the study and practice of the art of writing, and I hear that the Council of the Institute has been seriously perturbed at the consistently low standard of the examinees in grammar and syntax.

To give point to this matter an address was given recently by Mr. Cyril Harvey to the London Branch Students' Society of the Institute in which he emphasized that the art of writing transcended in importance every other desirable attribute of the good secretary. Few, if any, would be prepared to deny this assertion, for in all official communications the secretary acts as the mouthpiece of his board and any failure to use good English must lower the prestige of the company in the eyes of the business world.

Chamber of Commerce Journal **1949**

STOP! – *that's Bobby's milk*

You may have heard someone say " Oh, we're all right for milk ; you see, we have two children." But it's a crime to use the children's milk for anybody but the child on whose ration book you get it—it's like robbing a blind person. The children need every drop of their priority milk to build strong bones and healthy bodies.

Every child under five should have his pint of milk a day, and every over-five should have half a pint, plus what he gets at school. Don't let the children's milk reach *your* jug. Pour it straight into the children's mugs and let them have it at breakfast and tea. They need their share of canned and household milk also, for these, too, are fine body builders. Use them for the children's puddings and other milk dishes.

children's MILK priorities

Every holder of a child's Ration Book (R.B.2) gets a pint of milk a day at 1½d. a pint, or, in certain cases, free. Holders of the Junior Ration Book (R.B.4) get half a pint of milk a day in addition to any they may have at school. Children between 5 and 14 who are not attending school (excluding those temporarily absent during school holidays and absent through sickness) are authorised to obtain 5 pints of milk each week on application to the Food Office. Children temporarily absent from school through sickness are authorised to obtain one pint of milk a day on presentation of a doctor's certificate at the Food Office.

some ways with milk

The best way to make certain that children take every drop of their priority milk is to see that they drink it or have it with cereal or bread-and-milk. If children are difficult about drinking milk, vary the flavour and appearance as much as possible, for example :

Stir in a big spoonful of jam. Red jam is best as it gives colour as well as flavour.
Some children have a distinctly savoury tooth and prefer milk flavoured with a little vegetable or meat extract.

Add a few drops of cochineal or other cooking colouring.
Make cocoa with milk, whisk it well, or pour on the hot milk from a height, so that the cocoa becomes frothy.

ISSUED BY THE MINISTRY OF FOOD (S.156)

Woman's Journal 1947

JUDGE SETS FREE A 'JOYLESS' WOMAN

MR. JUSTICE OLIVER at York Assizes yesterday told Mrs. Eliza Windley, aged 36, of Dunnington, York, who pleaded guilty to forging a copy of her son's birth certificate to make it appear that he was 14 instead of 13:

"I have not the heart to say much to you or to pass any sentence on you."

An N.S.P.C.C. inspector said Mrs. Windley had been driven to desperation to supplement her meagre allowance so that she might do better for her children. She had had ten children and eight were living, aged from 14 years to six months.

The Judge imposed a nominal sentence of three days' imprisonment, which meant Mrs. Windley's immediate release.

"When one hears a story like yours one appreciates that some people have to live joyless lives and have to undergo hardship which few people in the country have to face," he said.

Daily Sketch 1946

CHILDREN TO VISIT B.A.O.R. PARENTS

A party of 27 children, aged eight to 17, leave Tilbury on Friday to spend the Christmas holidays with their parents in Germany. The scheme is being run by the British Air Forces of Occupation and transport passports and military entry permits have been arranged by the Air Ministry.

The children will sail in the Empire Halliday for Cuxhaven. Seven other children will leave Victoria on the same day to visit their parents in Austria and Italy.

Sunday Times 1946

YOUNG WALLINGFORD JOCKEY'S SUCCESS.

Alan Honeybone, aged 15, son of Mr. and Mrs. Owen Honeybone, of St Nicholas-road, Wallingford, an apprentice at Major Goldsmith's stables at Aston Tirrold, on Monday won an apprentices' race at Birmingham. Finishing first on Le Jacobin, he beat the odds-on favourite in a great struggle. This is only his third race.

Honeybone, whose grandfather is a saddler in Wallingford, has won several cups in connection with the boxing tournaments arranged by the Wallingford Amateur Boxing Club.

North Berkshire Herald 1947

BOYS LOST IN OLD MINE

FROM OUR CORRESPONDENT
NORTHALLERTON, April 25

Two Middlesbrough schoolboys—John Abrams and Harry Lewis, both aged 13—lost their way yesterday while exploring the workings of an old jet mine at Osmotherley, near here.

As they entered the mine they unravelled a ball of string, one end of which was held by a companion outside the mine. When they tried to return by feeling along the string they found it had broken. Their companion ran to Osmotherley, where a search party was organized, and the boys were found four hours later.

The Times 1948

The ONLY child

You have to know when to give way, and when to be firm, says Dr. Janet Wise.

MANY misfits in life owe their unhappiness to over-protective parents. This is particularly noticeable in the case of an only child who has not been allowed to grow up and develop mentally. So often parents do not realize the harm they are causing by mistaken acts of kindness. They have a natural desire to shield a child from hurt, but over-indulgence is the worst way in which to prepare him for a full and happy adult life.

Misplaced kindness — as distinct from kindliness — may leave a child unprepared for the harsh realities of adult existence.

Never choose your child's friends. He needs to develop his own judgment, and if everyone with whom he comes in contact has first to be 'vetted' by his parents, he will never have any standard of his own by which to go. An advanced child will probably need older companions, because those of his own age are not equipped to provide him with adequate mental companionship; but sound training should help him to find suitable friends through the exercise of his own good taste.

After all, we learn only through our *own* mistakes, and parents who control a child's life prevent him from building up any fund of experience to draw on when he grows up. It would be interesting to know just how many marriages have failed through lack of a developed judgment in one or other of the partners, dating back to wrong control in childhood.

Too often the desire of parents that their child should look only to them for help and advice is an extension of their own egos and a form of emotional tyranny. This possessiveness takes two different forms — either the parents seek to hold the child's affection by giving in to his every whim, thus making him selfish and unruly, or they keep a firm hold on his every action, making him timid and lacking in personality. In both cases it leads to difficulties at school. Too often a child who has never learned to stand on his own feet, or to mix easily and naturally with others, will be left out of games, and be hurt by the cheerful joking of other young things.

This is why day nurseries and nursery schools are of such tremendous advantage to an only child. There he will find companionship from an early age, and so will learn to give and take in easy friendship, without grasping or timidity.

Every child must work out his own problems in life, and so long as parents give advice and — perhaps, even more important — encouragement, when guidance is really necessary, their children will always have a sound basis on which to form personal judgments.

Woman's Own 1948

Danger to Baby

I have often wondered how many young mothers realize the danger to their baby's eyesight caused by having rattles, woolly balls and toys dangling from the pram or cot head. An eye specialist told me recently that this can put great strain on the child's eye muscles.—D. B., NOTTINGHAM.

(We're glad you mentioned this—Dr. Janet Wise confirms it too.)

Woman's Own 1948

SCHOOL TILL FIFTEEN

ANOTHER STEP ON A LONG ROAD

The raising of compulsory school age to 15 from last Tuesday is correctly viewed less as a striking measure of reform in itself than as a small and belated step forward in the advance which began on August 9, 1870.

Forster's Elementary Education Act did not enforce compulsory attendance at school. That was not possible at the time. To-day's accommodation problems, grievous though they are, look slight beside the million and a half places for children between six and 12 which the newly constituted School Boards had to provide.

*Times Educational
Supplement* 1947

Times and Opinions Change

THE policy in regard to exclusion of contacts of the common infectious diseases has greatly changed since Medical Inspection was introduced.

This was clearly emphasised by experiences recalled by officials of the Union who were formerly teachers, when glancing through the latest Report. They remember when schools were closed because of epidemics which do not now involve the exclusion of contacts.

The recently issued *Health of the School Child* refers to an addendum issued in 1942 to the memorandum published jointly by the Ministry of Health and the Board of Education in 1927. This addendum suggests that all exclusion of contacts of German measles, mumps and chicken-pox should be discontinued. Even the exclusion of contacts of scarlet fever, diphtheria, measles and small-pox should be less rigorous than formerly.

Schoolmaster 1948

PAN-CAKE DAY.

It's fun in the kitch-en,
　Anne can't come to play.
She's mix-ing the bat-ter
　For pan-cakes to-day!

Plip-ity plop, plop plop!
　Round goes the big spoon.
The smooth gold-en bat-ter
　Will be read-y soon.

" Oh, what a loud siz-zle ! "
　Anne cries in de-light.
" Look, mum-my ! I toss-ed it,
　And caught it—just right.

" Now hur-ry up, dad-dy,
　We real-ly can't wait.
The pan-cakes are read-y
　So please don't be late ! "

Tiny Tots 1949

Return Journey

" WHAT did they teach you to-day ? " the mother asked her little son upon his return from his very first day in school.
" Not much," the youngster reported. " I've got to go again to-morrow."

Schoolmaster 1948

Wonder 1948

Baby Limbers up

HERE is something quite new—Dr. Janet Wise gives you exercises for your baby that will help his limbs to develop firmly and make his body as supple as that of the beautiful baby girl pictured here

Baby should start his gymnastics from the fourth month; they should be done before a meal and, preferably, before his morning bath.

Remember that each exercise must be done with the utmost gentleness.

This is a good exercise because the baby's body works continuously either by lifting up his head, turning it, or by moving his body to such an extent that his tummy and back muscles contract and relax rhythmically. Hold him by the calves near the ankles, leaving the ankle itself free to move; support the instep of the foot with your forefinger.

Hold your baby tightly by his calves with one hand put your other hand under his chest and make him 'swim' through the air. As he gets stronger he will lift his head a little more, and as he does so, move your hand from under his chest down to his tummy.

Now for an exercise to improve circulation and tone up the leg muscles. Grip baby's ankles so that your little finger lies along the sole of the foot, with your forefinger along the outer part of his leg. Bend and extend the legs gradually quickening the pace in a cycling movement.

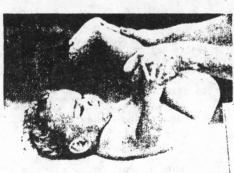

Grasp you baby's legs just below the knee. Keep the knees straight and very gently bend the legs from the hip, using slight forward pressure so that you will lift your baby's weight on to his shoulders. Repeat this exercise several times.

Woman's Own 1948

"WESTERN" PUT NEW LIFE IN RONNIE

EVIDENCE of the therapeutic value of a "Western" film is indicated in the story of Ronnie Maxfield, aged nine, who lives with his parents in Wynchcombe-avenue, Wolverhampton.

Last night a *Birmingham Gazette* reporter who visited the family met Ronnie at the gate. His eyes were shining and his cheeks were pink.

And he walked across the road to claim a £1 note which, when he was very ill, a neighbour had promised to him on condition that he collected it himself.

CAN'T EXPLAIN IT

Doctors cannot explain this "modern miracle," and his aunt said: "They still don't know what was the matter with him. He became listless and was taken to hospital and when the doctors gave up all hope for him, his mother brought him home and gratified his every wish, no matter what it entailed."

Ronnie is a cinema fan. He goes regularly to Penn cinema and he is very fond of cowboy films. A relative of the family, Mr. C. Moore, is chief operator at the cinema and one day, when he went to see how Ronnie was, he heard him tell his mother that he would like to see a film "My Pal Trigger" which he missed seeing at the cinema because he was too ill to go.

M.G.M. HELPED

Mr. Moore told his manager, Mr. H. Shawcroft, who said: "What about taking him a film and showing it to him at his home? It might do him some good."

Last night Mr. Shawcroft said: "I contacted British Lion, but they said there was no 16mm. copy of the film available. The firm got into touch with the managing director of M.G.M. London. He could not get a copy either but he was able to get hold of a new 16mm copy of another cowboy film, 'The Cowboy and the Senorita' and sent it along.

"The local education authority lent a talkie projector, and Mr. Moore took it to Ronnie's home and showed the film to him as he lay in bed. Meanwhile I took Mr. Moore's place as operator of the cinema. Ronnie was 'tickled pink'."

Last night Ronnie, who is a gentle-mannered little boy, said: "It was silly and it made me feel a lot better."

His aunt broke in: "And some days later he was able to get up."

Birmingham Gazette
1947

Silver Cross

The world's most exclusive

BABY COACH

Vogue 1949

Father does 400 lines

Mr. and Mrs. Cuthbert Sykes objected to their son Gerald, aged 13, having to write "I must learn to play the game" 400 times as a school imposition for a prank. So they wrote the lines for him.

Brother Lennon, headmaster of St. Brendan's College, Bristol, a Christian Brothers' School, refused to accept the lines. He says that if Mr Sykes does not let Gerald write them, Gerald cannot go back to school next term.

Daily Express 1949

TOURIST TRADE

Sir George urged that Ludlow, which he described as a most attractive place, should be got into shape to receive tourists, particularly American tourists, as the spending of American dollars would increase our buying power. He said that he had spent the night at a very nice hotel, but he found that when he got into bed, it was necessary to get out again to put out the light. Modern fittings were essential, as Ludlow would be in competition with other great world beauty spots such as in Italy, which he had recently visited to interview the Pope on the world crisis.

Sir George revealed that he had 15 grandchildren and he was going to do everything in his power to see that they did not starve. It was necessary to apply our Christian principles to governments, if we could get governments to act in a Christian-like manner for the good of the whole world. Instead of being in continual competition we should create friends instead of enemies fulfilling the hope of the great Father of Mankind, who would see the world in the manner that he wished it.

Several Rotarians questioned the speaker and Rotn. Bishop E. W. Sara, D.D. thanked the speaker.

Tenbury Wells
Advertiser 1947

THE NEW YEAR'S WEL-COME

"How kind of you to meet me,"
Said nine-teen for-ty nine,
When Jan, the snow-man, met him,
One night by bright moon-shine.

The snow lay thick a-round them,
Frost glist-en-ed on the trees,
The mer-ry sound of chim-ing bells
Was car-ried on the breeze.

The New Year felt quite ner-vous,
"I'm strange," said he, "and small,
And if the folk will like me,
I do not know at all."

Said Snow-man Jan : "Don't wor-ry,
The chim-ing bells you hear
Are ring-ing out their mer-ry peal,
To wel-come you, New Year!"

C. K. L.

Chick's Own **1949**

LESLIE MEETS LESAOAMA

Last Saturday morning, Leslie took a sixpenny trip to Basutoland—all from his seat at the Children's Cinema Club. Though he laughs at the cartoon and thrills at the serial he likes best to see how boys and girls live in other lands.

The Magic Globe is typical of the special films now being made for children. When the Odeon and Gaumont Children's Cinema Clubs were started three years ago few suitable films existed.

If children will go to the pictures, how can they be prevented from seeing unsuitable ones ? These clubs gave the answer by providing non-profit-making performances of carefully chosen films on Saturday mornings, when schools are closed and mothers out shopping.

At first the difficulty was the shortage of suitable pictures. But the movement has grown so rapidly that now a Children's Entertainment Film Department has been formed to make special films for the clubs : features, cartoons, serials and instructive 'shorts' such as *The Magic Globe*.

Leslie's teacher calls this geography, but to Leslie it's a new way of making friends.

 J. ARTHUR RANK ORGANISATION LIMITED

Leader **1947**

DECORATED BY THE KING: DAVID WESTERN WEARING HIS ALBERT MEDAL.

On November 2 eleven-year-old David Western, of Acton, went to Buckingham Palace, where he was invested by the King with the Albert Medal. In February, David, who is a Boy Scout, made gallant efforts to rescue some boys from a frozen lake in Osterley Park and spent some time in the icy water.

Illustrated London News **1948**

The Schoolboy

A MONTH ago, Mrs. Harrison bought two hundred coupons at one-and-nine each.

"Three years ago I would have thought it unpatriotic. A year ago I might have hesitated because it is illegal. This year I have no choice, and my only complaint is the expense."

Mrs. Harrison produces a long sheet of foolscap.

"Have a look at this ! I've just sent my boy off for his first term at school. This is the clothing list the school sent me. For a child of seven !"

The list is typewritten and single-spaced. There are forty-eight items. It would cost 260

260 COUPONS

coupons to get him the lot; more than four years' supply for a growing boy.

"It was no use getting the boy off to a bad start, being dressed differently from the others, so I raised thirty coupons of my own and bought two hundred. It broke my heart to do it."

Leader **1947**

Same Bodies—

Similar Lives?

THE problem of twins is one of those ancient chestnuts that is served up to the serious astrologer by the very tyro in the science. Those of us who have ever given public talks on Astrology can almost spot the man or woman who is likely to bob up in the first five minutes after one has ceased speaking, with the old poser— " Ah, but what about twins ! "

Well, of course, questions of this kind are a little off the mark : as most observers of human nature will know, twins are often what is called "identical"—i.e., resemble each other uncannily in features, habits, outlook—and can almost be considered astrologically as two facets of the same personality. Such births probably occur within a very short time of each other.

But there are always the exceptions—twins who differ in personality and sometimes to a striking extent in looks and superficial characteristics. It is at the risk of repeating what many readers of PREDICTION already know that I should point out that the explanation of such a difference is probably that between the arrival of one twin and that of the second, the Ascendant or "Rising Sign" may have changed or some powerful planet have passed from the Ascendant to the Twelfth House of the chart, or from the Midheaven to the Ninth House. That is, certain factors that condition the appearance of one twin may, in the case of the second, have worked out mentally and psychically rather than physically.

Hence it is possible to have twins of whom, say, the first arrival has a Scorpio Ascendant, is thick-set, dark, reserved, deeply emotional, while the second twin arrives with Sagittarius on the Ascendant and exhibits all the characteristics of that Sign—versatility, bonhommie, a love of travel and philosophy.

But one cannot get away from the fact that unless a freak birth occurs and twins are born up to two days apart, fundamentally to be born one of twins is to enter the world with another entity more closely allied to one's self than any other individual is ever likely to be. Special problems confront twins when they marry or separate : in a number of instances I know that it has been a major problem for identical twins to develop lives of their own.

WITH characteristic thoroughness, German medical scientists were exploring the problem of twins in the years immediately before the war. Probably the results of their investigations will be available to the English reading public in a few years time and will give us some valuable data on which to base our studies of twin birth and mentality. Teutonic thoroughness had gathered together an amazing number of instances of twin births and their subsequent lives. From what I remember of their tentative conclusions, there was striking evidence in favour of astrological science. For in an amazing number of instances twin lives were found to have run an identical course as regards health, career and marriage. Possibly because such statistics were easily available, the investigators had dealt with the birth dates of twin criminals or twins who were the subject of clinical observation.

Prediction 1949

Jingles 1950

Sleeping baby taken from cot

Police searched yesterday in the densely wooded countryside round Loch Lomond for a man who seized a sleeping baby from her cot early on Saturday morning.

The child, 15-month-old Jean Thomasset, is in Glasgow Children's Hospital, and last night was said to be " comfortable."

Jean's mother and her grandmother, Mrs. Edge. were asleep in the same room as the baby at the Loch Lomond youth hostel Mrs. Edge awoke to see a shadowy figure moving in the room. Later she saw the cot was empty.

After a short search the baby was found in the conservatory on the ground floor.

News Chronicle 1951

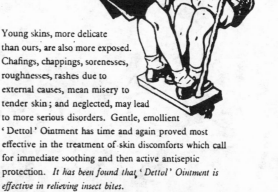

Girls will be boys

Young skins, more delicate than ours, are also more exposed. Chafings, chappings, sorenesses, roughnesses, rashes due to external causes, mean misery to tender skin; and neglected, may lead to more serious disorders. Gentle, emollient ' Dettol ' Ointment has time and again proved most effective in the treatment of skin discomforts which call for immediate soothing and then active antiseptic protection. *It has been found that ' Dettol ' Ointment is effective in relieving insect bites.*

'DETTOL' OINTMENT

Soothing and actively Antiseptic

BECKITT & COLMAN LTD., HULL AND LONDON 'PHARMACEUTICAL DEPT., HULL'

Woman 1950

Gramophone 1951

BRITTEN : MOZART. The Birds. Alleluja from " Exsultate Jubilate. K.165. Sung in Latin. **Master Billy Neely** (boy soprano), **Gerald Moore** (piano). H.M.V. B10041 (10 in., 5s. 4½d.).

Master Billy Neely gives a charming performance of Britten's setting of Belloc's lovely little poem and I commend him for his clear enunciation. (It is a pity that no one told him how to pronounce the first vowel of *creasti*). How imaginatively Britten has set the last two lines of the poem :

" Bless mine hands and fill mine eyes,
And bring my soul to Paradise."

The inconclusive end, and the way Master Neely sings it, exactly suggests the child, hands clasped in prayer, looking up to Heaven, but not perfectly sure his petition has been properly heard !

The young singer cannot quite give the Mozart *Alleluia* its joyful lilt, and even Gerald Moore, admirable in the previous song, seems affected by this. The runs are fairly well done, but the music never gets off the ground. The other side, however, makes the purchase price well worth while. A.R.

HANDEL. I know that my Redeemer liveth, from " The Messiah." **Mansel Squire** (boy soprano), **Felton Rapley** (organ). Decca X420 (12 in., 9s. 8½d.).

A young girl soprano of the Kirkintilloch Junior Choir recorded a truncated version of Handel's famous air in October 1950 Parlo. 11477) and, apart from any local interest, there seems to be little reason in letting young Mansel Squire sing the whole thing with organ accompaniment. The organ, however well played, lends a dreary, musty, hymn-book flavour to music that requires the orchestra ! And I am, it must be confessed, peculiarly allergic to this kind of accompanying. The boy has a pleasant and clear voice and the recording is adequate, but the fact remains that there has been only one Master Lough in our time.

in TENBRALAIR—
the new knit-weave Nighties and Pyjamas which stand up to any amount of washing and wear and they're warm .. warm .. warm.

every BODY needs *Tenbra*

★ TESTED UNDERWEAR FOR EVERY BODY IN THE FAMILY

News Chronicle 1951

Champion 1951

"You know who's paying for all this tuck, don't you ?" Ginger grinned at Jumbo. "It's YOU!" The news staggered the tubby Fourth-Former. But Jumbo would have been even more amazed if he'd known that this was all part of a plan to cure him of being a snob!

A Puzzling Mixture Of Ignorance, Hardihood And Crudeness

Approved School Boys Crave For Affection

WHAT are boys at approved schools really like? That is one of the questions that Mr. John Gittins, 42-years-old headmaster of Aycliffe Approved School, near Darlington, sets out to answer in his book "Approved School Boys," written for the Home Office.

Mr. Gittins meets his boys immediately after they have been ordered to an approved school, for

By DEREK MOON

Aycliffe is a classifying school where boys between the ages of eight and 17 are observed for several weeks before being sent to an appropriate training school.

Since Aycliffe was opened nine years ago, and Mr. Gittins has been there all that time, nearly 5,000 boys have passed through it, most of them after committing a number of crimes, but some being sent to the school as being either "in need of care and protection" or "beyond control."

Physically the boys seem normal, but have a characteristic round-shouldered earthbound gait, walking with their heads down, and dragging their feet. Their movements are jerky and unco-ordinated, their posture poor, but their stamina and endurance are good, their physical hardihood remarkable.

The intelligence of the approved school boy is below average. Their vocabulary is small and mental capacity limited. A boy will listen with attention and yet immediately afterwards be genuinely unable to remember what was said.

At the time of the General Election only one or two boys knew the names of even the main political parties, no boy had ever heard of G. Bernard Shaw, only a tiny minority could name three First Division soccer teams, hardly any knew the names of more than a couple of Test cricketers.

Liverpool Echo **1952**

Baby trapped in brass bowl

Mrs. Noreen Marjorie Kifford was putting her 20 months' old baby Judy to bed last night in Hanover Terrace, Brighton, when the child grasped a brass bowl and put it on her head. The bowl stuck and Mrs Kifford could not get it off.

Screaming, the child was hurried to hospital in a police car. It took a doctor and three nurses 20 minutes to get the bowl off

News Chronicle **1952**

60 schoolboys ill

Sixty of 250 boarders at Brentwood School, Essex, were reported yesterday to have had a mild form of food poisoning. Said the headmaster: "They had something for tea which did not agree with them. All have recovered."

Daily Express **1952**

Drifting boy search fails

A three-hour search by Minehead lifeboat failed last night to find Denis Eastman, aged 14, adrift in the Bristol Channel in a rowboat.

Denis of Bleadon, Somerset, disappeared after leaving a note for his mother saying he had taken food for a week. A pilot of a low-flying plane reported him eight miles off the coast at Watchet.

Daily Express **1952**

BEKONSCOT'S OWN FESTIVAL YEAR FUN FAIR: A VIEW SHOWING THE SWING-BOATS, GREAT WHEEL, MERRY-GO-ROUND, AND SO FORTH, WITH TWO CHILDREN ADMIRING THEM.

Illustrated London News **1951**

SEARCH FOR ARCHIE ANDREWS

Peter Brough doubles reward for the lost dummy

NEWS CHRONICLE REPORTER

ARCHIE ANDREWS, the £30,000-a-year star without a voice of his own, was being sought throughout England yesterday.

The "price" on his wooden head jumped from £500 to £1,000 and ventriloquist Peter Brough appealed to anyone who has Archie to return him at once.

For Archie—who disappeared during a railway journey to Leeds on Friday—is a star without a stand-in.

Without him Peter Brough will not be able to fulfil stage engagements booked months in advance. Nor will he be able to give next Sunday's show in the B.B.C. series "Educating Archie."

Archie, in his suitcase, was being taken to Leeds to compere televised Northern Music Hall at the Theatre Royal, Leeds. While Brough was dining the carriage in which he had been sitting was taken off and went to Bradford.

A check later failed to locate Archie. People who had heard of the disappearance waited outside the theatre for news.

Inside Brough went through a revised script without his protege.

Archie Andrews, wearing his "old school" blazer and scarf, in trouble—with Peter Brough

News Chronicle 1951

"I am lost"

Yesterday Brough waited for news at home in Aston Road, Moor Park, Northwood, Middlesex, and said: "I am lost without Archie. I have no plans. All I can do is hope that whoever has Archie will realise what a spot I am in.

"There has only been one Archie, and the mould from which he was made in 1942 was destroyed in the London blitz.

"I have tried other dummies, but it is no good. Without Archie it isn't the same. Apart from the controls being different, the whole illusion would be destroyed."

His worth

Archie is an expensive doll. His head alone cost £250. Until last year he was insured for £1,000. Then it was increased to £10,000.

He is dressed by West End tailors and has half-a-dozen suits—some of them costing 20 guineas.

He has been lost before: once in 1947, when Peter Brough's car was stolen in Lower Regent Street, London. Two days later Archie was found in a garden at Paddington.

On another occasion he was left in the rack of a railway carriage at Chatham, but a railway porter sent him back by taxi in time for his show.

To millions of radio listeners Archie is human. They send him fan mail and once he got an income-tax notice.

No Corns

DO your children have corns on their toes? A woman doctor says that in children over 10 years of age, a corn on the fifth toe is almost universal. Is that your experience? She suggests that children's shoes should be checked every fortnight to see they are not becoming too small.

I imagine most mothers check their children's shoes almost daily, primarily to see how they are wearing. The shoe bill for growing children is one of the biggest headaches parents have these days, the shoes in the first place costing so much, and the soles wearing through so quickly —apart from the important fact that children seem to grow out of their shoes in less than no time.

Three months is the time limit among the small members of my family.

Liverpool Echo 1952

Very great grandpa

MY father, Mr. H. Whitear, of Olnesford-road, Winchester, has been 14 times a father, 32 times a grandfather, and 43 times a great-grandpa.—(Mrs.) B. V. Hutchins, Sturminster Marshall, Wimborne, Dorset.

Daily Herald 1954

BRUMAS MAY HAVE A BROTHER

Daily Graphic 1952

Brumas keeps cool despite exciting rumours. It is whispered at London Zoo that her mother, Ivy may soon have another cub, or may be twins. But until that happy day Brumas goes on, enjoying the lime-light.

Boy told 'Don't worry over your sums'

A 12-year-old boy charged with attempted suicide was told by a Hull magistrate yesterday, "Don't worry about your sums."

The boy, who broke away in the courtroom, had taken pheno-barbitone tablets. He was sent to a remand home.

Daily Herald 1953

Woman's World 1952

CHILDREN'S CRIME?—STOP PUTTING BLAME ON FILMS

A noose killed boy with Wild West magazine

By Daily Graphic Reporter

NEAR a 15-year-old boy found lying dead on the stairs at his home were a box of crayons and a cowboy magazine open at the story of a man who was hanged.

Loosely fastened round the boy's throat was a red neckerchief and tied to this was a rope with a noose, which hung round the post at the top of the stairs.

★ ★ ★

But the boy, Michael John Tulip, of Deneford - road, Didsbury, was not hanged. It was disclosed at the Manchester inquest yesterday.

He died from shock when the neckerchief pulled tightly on his throat, a doctor told the city Coroner, Mr. Jessel Rycroft.

"Having regard to the nature of the magazine, I think he might have been trying some experiment," said Mr. Rycroft.

★ ★ ★

The parents of the boy—an only child—found him when they returned from a car drive.

Mr. Rycroft said: "I think accidental death is the proper verdict."

SAY TWO EXPERTS

By Daily Graphic Parliamentary Correspondent

TWO men who ought to know said last night the cinema was, not a prime cause of children's crime.

One was Sir David Maxwell Fyfe, Home Secretary, and the other was Mr. Chuter Ede, who was Home Secretary in the Socialist Government.

Sir David, speaking in the House of Commons on the Cinematograph Bill, which proposes wider control over film shows, said:

"It is all to easy to regard the cinema's influences on children as wholly bad and to see in it causes of juvenile delinquency, which in reality go much deeper."

Mr. Chuter Ede said: "All my life, whatever a boy has wanted to do has been the cause of juvenile delinquency.

"In my youth it was the 'penny blood.' The worst hiding I had was given me by a schoolmaster for reading 'Treasure Island,' which he called a 'blood'—and if there is a bloodier blood I would like to read it."

Hide faces

Because a boy liked to read some of the comics which were the subject of considerable talk, he did not think he was likely to go wrong.

M.P.s learned from Mr. A. Woodburn (Soc., Clackmannan) that in Inverness audiences booed kissing.

Children were bored by that sort of thing, too, he said. Mr. H. M. King (Soc., Test, Southampton) said he saw infra-red photographs of the behaviour of children at a Saturday morning cinema show.

"We saw children in the dark and intimate secrecy of the cinema register terror, shrinking away, hiding their faces and peeping through their fingers, seeing something they were frightened to see and were yet drawn to see," he said.

Aiding the law

The Bill, in addition to giving local authorities more control over children's film shows, enables the law to catch up with the development of non-inflammable films.

The Act of 1909 made only inflammable film shows subject to licence—for safety's sake. The new Bill brings all shows into the net.

Fears that it would mean the end of 16mm. film shows in such places as village and church halls, hospitals and schools were removed by Sir David Maxwell Fyfe.

He said the Government had no intention of imposing onerous and expensive safety requirements for non-commercial film exhibitions.

They would be confined to simple precautions which, he had no doubt, were already being used.

Daily Graphic 1952

Carrying on the adoption theme ...

A child knows —what then?

COUPLES who adopt children are more and more following the advice quoted in the last Home Page, to tell the children from the earliest moment that they *are* adopted.

How do most children feel in later years towards the adoptive parents who have given them a home, an upbringing, and the love that might otherwise have been denied them?

The question was posed last night by a woman who adopted a nine-day-old baby girl.

The girl is now three and a half years old. From the earliest days her adoptive mother has told her she was specially chosen from lots of other babies.

She was told so early because the woman who adopted her remembered another adopted girl who, when she was suddenly confronted with the truth, changed completely in character.

This, the woman determined, would never happen to *her* child.

"But," she asks, "how will my child feel towards me as she grows up?"

THE HOME PAGE of the Daily Express asks readers who are themselves adopted children to answer this question from their own experience. Address : "Adopted," Home Page, Daily Express, E.C.4.

Daily Express 1952

Use this to help them add quickly

DARTBOARDS in schools to help children with their arithmetic were suggested by Mr. A. A. Bloom, headmaster of St. Georges-in-the-East School, at a conference of East London teachers on Saturday.

"Why cannot children have dartboards in schools?" he asked. "Grown men have them in public-houses. They add and subtract their scores far quicker than I can ever hope to do—and I am supposed to be a much better educated man."

Daily Herald 1953

11 YEARS OF SWEET RATIONING ENDED AT MIDNIGHT

Collins Magazine 1952

Target for To-morrow

THE BOY WHO WANTS TO PLAY HAMLET

THE 'target' for 14-year-old Terry Wale is not an unusual one for an actor. He wants to play Hamlet. Most actors want to play Hamlet, and who could blame them, since it is probably the best acting part ever written?

Terry, who lives at Kensal Rise, London, says he has been interested in theatricals since 'an early age'. He joined Kilburn Grammar School when he was eleven, was keen to go in for school dramatics, and at Christmas, 1950, was fortunate enough to be chosen to play Ariel in *The Tempest*. He says he was given to understand that he was something of a success.

That must have been so, for the following summer Bernard Miles asked if Terry would like to play Ariel again, this time at Mr. Miles's private theatre, a well-known place among theatrical people. By Christmas, 1951, he had risen as far as the famous 'Old Vic', where he played Puck in *A Midsummer Night's Dream*.

After that he appeared as Chippie in the television play *Young Chippie*, and he is now understudying film actor Jeremy Spenser in the stage production of *The Innocents*.

Terry admits to not having been a very ardent theatregoer, but he tries to see as many Old Vic productions as possible.

He says his parents don't want him to take up acting as a career but he hopes, eventually, to do so. His favourite actor is Laurence Olivier, and his favourite actress Flora Robson. We hope that one day *he* will be the favourite actor of some other boy with a target.

Collins Magazine 1952

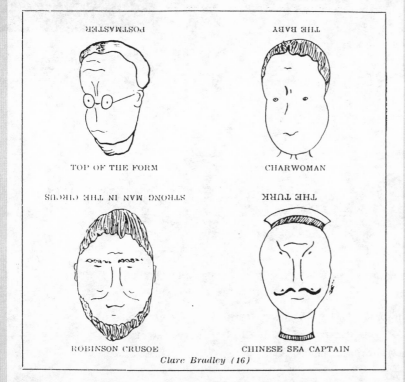

POSTMASTER
TOP OF THE FORM

THE BABY
CHARWOMAN

STRONG MAN IN THE CIRCUS
ROBINSON CRUSOE

THE TURK
CHINESE SEA CAPTAIN

Clare Bradley (16)

SWEETS came off the ration for good at midnight. Price control also ended then.

The Minister of Food (Major Gwilym Lloyd-George) made the surprise announcement in the House of Commons yesterday following advice given to him by manufacturers.

The snap statement was made because it was felt that to announce the actual date of de-rationing in advance would only encourage people to wait and then make a big rush on the shops.

A spokesman for the manufacturers organisation, the Cocoa Chocolate and Confectionery Alliance said yesterday, "When Mr. Strachey, the former Food Minister, announced well in advance that sweets would be de-rationed in April, 1949, children and others saved money for a long time and the shops were emptied.

Plentiful stocks

"Our advice to the Minister was that he would have a far better chance of ending sweets rationing now than Mr. Strachey had in 1949.

"Stocks are plentiful in the shops because the present ration of six ounces a week has not been taken up fully for many months."

Supplies of sugar to manufacturers are not being derationed, and they will receive no additional sugar allocation apart from a small one to help during the transition.

Derationing will mean a saving of some 500 Ministry of Food staff and for the sweet industry a saving of about 1,000.

Slot machines

Hundreds of automatic chocolate machines will once more be put into use.

In July, 1942, Lord Woolton, the then Food Minister, imposed a weekly 2oz. ration of sweets.

Mr. Strachey's ill-fated derationing attempt in 1949 lasted 15 weeks.

Footnote.—Fifty minutes after the Minister of Food's announcement in the House of Commons a shop in Fleet-street, London, was selling sweets off the ration.

Western Mail 1953

CHARLES AND ANNE SHOP FOR MUMMY

PRINCE CHARLES and Princess Anne went shopping yesterday—feeling so grown-up with two nannies accompanying them—to buy presents for Mummy and Daddy.

They looked at butter dishes, plaques and brooches in a Windsor shop. And on many of them were pictures of the Queen and the Duke of Edinburgh.

Daily Mirror 1953

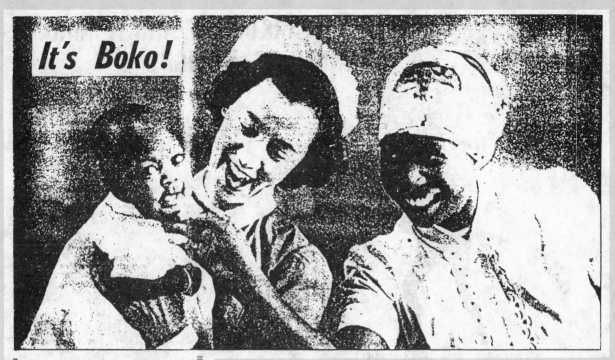

It's Boko!

Last night's picture— and she's the

BABY OF THE YEAR

THE "Daily Mirror" chooses **BOKO** survivor of the Siamese twins, as The Baby of the Year.

She is seen here last night in this first picture of her out of bed, taken at Hammersmith Hospital, London, where the operation separating her from her twin sister was performed fourteen days ago.

It is a picture showing that Boko is doing well—a happy, gurgling baby as, held by Sister Fletcher, she produces a radiant smile for her mother, twenty-year-old Mrs. Veronica Davies, from Nigeria. If Boko maintains her progress Mrs. Davies hopes to take her home in January.

Daily Mirror 1953

IN "WESTERN" STYLE

For little girls who like to play at cowboys, there are the Roy Rogers cowgirl outfits, made by J. and L. Randall Ltd. The outfit shown, minus shirt, costs 59s. 3d. and is made for 5- to 7-year-olds and 8- to 10-year-olds. The skirt is made in black suedeen and the bolero in white leather cloth, both trimmed with gold fringing. The Western style felt hat has a Roy Rogers hatband. A jewelled toggle and kerchief are worn at the neck. With red skirt edged in yellow the outfit costs 72s. 3d. Another version costing 44s. 11d. consists of red bolero edged in yellow with motifs and pockets, black suedeen skirt, felt hat and Roy Rogers badge and cuffs. For an extra 13s. a gingham shirt is included.

Nursery World 1953

First at the winning post that popular 'old salt', Arthur Ransome; a few paces behind him adventurer Stevenson; on his heels that man of parts, Charles Dickens; at his coat tails, the creator of Sherlock Holmes; and swishing along at his heels, Pamela Brown

Young Elizabethan 1953

TWINS HEAD WELSH C-DAY 'BOUNTY' BABIES

Twins, born to Mrs. Jack Muff, of Vale-road, Rhyl, head the list of Welsh "bounty" babies arriving on Coronation morning.

They are accommodated in a specially decorated cot at St. Asaph Maternity Hospital, Rhyl, where they were born.

There was great excitement among the staff at the hospital when it was realised the twins were due in the early hours of C-Day.

The first baby, a boy, weighing 6lb. 2oz., was born at one a.m., and the second, a girl, weighing 6lb. 8oz., was born half and hour later. Both are doing splendidly.

The twins will be claimants to a prize of £5 in Savings Certificates offered by the chairman of Rhyl Council to the first child born of Rhyl parents on Coronation Day and also to a prize of two guineas for the first baby born in the area after midnight on June 1.

Rhyl Council are presenting a silver spoon to each baby born of Rhyl parents during Coronation week.

Mr. Muff, father of the twins, is in business as a butcher in Vale-road, Rhyl. He and his wife have three other children aged nine, eight, and four. Nurses at the hospital have already "named" the twins Philip and Elizabeth.

Popular "Charles"

The Mayoress of Pembroke Dock (Mrs. Darrell Rees) was present at Riverside Hospital, Pembroke Dock, when a baby boy was born to Mrs. Mayhew, of Victoria-terrace, Pembroke. He was named Wilfred Charles.

A baby boy, who was named Philip Charles, was born to Mrs. T. Hughes at Castlemartin.

At Panteg County Hospital on Coronation Day at 3.30 a.m. a baby girl was born to Mrs. Catherine Mary Jarvis, of St. Julian's - road, Newport. The baby is named Helen Mary, and is to receive a suit from the matron, Miss A. E. Noot.

First at 12.10 a.m..

First baby to be born in Cardiff on Coronation Day was the daughter of Mr. and Mrs. Gordon Thomas Mace, of Sloper-road, Cardiff. Born at St. David's Hospital at 12.10 a.m. the baby girl weighs 8lb. 8oz. The parents have not decided on Christian names, but they will probably include Elizabeth.

Another Coronation Day baby was a 5¾lb. boy to Mr. and Mrs. Charles Herbert Williams, of Kingsland-road, Canton, Cardiff. The birth was at 5.40 a.m.

A 7½lb. girl, to be named Elizabeth Maud, Elizabeth after the Queen, and Maud after the baby's maternal grandmother, was born to Mrs. Audrey Nellie Marshall at her home in Ninian Park-road, Cardiff. The father, Mr. Marshall, aged 25, is a regular soldier doing duty as a driver with the 53rd Welsh Infantry Division at the Drill-hall, Penarth. Mrs. Marshall is 20.

Savings Certificates

All the Cardiff Coronation babies will receive a 15s. Savings Certificate from Cardiff Savings Committee.

Awards will be made when the births have been confirmed by the Registrar and parents should apply to: The Cardiff Savings Committee, Savings Centre, Great Western Hotel Buildings, Cardiff.

The Mid-Rhondda Coronation Committee have decided to give one guinea to every baby born in the area between May 31 and June 7. Birth certificates must be produced not later than June 14 to Mr. A. F. Thomas, Midland Bank, Tonypandy.

English triplets

Triplets—a boy and two girls— were born yesterday to Mrs. Hilda Verity, who is 41, at Hillingdon Hospital, Hayes, Middlesex.

The babies are to be called Elizabeth, Margaret and Philip. Their father, Mr. William Verity, school caretaker, also aged 41, of Orchard-road, Hayes, only heard the news when he telephoned the hospital at midday. "I had a hard time believing it for the moment. I only expected one baby," he said.

Coronation Day twins were born at St. Leonards (Sussex) to Mrs. O'Neill, of Carisbrooke-road. Each weighed 6lb. The children, a boy and a girl, are to be named Norman Philip and Norma Elizabeth.

A son born to Mrs. Ceridwen Davies, of Station-street, Holyhead, at two a.m. yesterday at the Gors Maternity Home, Holyhead, will be called Philip.

Western Mail 1953

Steps needed to preserve Welsh language

A SUGGESTION that the Welsh language is dying out and that vigorous steps must be taken if it is to be kept alive, is made by the Central Advisory Council for Education (Wales), in a report published to-day, entitled, "The Place of Welsh and English in the Schools of Wales."

During the past 20 years the percentage of Welsh-speaking pupils has been maintained in only three Welsh counties. In all other areas it has declined.

In Merthyr and the Rhondda Valley the decline has been catastrophic. Both these areas were Welsh-speaking at the turn of the century but in 1950 the percentage of Welsh-speaking pupils had fallen to four in the Rhondda and 1.6 in Merthyr. Of the 329,408 pupils between five and 15 in Wales in 1950, only 69,275 (21 per cent.) could speak Welsh.

In the Council's view, the disappearance of the Welsh language would be an irreparable loss to Welsh culture, and the only feasible way in which it "can be kept alive and saved for posterity" is to see that the children of Wales and Monmouthshire are taught both Welsh and English.

Equal prestige

Equal prestige for the two languages must be secured but this can only be done if a sufficiently large majority of the people supports a bilingual policy. The schools can do much, but the support of Welshmen everywhere is necessary—parents, members of local education authorities, religious and political leaders. There must be many more Welsh-speaking teachers; the quality of the Welsh being taught must be improved; more text-books in both Welsh and English are needed and more books of light reading published in Welsh.

Dealing with the question of the second language, the report states that it should usually be introduced at the junior school stage and should be completely integrated within the pattern of primary school studies; every device should be used to exploit activities in the playground, the games field and the home as opportunities for learning it.

Present methods of teaching the second language are usually unsatisfactory.

It is found that for Wales as a whole, only 4 per cent. of English-speaking children have any real mastery of Welsh at the age of 11, but pupils whose first language is Welsh acquire English as a second language far more easily.

The Council are convinced that a satisfactory bilingual education can be provided for every child in Wales who can profit by it, but they stress that a bilingual policy can only succeed if it has full support, especially of the parents, who can determine the attitude of their children.

(More detailed extracts appear on page 3).

Western Mail 1953

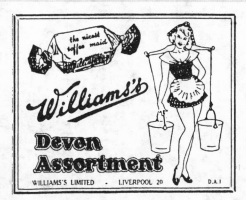
Daily Express 1954

Health and Happiness Beneath the Oaks

WITHIN the shade of ancient oaks set out in a horseshoe marking what used to be the archery grounds of Holt Hall of another age, 75 children from schools from various parts of the county are enjoying a holiday under canvas because of a far-sighted County Educational Authority and its enthusiastic officers.

In charge of this mixed camp, the first of two which will each last ten days, is Mr. J. Wilkinson, County Organiser for Physical Education, who is aided by Mr. J. Kendle and Miss Betty Smith, camp adjutants for the respective sexes, and nine other teachers, all volunteers. The children have the freedom of the lovely grounds of Holt Hall, and are having a well-organised and healthy holiday.

Mr. Wilkinson explained to a reporter that the camps began in 1946. They had as their aim the provision of a holiday for children who otherwise would probably not get one. "We have made a point of keeping the charge low—£2 per head—and arrangements exist whereby any child whose parents cannot afford the fee is provided with a holiday free," he said.

"A REAL SERVICE"

"The staff give their services absolutely free and give up part of their holiday because they have discovered that the work is worth while," he added.

Mr. J. Rutherford, H.M. Inspector of Schools, who was paying a visit, remarked: "It is a service they are doing."

The children's ages range from 13 to 18 years, and the present batch come from secondary grammar and secondary modern schools from Thorpe, Cromer, Dereham, Sprowston, King's Lynn, and Stalham. Children are not segregated by putting grammar school children together. Quite the reverse. When they arrive they are all mixed up, though care is taken in the lay-out of the camp to separate the sexes—the girls' lines, with women's staff tents at either end, running along one side of the ground, and the boys' lines similarly placed on another side.

The aim of the camp programme is to ensure plenty of organised activity for the youngsters, whose day begins at 7.30 a.m. and ends at 10 p.m. The mornings are devoted to tent-tidying and hygiene. One cwt. of potatoes are peeled daily, there is massed P.T., after which the boys go off to play one of many games, and the girls have country dancing on the Hall lawns.

TIME FOR REST

Lunch is followed by a rest hour, during which the children read books borrowed from the County Library service established in the camp. Afternoon programmes vary from sketching excursions, collecting flora and fungi for nature study, visits to the sea at Sheringham and Cromer, sports and other activities. The evenings usually produce a concert or social evening.

On Sundays the children attend, if they wish, early Holy Communion, and later in the morning a service, and at night one of the staff arranges a period of community hymn singing. There are outings in the afternoon and tabloid sports. On Saturday it will be parents' day.

Mr. Wilkinson explained that the children, who had never met before the camp soon became firm friends and quickly responded to the demands of community life. There are a few cases of early homesickness, but this soon disappears. "On Monday, when they leave, there will be tears because they have to go home," said one of the staff.

It was Mr. Rutherford who really summed up the true value of the modern approach to education and the advantages of it that have been won for the present-day pupils. He said as he watched a class of girls at country dancing: "Look at those youngsters. There is not a weak limb among them."

North Norfolk
News 1953

Vicar bans the youth club

News Chronicle Reporter

THE vicar of Christ Church, Bury, has severely reprimanded the youth club and suspended it from meeting at the school.

He says club members:

Used bad language.

Stole 39 bottles of mineral water.

Broke open a teacher's desk and damaged walls and pictures in the day school.

Boycotted a missionary meeting and played cards instead.

Disturbed a Conservative local election meeting by deliberately playing records so loudly in the next room that the candidates could not be heard.

The vicar, the Rev. M. T. Hagarty, an ex-R.A.F padre, explains it all in his parish magazine.

Three leaders quit

The 40 members of the club, aged 14 to 20, are so hard to control that three leaders have resigned in a row, he says.

"The club has been suspended from using the school premises until a new leader has been found. They have been extremely naughty, but I think it is a few bad ones who have led the rest astray.

"One of the members is a 'barracks' lawyer. He gives bad counsel and is a smart alec."

The girls' rounders team is continuing its matches. But the football team will not play until a new leader is found.

News Chronicle 1953

Nursery World 1953

DOIDY
COMPETITION RESULT
A NEW SLANT ON CUPS

The prize of £10 offered for the best photograph of a baby enjoying a drink from a DOIDY CUP has been won by Mr. & Mrs. Rose of Sundown Avenue, Sanderstead, Surrey, with a photograph of their 10-month-old baby Janet Verona. We take this opportunity of thanking all who entered this contest. In accordance with our rules a fee of £1.1.0 will be paid for any other photograph used.

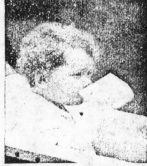

JANET VERONA ROSE

THE DOIDY CUP
IS A WINNER, TOO!

It wins praise wherever used. It is a joy for baby and a boon for mother or nurse. Contents in view all the time, and the special *slant* prevents spilling. No corners to harbour germs. Supplied in Pastel Pink, Blue and Cream from leading Chemists, Stores and Baby Shops everywhere. Price 3/11 each.

Awarded the Certificate of the Royal Institute of Public Health and Hygiene

They snuggle down quickly *with...*

DUNLOP
Hot Water Bottles

Daily Mail 1954

'We can't ban horror comics'

NEWSAGENTS spoke up yesterday against horror comics but they decided that it was the Government's place to ban them.

Members of the National Council of the Federation of Newsagents, Booksellers and Stationers, meeting at Stratford-on-Avon, argued that if they imposed a trade ban on comics it would lead to a black market in American pulp magazines.

Alderman Tom Singleton, ex-Mayor of Preston, said: "I'm amazed that people allow their children to read this type of material. It is being purchased by parents and handed on to children.

"I believe the Government is lax in taking action."

Alderman William Wood, of Hanley, Stoke-on-Trent, said it was time newsagents let the public know that they are dissatisfied at having to sell this horror comic literature.

Daily Herald 1954

A Bible each

Every child in Bedfordshire Education Committee schools is to be presented with an illustrated copy of the Bible on reaching 11 years of age.

News Chronicle 1954

Nursery World 1953

The boy from Syria

An 11-year-old Arab boy from Syria who is to have a delicate brain operation in a London hospital arrived at Stanstead Airport, Essex, yesterday, with his mother.

Doctors at Beirut decided that the operation was the only way of giving full sight to the boy, Rafic Mattar.

The operation will be done for nothing at the Maudsley Hospital, Denmark Hill, S.E., and the boy and his mother were flown to England free.

Daily Express 1954

CRIME AT CLUBLAND

THE morning papers yesterday contained melancholy news. It was the news of the vandalism at Clubland.

Clubland is perhaps the most famous British youth club. It is in Camberwell, a London suburb, and stands as the life-work of its founder, the Rev. J. Butterworth, a Methodist minister.

For more than 30 years it has been honoured and cherished by the boys and girls of the neighbourhood. Until now. Now, to the disgrace and shame of those who did it, Clubland has been wrecked and ravaged by young hooligans.

If this had been an isolated incident it would have caused less anxiety. It was not. Damage at Clubland has been going on for months. Not far away is Clapham Common, where last year a gang of youths were involved in murder.

The other day we said here that Britain had raised no finer generation than the present one. We believe that. The best of our young men and women are incomparable. But the worst are our shame and scandal.

Daily Mail 1954

Dundee Courier and Advertiser 1954

WHY BOY WORE THEM

Wet or fine

RAIN or fine, the people of High Spen, Durham, saw a 13-year-old grammar school boy wearing wellington boots and a mac. And always, even in the holidays, he carried a satchel.

Yesterday he told a juvenile court which was considering whether he was in need of care and attention that this was "unjust punishment" by his parents.

He was forced by his stepmother, he said, to wear the boots, coat and satchel because she accused him of stealing.

His father threatened to take him away from the grammar school if he did not do as he was told.

'SHABBY'

The stepmother said that he carried the satchel because he thought she was taking things from it.

He wore the raincoat because he wanted to hide his shabby trousers and the wellingtons because he wore out shoes in three weeks.

She denied he was forced to wear the things.

An N S P C C inspector said that the family had received anonymous letters complaining about the way the boy was treated.

The boy was put in the care of the local authority. Said the chairman, at Gateshead, Miss Ruth Cowan: "I hope you will be happier now."

Daily Herald 1954

TALES OF IMAGINATION

WILLIAM GOLDING: *Lord of the Flies.* Faber and Faber. 12s. 6d.
NEDRA TYRE: *Journey to Nowhere.* Collins. 9s. 6d.
JOSEPH HAYES: *The Desperate Hours.* André Deutsch. 10s. 6d.

During an atomic war an aircraft carrying a number of small boys crash-lands on a coral island. The crew have been killed, and the boys are left alone. There is fruit to eat for the picking, there is a clear pool for swimming, in the forest there are piglets to be caught and eaten. What will happen to these children, the youngest of them about six years old, the leaders perhaps twice that age? In a remarkable fantasy called *Lord of the Flies* Mr. William Golding answers that question. The story is fantastic in conception and setting: but with so much of strangeness granted, *Lord of the Flies*, like all successful fantasies, enlightens and horrifies by its nearness to, rather than its distance from, reality. Accept the idea of children being set down on an island in conditions that preclude the possibility of starvation, and this is really how they might behave. A leader is elected, Ralph; a boy honest, tenacious, not highly intelligent but aware that the first requirements are to build shelters and to keep a fire burning day and night. A routine of duties is arranged; there will be fire stokers, shelter builders, hunting parties to catch pigs. But the routine becomes tiresome and is not maintained; the smaller children believe that there is a beast in the forest, and it is only one step from belief in the beast to worship of it, one step more to the idea that the beast must be propitiated by a human sacrifice. A new chief is chosen who fulfils the children's desire for a reversion to primitivism, and the old chief becomes in the natural course of things a scapegoat.

Perhaps this makes *Lord of the Flies* sound too much like a variation on a Frazerian theme. It is that, incidentally; but taken purely as a story it is beautifully constructed and worked out, with the various children just sufficiently individuated and with tension built up steadily to the climax in which the scapegoat is hunted over the island.

Times Literary Supplement 1954

Daily Express 1955

FAMILY AT MRS. MUFFIN'S BEDSIDE

Express Staff Reporter

ANNETTE MILLS, who presents Muffin the Mule, TV's best-loved character, was critically ill early today.

Yesterday—when she was scheduled to appear in Children's Hour with her own glove-puppet Prudence Kitten —she was taken from a nursing home to the London Clinic for a major operation.

And early this morning her brother, actor John Mills, said:—

"All of us, her family, have been with her all day. And we are staying all night."

EXHAUSTED

Miss Mills became ill last November. It was said then that she was suffering from exhaustion.

She always appeared on TV as Muffin's human partner. While the puppets' creator, Miss Ann Hogarth, was out of sight, pulling the strings, Miss Mills played the piano, sang, and talked to Muffin. His stage was the top of her grand piano.

She composed all the songs for the show, more than 400 of them. The theme song opened:—

Here comes Muffin, Muffin the Mule.
Dear old Muffin, playing the fool.

Miss Mills, who started on the stage as a dancer, wrote popular songs too. And of these, the one like most was "Boomps-a-Daisy."

She has written several Muffin story books, all best sellers with the children.

ANNETTE MILLS
With Muffin the Mule

Mother and babies fall under express

A woman with a baby in her arms, and holding another by the hand, fell in front of the Devonian express at Derby Station last night.

After the train had passed over them, they were brought to the platform.

All three were taken to hospital. They are not believed to be seriously injured.

The woman is Mrs Dorothy Louise Pedley (27), Ryknell Road, Littleover, Derby.

In her arms was her seven-month-old daughter, Jane. She was holding by the hand her other daughter, Susan, aged four.

A station official said, "People screamed as the woman and her children fell on to the track right in front of the train.

"We expected them all to be dead. But when we crawled under the train we found the eldest child under the tenth coach sitting up between the sleepers crying.

"The baby was also crying. All three were carried on to the platform.

"The woman appeared to have hurt her leg and to have a head injury, but there seemed little wrong with the children."

Dundee Courier and Advertiser 1954

You can't cuff a boy nowadays

THESE days, it was said in defence of a policeman yesterday, even parents hardly dare lay a hand on their own children.

Police-constable Walter Mowle, of Inverness-avenue, Southend, had separated two boys fighting in the street.

One was his son. The other, 12-year-old Peter North, of Brightwell-avenue, Southend, through his mother, summoned the policeman for assault.

Mr. J. C. Lamb, defending, said that in parting the boys Peter's shirt was ripped and he was slapped by Mowle. "Had this case been brought a generation ago it would have gone no further." said Mr. Lamb.

Mowle, who pleaded guilty, was given an absolute discharge at Southend. But he had to pay £1 1s. costs.

Daily Herald 1954

OVERWHELMING HANDICAPS

A little child in our modern society certainly has the odds against it where drink has played a devastating role in the home. We are not in the mood for quoting statistics, but any intelligent observer knows today of the innumerable broken homes, of the divorces resulting from drink, of children who, because of godless, inebriate parents, are whipped in the race of life before they start.

The second dog that pursues the soul of innocent childhood belongs to our modern pernicious literature, these hell-raising, murderous comics, sexy movies, liquor advertisements in magazines and the vicious conscienceless propaganda poured into their young minds and souls through television.

CRIMINAL LACK OF RESPONSIBILITY

And what might be the third evil? It is the neglect, the thoughtlessness, the criminal lack of responsibility on the part of leaders, educators, preachers, fathers and mothers concerning rampant perils of the day. Belonging to it also is the belief that it is of no use to fight, that nothing can be done, that no reform is possible. We may rest in a state of lassitude but God will condemn us for our inactivity. There are some things to which we may become justifiably resigned, but if we do not exert ourselves to destroy the evils that dog the human soul, especially the moral interest of our children, how can we escape what will inevitably be poured out on such indifference in the Judgment Day?

British Sentinel 1954

National Baby Week

IN earlier years the National Baby Welfare Council was concerned with the physical aspects of child care, in view of the very high infant mortality rate which existed during and after the 1914-18 war, and it was largely because of this that the first National Baby Week was inaugurated. Now the infant mortality rate has been so reduced that the Council is devoting its attention to the equally important emotional needs of children and, consequently, the slogan of National Baby Week, which will take place this year from June 5th to 11th, is "Happy Homes Rear Happy Children." For it is only too true that a stable family background is very often lacking today and family life is sometimes conducted to a background of tension, disharmony and even irresponsibility.

As usual, national competitions are being organised in connection with Baby Week. A Sewing Competition, which started in March, will run until the end of August. Competitors may apply for a free pattern of one of six different baby garments and there will be a prize for each month of the Competition and a final prize for the best of all entries. Particulars may be obtained from the Secretary, National Baby Welfare Council, 31 Gloucester Place, London, W.1. (Do remember to enclose 1½d. stamp for reply.)

During National Baby Week the Council urges all parents to give some thought to home atmosphere and to consider whether they are providing the happy background, free of tension and built upon the solid foundations of affection and security, which is so necessary to all children.

Townswoman 1955

Main line clear

It started, as most Hornby railways do,
with a Hornby Train Set. But half the fun is adding
accessories and planning development to the system!
There are plenty of accessories to choose from — many
kinds of rolling stock, different track parts,
stations, turntables, level-crossings, etc. — all
made in strong metal to withstand the rigours of a
hard-working playroom railway.

HORNBY *Clockwork* TRAINS

MADE IN ENGLAND BY MECCANO LIMITED, BINNS ROAD, LIVERPOOL 13

Daily Express 1956

*Broadstairs
and St Peter's
Mail* 1955

BOY IMPALED ON RAILINGS

TRYING to reach a tame jackdaw in a tree, a 14-year-old boy slipped and impaled himself on iron railings at Minster on Sunday morning.

Dennis Sloane, of 4 Bradley-road, Ramsgate, sustained an injury to his groin. He was impaled on railings at the side of the road near Sevenscore Farm, Minster.

Dennis was helped off the railings by other boys and given attention by P.C. Hunt, who was on motorcycle duty. He was taken by ambulance to Ramsgate General Hospital but was not detained.

*Picture
Post* 1955

Dog at the doc's

I love dogs, but I feel that there are signs of dog worship being carried to extremes. I was recently waiting to see the doctor. There was

a woman with a baby and another with a peke on her lap. All the other women there were interested in the dog. They twiddled their fingers to attract its attention, tried to talk to it. But not one showed the slightest interest in the baby.

CHARLES ABRAMS,
WIMBLEDON.

Roxy 1959

HE CRUSHED ME JOYFULLY TO HIM. HIS LIPS PRESSED HARD ON MINE. AND I KNEW THEN WHAT IT MEANT FOR THE VERY HEART OF YOU TO FLOAT!

Townswoman 1955

" Comics and Your Children "

The " Comics Campaign Council " has produced a booklet entitled *Comics and Your Children*, in which the author, George H. Pumphrey, Headmaster of the County Primary School in Dover, compares traditional British comics with so-called American comics. Here are one or two of the statements made in the booklet which show that the problem is one of considerable importance : " Over 350,000,000 comics are sold annually in Britain, and each of these comics is said to have an average of eight readers." " Some of the comics available in this country are more horrible than they have ever been. . . . The latest development is the growth of ' horror comics,' which are quite nauseating in their use of phantasy to exploit violence and degradation." Practical evidence of this last point is given by reproduction of illustrations which have appeared in " horror comics." On the positive side the author analyses steps that have been and still need to be taken to deal with the menace. The booklet costs 6d. (7½d. post free from the " Comics Campaign Council," 23 Tillingbourne Gardens, London, N.3).

Film Strip

The National Union of Teachers has prepared a film strip with speaker's notes on the " Horror Comics " Exhibition which it held towards the end of last year. Copies of the strip may be purchased (price £1 11s. 3d.) or borrowed (free). Enquiries should be addressed to the National Union of Teachers, Hamilton House, Mabledon Place, London, W.C.1.

NEW CATALOGUES

THE METTOY CATALOGUE is always the first in the field every year. It's annual appearance is always cleverly timed in order that many of the firm's customers may receive it at the Harrogate Fair. For the benefit of those who have not yet received their copies, we would recommend that they do so immediately, for the catalogue itself should be in the hands of every first-class stockist.

There is an extensive variety of mobile toys, ranging from sparking tanks to paddling ducks, which, apart from running around, actually open and close their beaks and quack. There are a number of beautifully designed friction drive models and amongst the new novelties introduced there is a certain winner in "Jack and Jenny," a tortoise with a rotating and balancing monkey on its back, with a swinging arm. Attention will be attracted by the model Hoover washing machine, which has been set out in all mechanical detail. It is an exact replica of the real thing, and Mettoy are to be congratulated on producing such a wonderful model.

There is a galaxy of train sets which should please the most critical juvenile and the young lady about the house will really enjoy herself with any of the domestic toys, which include kitchen ranges, carpet sweepers and mechanical sewing machines. There is also an ample supply of cracking pistols and water pistols and a safety dart set, which should appeal to all marksmen.

It is pointed out that catalogues form a very valuable sales aid as they can be utilised as pocket showrooms by toy salesmen throughout the world. Look through the Mettoy catalogue thoroughly and you will agree with this statement in full.

British Toys 1955

TV COWBOY SAYS 'I QUIT THE RANGE'

By REG SCOTT

ROSS SALMON, the B.B.C. television cowboy, is to quit riding the range.

"Posing as a super-fit cowboy to children has been rather a fraud," he told me yesterday.

I haven't been fit for years.

"Now I'm packing up my ranch and all that it means to me. I shall never ride again."

Their Hero

Ross, owner of the Lazy "S"-ranch at Longdown, Devon, and hero to thousands of children who have heard his cowboy adventures on TV, was lying in bed at the Royal Devon and Exeter hospital, Exeter.

Thrown from his horse Faithful on Monday in Rattlebrook Valley on Dartmoor, he had crawled around for nineteen hours in five degrees of frost until he was rescued.

Thirty-four-year-old Ross said: "I'm the victim of an old man's disease—osteo-arthritis—following a plane crash in the South American jungle and have to wear a spinal jacket.

"I've been warned that in a few years I may be crippled."

[Osteo-arthritis is the medical term for inflammation of a joint.]

Ross added, bitterly: "Some people seem to have suggested that my ordeal on Dartmoor was a hoax, but it was no stunt, I assure you."

Miss J. Lieper, the hospital matron, said: "Although no bones were broken Mr. Salmon was shaken and shocked by his experience."

A private doctor who has attended Ross said: "He did the sensible thing in crawling rather than trying to walk."

Daily Mirror 1957

THE PRINCE? ABSENT, SIR

PRINCE CHARLES did not attend his preparatory school in Knightsbridge yesterday. The headmaster received a message from Buckingham Palace that the Prince would not be coming.

Said the headmaster last night: "I don't know why the Prince did not come to school. It would not be usual for me to be given an explanation. I expect him here tomorrow."

A Palace spokesman, when asked the reason for Prince Charles's absence, said: "I am sorry, I cannot help you."

News Chronicle 1957

Punch 1959

MOTHER ... when a bright lad seems dull

Maybe it's constipation that is dulling his wits and putting a damper on him.

That's when nature sometimes needs a little help, and the wise Mother relies on 'California Syrup of Figs'.

Here is a purely vegetable laxative containing extracts of senna and ripe figs. Its action, gentle yet effective, can be relied upon absolutely. Next time your boy is listless, bilious or off-his-food — or shows other signs of constipation—give pleasant tasting 'California Syrup of Figs' . . . it's grand for grown-ups, too.

'California Syrup of Figs'

The natural laxative

If a family laxative in the form of TABLETS is preferred, remember to ask for 'Califets' — pleasant tasting, easily chewed . . . 'CALIFETS'.

Woman and Home 1957

BIRMINGHAM YOUTHS PREFER CAPS

Headgear Poll Result

By a Woman Staff Reporter

Men's elegant headgear of many kinds lined the table when I visited the Hatters' Information Service headquarters in Birmingham yesterday.

I went there to learn the result of a check conducted in the city in which 500 youths and girls were interviewed to discover their tastes in hats.

I looked hopefully at a neat little trilby and with positive eagerness at a dashing Robin Hood type of hat with a feather. I even pointed at the sober homburg and the lightweight summer hat which was the national choice by the youth of the country. But no, there was the choice of Birmingham's youth at the far end—a cap.

Girls Agree

It was a smart cap—as caps go—but even the Hatters' Information Service officials agreed that it was an unexpected result for the second city of the country. The 400 boys between 15 and 20 interviewed were supported by the opinion of 100 girls of the same age group.

Only in Leeds did the cap also top the poll among the youths, but there the girls placed it fourth in order of selection. Youths in Manchester, Glasgow and Bristol chose a lightweight summer hat and in London and Edinburgh a lightweight sports Tyrolean-type hat.

" I think Birmingham's youth chose the cap possibly because it is such a big industrial area and because this particular age group is interested in sport," Mr. H. Chevalier, of the Service, told me.

Spanish-style Hat

I was just digesting that one when he gave me an even greater shock. Most of Birmingham's youths might vote for the prosaic cap, but they go wildly romantic in their choice of a hat style especially designed for young men.

Out of four such hats, they were the only ones in the country who choose the most original and unusual of them all — a Spanish - influenced flat-crowned lightweight snap brim, called " Mambo." The national choice was a green velour Tyrolean hat which looked almost plain against the " Mambo."

The question " What hat does your father usually wear ?" brought out the fact that in Birmingham the majority of fathers wore a cap, usual in most industrial towns. Those who had a hat also favoured the formal type of trilby.

In their choice of suit, the boys followed the rest of the country and selected a double-breasted light fawn flannel suit with wide lapels and medium narrow trousers.

Birmingham Post 1956

Topper 1957

AMBLESIDE SCHOOL PRESENTATIONS

At a ceremony at the infants' school, Ambleside, on Friday, Miss Mabel Shegog was presented with a VHF radio to mark her retirement after serving as headmistress for 16 years.

On the same day at the senior school, Mr. J. R. Ellerby, assistant master, who has been appointed headmaster of Grayrigg School, was presented with a wristlet watch and a tobacco pouch.

Both presentations were made on behalf of the managers, staff and scholars of the respective schools and among those present were the Bishop of Penrith, the Rt. Rev. S. C. Bulley and the Rev C. H. Jobson (curate).

Westmorland Gazette 1959

Dandy 1958

...The One-and-Only
RUPERT

NOW FOR THE FIRST TIME HE GOES TRAVELLING ALL OVER THE WORLD...

FOR the first time this Christmas the world-famous Rupert Annual will be on sale in substantial quantities in France and Germany, in Scandinavia, and across the Atlantic in Canada and America.

Thus a new chapter of achievement is added to the astonishing story of little Rupert Bear—for the circle of his admirers now spans the world.

No children's annual ever published has had such phenomenal success as Rupert.

And the reason for its stupendous success is simple.

For no character has ever stolen the hearts of children everywhere as Rupert has done. He has made himself the No. 1 Family Favourite in millions of homes.

His clothes

Take a look at the picture of this year's Rupert Annual, shown here. Rupert is the same jolly little bear that he was more than 35 years ago

when he first found a warm place in the children's affections.

He still strides out on adventure in his striped trousers, pullover, and muffler.

His friends

He still collects round him a cluster of little animal friends, lovable as himself, who follow him on land, sea, and in the air to the weird homes of the birds, of conjurers, professors, dragons.

★☆★☆★☆★☆★☆★☆★

KNIT HIM FOR CHRISTMAS

You'll find he's the star attraction in the stocking

Yes, he's easy to knit in time for Christmas — and wonderful when he's finished . . . in all the colours you find in the Rupert Annual. Knitting instructions and patterns free. Send to "Rupert Knitting-Leaflet," Daily Express, London, E.C.4, enclosing 2½d. stamp for postage.

★☆★☆★☆★☆★☆★☆★

or even Father Christmas himself.

Rupert—so homely, so full of mystery that thrills all children, of all ages, everywhere.

His eagerness has a quality they share; his despairs are something they can feel. He lives for them, and never fails them.

Rupert and his adventures in the all-colour RUPERT ANNUAL—now on sale in the shops—will be wanted by every child this Christmas.

In addition to the stories they will find in it a Painting Contest with cash prizes to the value of £200.

MAKE SURE OF YOUR COPY. Get it now while stocks are in the shops or ask your bookseller or newsagent to reserve a copy for you.

The Rupert Annual costs only 4s. 6d. It is this year's most wanted, least expensive Christmas gift book.

Here is Rupert as he will look when he is knitted...

Daily Express
1956

WORKING WITH CHILDREN

Right Method

Wrong Method

Punch
1959

Children play in the courtyard of a Gorbals tenement, Glasgow, 1958.

Q AND A ON POLIO VACCINE

Parents can withdraw children from scheme at any time

By John Waddell

PARENTS who have consented to their children being vaccinated with the new polio vaccine can still withdraw at any time even if they have agreed in writing.

That was one of the answers given by Mr. Turton, Health Minister, to 15 questions put to him by Mr. Peter Freeman (Lab., Newport) in the Commons yesterday.

Other points from Mr. Turton's replies:

Q.—Why is a second injection necessary?

A.—To increase immunity, it will be given at an interval of not less than three weeks. Where the injection is given after June 9, the second will be given in the autumn.

Q.—Will compensation be paid if the child dies or is ill after inoculation?

A.—No absolute guarantee can be given, so the question of compensation does not arise.

Q.—Is any alternative vaccine available?

A.—No.

Q.—Are children who have had tonsils and adenoids out,

or been inoculated with any other vaccine, more susceptible to polio?

A.—No: except in an area where there is a serious outbreak of the disease

Q.—Does the vaccine give children a mild form of the disease?

A.—No. No segregation after inoculation is necessary.

Q.—Is the danger of polio declining?

A.—There is no evidence to support that, but the vaccine will give considerable protection.

News Chronicle 1956

NOW every Dinky Toys enthusiast can have a Dinky Toys Collector's Licence, which in the Dinky Toys world is equivalent to the driving Licences of real motorists. All that he has to do to obtain his licence for the current year is to write for it to the Secretary of the Club at Binns Road, Liverpool 13.

The Dinky Toys Collector's Licence is the same size as a motor car driver's licence, so that holders will be able to carry them in their pockets, ready for use at any time. Each has a printed Registration Number, with space on the inside front cover for the holder's name and address. It becomes valid when he adds his

DINKY TOYS
COLLECTOR'S LICENCE

1958-9

The cover of the Dinky Toys Collector's Licence for 1958-9 looks like this, but is in an attractive colour. It is something that every Dinky Toys owner must have.

Meccano Magazine 1958

Chained to his bench

LIKE A GALLEY SLAVE!

THIS WAS HOW NICK MORROW SERVED HIS APPRENTICESHIP IN OLD LONDON.

But Nick didn't stay at his bench. YOU'LL SEE WHY NEXT WEEK IN THE GREAT NEW PICTURE-STORY—

QUICK NICK

THE LIGHTNING LOCK-PICKER OF LONDON.

Dandy 1958

A busy scene with the new Dinky Toys Hudson Hornet and Hillman Minx cars, with glazed windows, in a realistic and easy-to-arrange garage setting.

Meccano Magazine 1958

Concerts for Children

Then in 1923 they felt able to embark on a project that had been in Robert Mayer's mind for years — a series of concerts for children. And so there came into being the famous Robert Mayer Concerts for Children.

The first concerts were conducted by Sir (then Dr.) Adrian Boult. When Boult left London to take over the Birmingham Orchestra his place was taken by Malcolm Sargent, always an enthusiast for bringing music to young people. And Robert Mayer provided not only money but organisation, setting out to secure the co-operation of schools and local authorities, pushing and pestering and badgering officials for interest and support.

By 1928, when an illness forced Sargent to retire abroad for recuperation, the Robert Mayer concerts had spread all over England.

This was the time when the great upsurge in broadcasting and recording made many music lovers fearful for the future of 'live' music. Robert Mayer decided that the thing to do was not to fight radio and the gramophone, but to collaborate with them, to bring the best music at the lowest possible prices to thousands of up-and-coming music lovers all over the country, to give them in their impressionable years a knowledge of music and a feeling for its sound in the concert hall.

During the nineteen-thirties the number of concerts given under the scheme grew from 38 in a season to 65, in 25 different towns and cities all over the country. And children, first experiencing music in actual fact, gradually grew up to provide what became, during the war, the large group of people who found that they needed music in their lives—and who then demanded it.

For it is obvious that the widespread growth in musical interest in this country, during the war and the years that followed, had its germ in Robert Mayer's idea of bringing real, live music to hundreds of thousands of young people.

In 1937 Sir Robert and Lady Mayer again put their hands into their purses to found the Moulton-Mayer Award — a prize for young students, competed for annually at the Royal College of Music, and carrying with it the right to a London solo recital at the Wigmore Hall — the usual debut recital for a young artist, but which many find it impossible to afford. Many fine young artists have been, in this way, "discovered" and given their first chance to play or sing in public—at the expense of the Mayers.

In 1939, just before the war, teachers and music lovers all over England made representations to the authorities for some recognition of Mayer's work. The result was that he was knighted.

After the war conditions were different. Local authorities became more alive to the need for providing music, and local orchestras began their special schools concerts. Sir Robert and Lady Mayer decided to confine their activities to London, with the famous Robert Mayer concerts now being given regularly on Saturday mornings in the Festival Hall.

Music and Musicians
1959

A.I.D. 'not a sin' say Modern Churchmen

A.I.D. should not be regarded as a sin—at the worst it is "ill-advised," says the Modern Churchmen's Union in evidence submitted to the Home Office departmental committee on artificial insemination.

The committee has asked for a delegation from the union to meet it on Tuesday when the evidence will be discussed.

The union, whose president is the Bishop of Birmingham, Dr. John Wilson, says A.I.D. should be used only as a last resort.

'Enriching'

Some people envisaged A.I.D. as another step in the depersonalisation of human relationships and dreaded the perceptible drift towards an Orwellian 1984.

"Far from encouraging an Orwellian 1984, or a Huxley brave new world, the actual results of artificial insemination will be to humanise and enrich a number of lives that would otherwise be sterile and unfulfilled . . .

"We would object with all our might to legislation that turned the fulfilment of a woman's natural desire for a child into a crime."

Evening Standard 1959

Dandy 1958

Hardwearing, healthy, flexible, in high grade leather with finest plantation-finished crepe soles from 15/9

EAGLE sandals
as tough as the boys that wear them
Eagle Shoes Ltd. Anstey, Leicester

Woman and Home 1957

ZIP-UPS FOR LIVELY YOUNGSTERS

Boys are more colour conscious these days, so we suggest Elizabethan red, cognac, fir green or royal blue for their lumber jackets.

Woman's Weekly **1960**

THE SAD STORY OF A LETTER

"Dear Mr. Editor," nine-year-old Gea Austen wrote to the Express & News, "last Friday morning I went to buy my mummy a present for Mother's day, but on the way from Lambolle Road to Swiss Cottage I lost my purse, with all the money I have saved this year.

"The purse was gold plastic, and if anybody finds it please telephone me and I will come and get it. My number is SWIss Cottage 4809."

"She was very upset," said Mrs. Irena Ford, who shares a flat in Lambolle Road, Hampstead, with Gea's mother. "She had 25s. in her purse, 5s. belonging to my seven-year-old daughter Veronica, who had asked Gea to choose something for me. But there is still hope that somebody will find the purse and return it."

Hampstead and Highgate Express **1961**

EXTRA DAY. — The 300 children attending the Junior School in Margaret Road, Headington, had an extra day's holiday because a boiler burst They were to have gone back to school on Wednesday, but a notice was posted warning ther to stay away until yesterday

Oxford Times **1961**

WHILE I WAS OUT visiting a sick relative on Christmas Eve someone stole my child's pram from outside my door.— (Mrs.) F. E. BRIDGES, St. Leonard's - road, Poplar.

Evening News **1960**

SUNBEAM AND THE SEVEN DWARFS

Raleigh Industries Limited, of Nottingham, have recently supplied seven bicycles from their Sunbeam range of toys, for use in a production of "Snow White and the Seven Dwarfs" which is now touring the country.

The bicycles are ridden by seven midgets who play the dwarfs; singer Ruby Murray, plays the title role.

In each town visited by the theatre company, a nominated Sunbeam dealer is arranging for a special window display to be mounted and, early in each week, Snow White and her Dwarfs are visiting the shops to sign autographs.

Toy dealers in Southsea, Liverpool, Nottingham and Bradford and Newcastle, have already co-operated in this joint publicity venture and similar arrangements have been made for Cardiff, Bristol and Weymouth.

British Toys **1962**

Wise couples know that complete family happiness does not come about by chance. The happiest are those that have carefully and thoughtfully *planned* their families.

These days, more people than ever realise the wisdom of modern family planning, and appreciate the vital difference it can make to their whole future —and that of their children too.

For Family Planning is, after all, the surest safeguard of a family's lasting happiness. Why not find out more about it— today?

POST THIS COUPON NOW!

Woman's Weekly 1960

QUADS ON THE WAY

BLONDE Mrs. Rachel Sands, aged 27, was told yesterday : " The baby you are expecting in three months' time will be QUADS."
Mrs. Sands, of Castlemilk, Glasgow, already has four children.

Sunday Dispatch
1961

—by a 14-year-old girl in an essay written for the Bournemouth Civic Shield competition:

THE first few years of married life are deliriously happy and the couple feel they want of nothing but each other's company. Some, however, visit libraries or reference rooms. Others seek more active pastimes, such as bingo or whist.

Daily Express
1962

NOW MICHAEL (17) HAS HIS OWN STEAM ENGINE

AFTER SAVING UP FOR YEARS

For years Michael Thexton (17) of The Cottage, Perry's Lane, Wroughton, has been saving up to buy a steam traction engine.

Now he has achieved his ambition. He has bought the one which for many years was a familiar sight at the side of the old Malmesbury Road at Coped Hall crossroads — a five-ton Burrell, built in 1916, which belonged to Mr. Lea, of Wootton Bassett.

The big day for Michael was Saturday, when another traction engine owner, Mr. Joe Powell of Ashton Keynes, drove his Garrett 1919 model from Ashton Keynes to Lydiard Plain, Braydon, where the Burrell was waiting to be collected. From there it was towed by the Garrett via Coped Hall and Hay Lane, to Berkeley Farm, Wroughton, near Michael's home, where the farmer, Mr. F. J. Gosling, is letting Michael "garage" it.

TAKING IT TO PIECES
With the help of fellow traction engine enthusiasts, Michael will be spending his spare time for the next two years, taking the Burrell to bits, overhauling everything and putting it together again.

With Michael and Joe on Saturday was Mr. John Plaister (28) of 133 Faringdon Road, Swindon, who owns a 1919 Marshall traction engine. He bought his 18 months ago and has just completed its overhaul and refit.

The other expert enthusiast with them was Mr. Graham Neate (21) a fitter and turner in Swindon railway locomotive works, of 63 Kitchener Street, Swindon, who did the re-tubing work on Mr. Plaister's engine.

Mr. Powell, who is a diesel engine parts manufacturer, bought his Garrett in 1951 and refitted it himself. Then he bought another in 1953 and is refitting that, too.

CREW OF FOUR
All four men manned the Garrett and Michael's Burrell for the seven-mile tow to Wroughton, and later they did the 14-mile return journey to Ashton Keynes in the Garrett.

Note: Mr. Powell's Garrett does about 200 yards to the gallon (water) and a similiar distance to the pound (coal).

Wiltshire Gazette and Herald 1960

SECOND BABY FOR DUCHESS IN JUNE

The Duchess of Rutland, who gave birth to her first child, a boy, in May of last year, is expecting another baby in June.

She and her husband are both hoping for a second son.

Their first child, the Marquis of Granby, was born at Westminster Hospital, London, and was named David Charles Robert Manners.

Leicester Advertiser 1962

What's your WORRY?

Helping with Homework

Q. My little sister wants me to help her with her homework. Do you think I should?

A. Certainly give her any help she needs to get on with it. But that doesn't mean do it for her.

Warm Welcome

Q. A girl and a boy have just moved in down my road and I would like to be friendly with them. What should I do?

A. We think it is a splendid idea to offer a real welcome to newcomers in the district. One way to do this would be for you and a friend to invite the boy and girl to join in at one of your homes for some games, listening to records, or something of that kind.

Should we go?

Q. We are three 13-year-old girls and we have been asked by three boys we met to go to the cinema with them. We don't know whether we should go or not. What do you think?

A. We think definitely NOT unless you know the boys well and your parents approve of the cinema party.

Renewing a friendship

Q. I have broken friends with a girl in my form. We were very close friends before. Now she wants to make friends again. Do you think that I should?

A. It depends why the friendship broke up. If your friendship was beginning to get dull and stale, we don't think there is any point in trying to start it up again.

Too possessive

Q. Some time ago I met a boy at a fair and liked him very much. I often saw him after that because he lives near to us. One day I saw him with another girl. Now I am very unhappy. Could you tell me what to do?

A. You really must stop being so possessive, you know. Just because you like this boy you cannot expect him to show no interest in any other girl. If you find him attractive, it stands to reason that some other girls will find him attractive too.

Girl 1961

Biggest Ever Publicity for Rosebud Dolls

Two outstanding dolls will be the subject of a major campaign this year and the manufacturers will be punching home their story through the medium of television, national press advertising and point-of-sale displays.

The two dolls are the Wonder Bay and the Chatty-Cathy talking doll, both of which are the products of Rosebud Dolls Ltd., The manufacturers boast that no celebrity has ever been accorded a press and television coverage as large as that being accorded to their two protegés.

A television advertising campaign will commence in September and run for three months during the peak selling period to cover all I.T.V. stations in

The Rosebud "Wonder Baby."

Great Britain, and it will be put over at a time which is just right for the children, i.e. 5 p.m. to 5.30 p.m. It will also be backed up by advertising in the mass circulation women's magazines.

In addition, free of charge, for retailers there will be sales-winning window display ads. The displays are available immediately upon application to the manufacturers.

The Rosebud Wonder Baby retails at £4 19s. 6d. and has a small clockwork unit which is easy to wind up and is unbreakable. She is 20in. in length and is dressed in an attractive blue and white knitted romper suit. She moves her head, wriggles, puts her thumb in her mouth, and holds her toes. Each of these movements is completely natural, smooth and unjerked.

Chatty Cathy is a talking doll made under exclusive patent with a voice that is natural and childlike and speaks ten separate phrases. She is 21in. tall and is dressed in an attractive blouse and pinafore dress available in a choice of two colours. She retails at £5 19s. 6d.

There is, of course, a large range of Rosebud Dolls and these two winners will stimulate sales for the whole of the range.

British Toys 1962

Ideal Home 1963

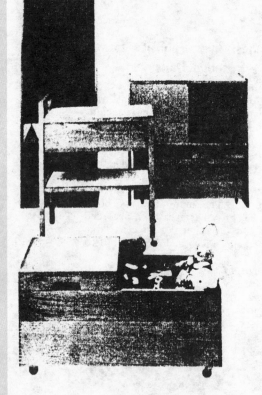

Fresh approach to children's furniture comes from technical college students. Barely out of their teens themselves, they appreciate robust construction and simple designs. The four prototype pieces (left) will be sold by the John Lewis Partnership. Another charming new design (below) at Denmark's Joinery Fair is the nursery seat and table unit that turns on its side to become a rocker, for a small child

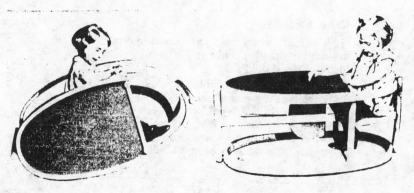

practical child's play

Victor 1961

Can children ever be made to order?

Marriageability: It is the secret ambition of every properly brought-up girl to become a duchess, failing that a marchioness, or, if the worst comes to the worst, the wife of a millionaire. And many pursue their aims with extraordinary single-mindedness. For example Jessica Mitford tells in *Hons and Rebels* how her sister Deborah – now the Duchess of Devonshire – stated her intention to fall in love with a duke when still the junior member of the Mitford Hons Cupboard and afterwards never doubted for a minute that she would reach her objective. She used to sing to herself: 'One day he'll come along. The Duke I love. . .' By the time she was 20 she had duly fallen in love with her young bachelor duke.

Town 1962

Daily Mirror 1962

CHARLES IS TICKED OFF OVER A QUICK ONE

PRINCE CHARLES bought himself a drink in a hotel cocktail bar yesterday . . . and was ticked off by his bodyguard.

For the 14-year-old Prince had ordered a cherry brandy.

It happened after he arrived in Stornoway, Isle of Lewis, aboard the yacht Pinta—training ship of his school, Gordonstoun.

Mr. Harris Mackenzie, a former Gordonstoun pupil, met him and took him into the Crown Hotel.

As Prince Charles sat in the cocktail bar with his drink in front of him, in walked his bodyguard, Detective - Inspector Green. He asked the Prince: "What are you doing in here?"

Cinema

The Prince turned, got off the stool and walked out of the bar with his bodyguard. The barmaid, Miss Christina Matheson, was asked:

"Do you know who that was?" She replied: "No, who is he anyway? Is it somebody important?"

After dining at the hotel, Prince Charles went to a cinema and saw Jayne Mansfield in "It Happened In Athens."

SOON, scientists expect, it will be possible not only to choose the sex of a child in advance but also to select strains that will make it superior in body and mind. In other words, to breed "fit, physically well-developed clever devils", as one authority put it.

This is fine for heredity, but what about environment? How far does one cancel out the other? Is it what we are or what we have that matters? Is success due to natural gifts or to the background our parents provided? In spite of the fantastic scientific advances we still know very little about this problem.

Our entire heredity is contained in the tiny cell formed at the moment of conception. Each parent gives the cell 24 chromosomes composed of genes that carry physical qualities such as blood-group and colour of eyes. It is here that scientists hope to interrupt the natural programme.

Yet even at this stage environment is confusing the picture. The mother's health and habits react on the unborn child which, by the time it is born, is already a complex product of both heredity and background.

We often comment on the differences between brothers and sisters. Environment causes many of these. Although parents insist they were all treated the same, a child's position in the family affects the way he is handled. A first child may be given responsibilities that make him old before his time. The youngest 50 years later may still demand from his wife and children the indulgence he had as the baby of the family.

Temperament, which may be inherited, impels each of us to take from our environment what we specially need. So an only boy may be allowed to dominate the household, an only girl may find that being helpless is an admirable

way of getting along in life. This is a case of heredity distorting itself.

Intelligence is not always inherited. In fact brilliant parents tend to have less bright, and dull parents brighter children. Yet again environment can affect ability. Intelligent parents are more aware of the importance of good education and of providing stimulating interests at home. It is also true that natural ability goes to seed in an atmosphere of unhappiness.

Personality is acquired, not inherited. Adopted children, for instance, are often like their parents. Children learn by imitation and take over a mother's happy nature or a father's irritability, though they may express it in a different way. An aggressive father may produce a forceful son or another who, overpowered by his father, shows his aggression in spiteful or underhand ways.

Special gifts—say, for music or science—are more likely caused by environment than heredity. In spite of the Bachs, Darwins and Huxleys it is far more common for a father's genius to die with him. His son may inherit some of the talent but not necessarily the background and surroundings that made it flourish. Greatness depends on so many factors.

Even those gifts that we consider belong only to one sex are open to question. Boys may be superior mechanically and girls in cooking but this is mostly because we train them that way. Nearly everything can be done equally well by both sexes. In some primitive tribes it is the males who are responsible for child-rearing.

Environment, then, may make nonsense of our blueprints for selective breeding. Who we are still depends so much on our surroundings.

Phyllis Hostler, M.A., Dip. Psych.

Ideal Home 1963

Octogenarian Hit By Pram

Mrs. Charlotte Swift, 82, of Fawe Park-road, Putney, had put down a can of paraffin on the footway of Putney Bridge-road, Wandsworth, on Wednesday, last week, when she was accidentally hit by a pram pushed by a woman and knocked down. She was treated in hospital for grazes to face, elbow and knee.

Wandsworth Borough News 1962

at CHILDREN PARTIES

Key your children's party to a special theme and work up (after an earnest interval for eating) to a grand finale

ALMOST ALWAYS, CHILDREN arrive bang on time for a party—and most of them are reluctant to leave at the end. It is wise then to be fully prepared for the event well before the time, and ease the parting by a spectacular finale or by presenting favours to the young guests as they file out.

Décor is of tremendous importance. A party will gain in significance if it is keyed to a specific theme—carried through décor, costume, games and food. One Mama arranged a Pink Party for her small daughter, with pink and white streamers, roses and balloons to decorate, raspberry milk shakes to drink, shrimp paste sandwiches and sponge cake with cherry jam, cakes with pink icing, and meringues Chantilly coloured pink to eat. Between games of collecting rose petals and hunting a pink slipper, strawberry ices were served to a bunch of pink-cheeked children each wearing *something* pink.

The theme might well be zoo animals, Cowboys and Indians, or fairies and pixies, with suitable decorations kept simple and functional. The over-sevens especially appreciate a gimmick and remember the occasion long after they have forgotten an ordinary affair.

Although most young social whirlers will mix in together, there is no doubt that children enjoy the company of their own age group more than older, or younger, friends. If possible, keep a party to children of much the same age.

Tea is the obvious high spot and should have some element of surprise about it. Children, like adults, remember food that is different and personal. Guests' names iced on to plain biscuits, or piped in cream on individual jellies have compulsive appeal.

One startling decoration fairly easy to make is a cooky-cake. This is a great four (or five) tier "cake" made of silver-covered cardboard or assorted cake boards. Each layer is decorated with cookies, star-shaped biscuits, ginger-breadmen, lolly-pops and chocolate fingers. Fasten the goodies to the sides of the "cake" with toothpicks or Scotch tape. Stud between the cookies with jelly sweets in jewel colours and trim with bright ribbon.

If you are tight on dining-room accommodation, children will welcome the opportunity to sit on the floor with individual boxed meals. Decorate shoe boxes and tie them up with gay ribbons. Party fare should be simple—sandwiches, selection of biscuits (cheese straws are more popular than sugary ones), a little iced cake and perhaps a jelly. The box should hold a pretty paper napkin and a picnic beaker for milk or fruit juice served separately by a senior child.

For a really spectacular finale there is little to beat an explosion of little gifts from a large papier mâché Christmas bell or cornucopia. This is filled with goodies and trinkets, sealed and hung from the ceiling until the end of the evening. At the crucial moment, the paper seal should be ripped open by pulling two crossed ribbons and the small items should spill over the departing guests.

Little toys can be attached to different lengths of tinsel so that they will drop and hang. The whole cascade should be as gay, sparkling and fairylike as possible while a packet or so of confetti sprinkled over the whole contents adds to the fun.

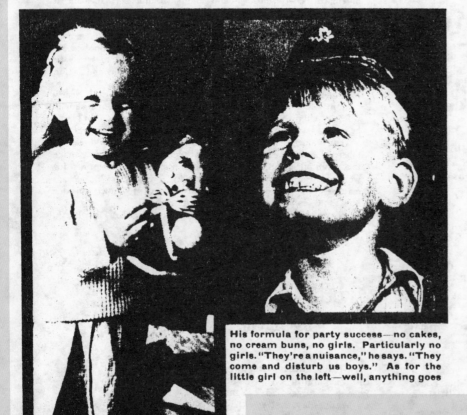

His formula for party success—no cakes, no cream buns, no girls. Particularly no girls. "They're a nuisance," he says. "They come and disturb us boys." As for the little girl on the left—well, anything goes

Ideal Home
1963

TV TOTS

CHILDREN are imitative, credulous and easily influenced. To protect them from their own natural characteristics, the I.T.A. have listed a number of new principles for TV advertisements.

Children must not be shown in situations of danger such as playing in the road, carelessly stepping off pavements, leaning dangerously out of windows or over cliffs, and handling matches.

These are excellent. So are the rules which forbid advertisers to suggest that if children do not buy a certain product they will be inferior to others, or will be letting someone down.

Such a code is not hard to apply. But one would think it more difficult to ensure that in free-gift advertising children do not "make a nuisance of themselves." How do you stop that?

Another principle is that "children seen in advertisements should be reasonably well-mannered and well-behaved." A great deal depends on "reasonably"— as every parent knows.

The darlings must not be encouraged to run wild, but we do not want to raise a breed of good little Erics.

Daily Mail 1963

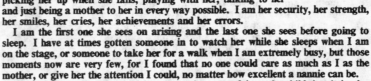

DENISE ROBINS,

confidante of thousands, author of 131 romantic novels, answers your personal problems **Straight from the shoulder**

KITT ON BABIES

SPRING is almost with us in England; and from California there comes a fascinating warmth and wealth of maternal feeling from that great artist, Eartha Kitt. She has a child and a job—an exacting one, as she is a famous international star, so I thought the following problem would interest her.

Q. *More and more young mothers today are going to work and leaving their children in crèches, or with neighbours, etc. Do you think this unfair to the children or does the extra money earned justify it?*

She answered:

Many people seem to have this problem today and though I can understand the necessity for it, I do not think it can compensate, no matter how much money is to be gained, for the love and attention the mother can give the child.

I have seen the difference in my child compared with children cared for by nannies and the like. Baby Kitt is a content, happy and well-adjusted baby, not in any way nervous, and able to take life in her stride.

I have spent many hours from the time she awakes in the morning until she goes to bed at night, doing everything for her, loving her and caring for her, changing her nappies, feeding, picking her up when she falls, playing with her, talking to her and just being a mother to her in every way possible. I am her security, her strength, her smiles, her cries, her achievements and her errors.

I am the first one she sees on arising and the last one she sees before going to sleep. I have at times gotten someone in to watch her while she sleeps when I am on the stage, or someone to take her for a walk when I am extremely busy, but those moments now are very few, for I found that no one could care as much as I as the mother, or give her the attention I could, no matter how excellent a nannie can be.

Not only is leaving the child in someone's care unfair to the child, but it is also unfair to the mother because she may never realise the true values of being a mother from the very beginning to the very end of the child's infanthood. No mother in the world should be denied this pleasure for it makes her aware of her own achievement of bringing this little thing into the world.

I have for the past year, slept on average five hours a night. Though I have gotten so tired I thought I could not possibly make it through the night's work, I did. And continue to do so in order that Kitt can be assured of the most important thing in her life; the love and affection and personal care of her mother. When she is old enough to understand she will be secure emotionally, I feel. For I was always there and will always be there.

I think it all goes back to the emancipation of women. They have stepped out of character. They were born to be wives and mothers. But they have entered the field of men and become business women. Extremely good ones, let's face it. Nevertheless I am sure it isn't what God created a woman for. Her natural function is to bring forth children and care for them. And the children must suffer if both parents are busy following exacting careers, or even in minor positions.

Eartha has said it all—I need not repeat her words—but I am sure that a child deprived of a mother's care suffers, psychologically. I don't approve of crèches, or children's homes, or paid sitters-in all day every day. I think such means justified only when the child's father is ill, or if she is widowed or deserted. I have deep respect for women who through sheer necessity combine the task of being a mother with that of being the only breadwinner. But to abandon her baby just in order to purchase that TV or some other extra luxury—no!

She
1963

ROEHAMPTON GIRL IN

FILM OF BALLET

Miss Suzanna Smith, 18-year-old Roehampton girl, of Nepean-street, whose successful career as a ballet student was told in a "Local People" story, has just completed work on a full-length film called "La Fille Mal Gardé."

This is a picture devoted to ballet dancing in which Suzanna Smith takes the part of a "chicken," a character which is an important part of the whole action.

Wandsworth Borough News 1962

A BOY'S-eye view of a GIRL'S world

"HE says I'm fab. He also says I'm the smartest girl for miles around and can cook, sew and darn with the best. When it comes to dancing I should be on the stage—and I'm sick of it all. Why? It's my father talking not a boyfriend. He scares them away!"

That's Pauline of Southampton writing. It's some problem she has to cope with but any boy she dates has a real king-sized headache.

A boy can be really keen on a girl but if Dad says it's no go because he's not good enough then nine times out of ten out goes that guy. The girl may regret it but—Dad is Dad after all.

Now, I'm not saying there should be a general rebellion against all the Dads but the time comes when they have to be checked. A girl may need kid glove tact but she should explain that her father can't live her life for her. She has to have a private life and only by trial and error will she meet the man she'll one day marry.

It might be a shrewd move to remind him of the fathers *he* had to cope with during his sweet-heart days.

Try to imagine how Dad feels, too, if you're handling this kind of problem. It may hurt him a little to realise you're no longer the little girl who needs to lean on him. That's why he rejects the fact you're now a self-reliant girl bringing home a wage packet full of new-found independence. So bring the facts home gently and he'll soon get over it.

Just don't let Dad down — you could break his heart. So you see in the end it all depends on you.

Mirabelle 1964

RECORDS

By Stylus

After 35 years his voice still thrills

PERHAPS it is a sign of my age, but in my listening this week what has thrilled me most has been a record of singing by a young choirboy 35 years ago.

I wonder how many of my readers remember the deep impression that was caused by the recorded singing of Ernest Lough and the choir of the Temple Church, London with Dr. George Thalben-Ball at the organ?

ERNEST LOUGH

Nostalgic memories stirred in me as I played this week a new album from H.M.V. entitled "My Life in Music," in which Ernest Lough's more famous treble solos are reproduced — I imagine in connection with the presentation to him and Dr. Thalben-Ball of a golden disc to mark the 35th anniversary of the recording of "Hear my prayer" and of so many years' association between the Temple Church and His Master's Voice.

Listening to that choirboy singing "Hear my prayer,"

"O for the wings of a dove," "O come, everyone that thirsteth," "Hear ye, Israel" and "I know that my Redeemer liveth," I marvelled at his effortless production, wide range and purity of tone.

There was a spiritual quality about his voice — and it moves the listener as deeply to-day as it did all those years ago.

In addition to the solos mentioned, this album includes a lovely duet, "I waited for the Lord," by Ernest Lough and Ronald Mallett (whose treble voice one also remembers so well), and a first issue of "I will sing of Thy great mercies" —made in 1928, but not used because the chorister's voice began to show signs of breaking before he could make a recording for the reverse side!

There are also two of Schubert's songs, "Hark! Hark! The Lark" and "Who is Sylvia?" and then comes the climax of the record — the singing by Ernest Lough —baritone—of Monk's setting of "Abide with me," supported by the Temple Church choir; and, finally, his singing of the baritone solo part in "For the beauty of the earth," with his son, Robin, taking the treble solo.

These last two items were, of course, recorded with modern techniques and are therefore more "brilliant" than the earlier work, but even this does not diminish the effect of re-hearing that lovely voice we enjoyed so many years ago.

THE ERNEST LOUGH ALBUM: "MY LIFE IN MUSIC"

H.M.V.: CLP1675 (mono only)

Kentish Times 1963

Universe 1965

THEY'LL be putting extra postmen on soon to bring you your Christmas mail. So now is the time to start a collection which will give you years of interest.

It is almost impossible for you to make a unique collection of stamps - but you can make your very own special collection of cancellation marks.

These are issued for a very limited period or a special occasion - once they are with-drawn they are not usually repeated.

HERE'S A NEW HOBBY

RELAXED APPROACH IN NEW TV SERVICE

By Gabriela Marik

Signs so far indicate that B.B.C.-2 is possibly to become all that B.B.C.-1 would have become had the presence of ITV not forced it into competition. It is less topical (apart from the news and only one current affairs programme so far, late Friday night) and more programmes are on a family level.

This in itself should not limit scope or variety. All it really means is that most of the programmes—whether drama, social documentary, educational series of a supplementary nature, even "Playschool" (the morning programme for toddlers)—have a style, as distinct from a content, which can be comprehended and enjoyed by people of different age-groups.

A reflection of this is the leisured atmosphere, as yet obviously contrived, beginning each evening with "Line-up," a chatty ten-minute preview of what's to come. Visible announcers introduce the evening's fare.

One of them is a girl, and a Scots girl at that. Pamela Donald, with that pleasant lilt in her voice, would cheer up anyone's lonely bed-sitter, where the telly is the only company.

Informality prevails throughout the evening. People keep "dropping in," telling you about later programmes. Some London sophisticates are irritated by this; provided the occasional condescension is eliminated, I hope the B.B.C. will not discard, only improve the idea.

Relief from sport

While 30-minute programmes abound on the other channels, on B.B.C.-2 they are the exception. But within a two-hour programme tied to a single subject one finds separate short items, complete in themselves. Saturday afternoon's alternative to sport, "Open House," a kind of loosened-up-Tonight-cum-pop session, is a case in point.

Watching the new channel last week, it was almost possible to forget the hectic world outside.

Scotsman 1964

A New Series of
Top of the Form

1

6.40

THE battle of the sexes is over. The two sides war no more, but stand united. On *Top of the Form* that is. Although the transworld edition of the programme between Britain and Australia, seen earlier this year, was fought out by teams each consisting of two boys and two girls, it is the first time that mixed teams have taken part in the domestic contest.

Another 'first' for this new series, is that all the English schools taking part are comprehensives. The schools from Scotland and Northern Ireland are as nearly equivalent to the English comprehensives as the difference in educational systems allows. And many of the schools are only a few years old.

The only difference the comprehensives will make to the form of the programme is to the older team-members. Some may be specialising in art, or a trade skill, others in academic subjects, so Boswell Taylor has had to find questions for a very wide range of topics! The fact that comprehensive schools are 'area' schools has also had some effect on the questions set. Children in rural Tavistock and those in the heart of a huge new estate in Liverpool wouldn't consider the same things 'general' knowledge.

The question-masters for this series are once again Geoffrey Wheeler and John Edmunds, and they are joined by a new scorer, Jon Kelley.

Radio Times 1964

Baby Circle
by MARY OWEN, S.R.N., H.V.

LET YOUR HUSBAND HELP WITH BABY

A NEW stage in your marriage starts on the day you bring your first baby home from hospital. He may be small and helpless, but his arrival can make or mar relations with your husband.

Your marriage will be strengthened and enriched if, from the very start, the baby belongs to *both* of you. This means that your husband takes some part in the simple jobs like bath-time and even nappy changes, and that playing with baby isn't just something for you to do— both of you will play with him together.

This will help your husband to feel that the baby has not become more important to you than he is, which is essential when so much of your time and emotions must be directed to your child.

Your baby might come between you both if you treat him as your private property—too delicate to be handled by a clumsy man. When a mother complains to me that her husband goes out alone far more after their first baby arrived than before, it is usually because he feels unwanted and in the way at home.

Besides sharing your baby as much as you can, do try to get out alone with your husband regularly. If you have no baby-sitter, the clinic may be able to put you in touch with another mother who would be glad to take turns with you, to enable her to have more free time too.

A baby can be a great bond in a marriage. But he shouldn't mean the end of those close occasions or those happy outings which you and your husband used to enjoy together before the first baby was born.

Woman's Realm
1964

Good speech plea
DAME EDITH EVANS OPENS TOYNBEE HALL THEATRE

THE importance of good speech was stressed by the famous Shakespearian actress, Dame Edith Evans, D.B.E., when she officially opened Toynbee Theatre, the L.C.C's new educational drama centre in Commercial-street, Spitalfields.

"I think that we all ought to see that our children speak this very beautiful language of ours well," she declared. Praising the new centre and its social importance, she continued: "I have heard such awfully bad things that have been done by school-children lately, and I cannot help but think that if they had had something interesting to do, they would not have been so naughty and sometimes so wicked."

Dame Edith said that the theatre had the blessing of an actress who was many years ago a small girl in London.

Proposing the vote of thanks, Mrs. Helen Bentwich, chairman of the L.C.C. Primary and Secondary Schools Sub-Committee, said: "We all agree so much with Dame Edith when she says that it is important that children speak correctly. . . . One of the things that the L.C.C. can be proud of is to have helped someone so wonderful as Dame Edith in her profession."

The opening was marked by a performance of "Spectrum," by the Minerva Players, which they themselves wrote.

Hackney Gazette
1964

No joke

MANY children are now enjoying a holiday because of chicken pox, but for adults the infection is no joke. I have contracted it from my young daughters and look like a monster from out of space. I also feel as if I am being eaten by ants.

Moral: Let children get children's ailments when they are children.

DONALD V. GRACE,
Minster, Sheppey, Kent.

Science reporter Henry Stanhope writes: Doctors agree. In most cases, childhood ailments are far worse when contracted by adults. It is possible for an adult who had chicken pox as a child to catch it again, but this is uncommon.

Sun
1966

Vocations stand at Olympia exhibition

THE schoolboys and schoolgirls exhibition which annually draws hundreds of thousands of children to Olympia at Christmastime has this year invited the Church to take part.

The Council of Major Religious Superiors in Britain has agreed to take on the stand and has appointed Fr. Bernard Slevin C.S.Sp., as secretary

Fr Slevin was organising secretary of Challenge '65, the vocations exhibition at Earls Court earlier this year.

The exhibition, sponsored by the "Daily Mail", will run from December 27 to January 8.

The stand will be in a special section on careers. It will be called "Vocations: priests, brothers, nuns."

Universe
1965

The child bride of Prince in the Tower

A SMALL lead coffin unearthed by builders in Clare Street, Stepney, has given dozens of historians and scientists 'detective work' that will last them for at least the next six months.

For the coffin has been found to contain the body of Anne Mowbray, Duchess of York, child bride of Richard, one of the Princes in the Tower.

It is already known that Ann was only a few weeks short of her ninth birthday when she died. It has also been established that she had fair hair, and was wrapped in linen before being entombed in her lead case.

The experts hope, by analysing every drop of liquid and every particle of matter in the coffin, to discover more, perhaps, for example, what her blood group was. They are even going to attempt to reconstruct her features. But one matter is, and will probably remain, a mystery.

HOW DID SHE DIE?

That is: How did the little Duchess die?

"There is no evidence to suggest that the little girl died as the result of poison," said Dr. D. B. Harden, director of the London Museum, where the coffin was opened.

"Detection of any poison would be virtually impossible."

Dr. Francis Celoria, the museum's archaeologist, added: "It was probably from any infectious disease that can affect a child."

Anne's sarcophagus was discovered in a small vaulted chamber on a building site. The builders who found it lifted the hundredweight coffin out of its tomb, and then phoned the police, who took it to Leman Street station. It was there that a museum field officer saw it an hour later, with a "Found Property" label round its neck.

PERMISSION FROM THE CORONER

Commented Dr. Celoria: "When we eventually opened it we found the pelvis had been broken by mishandling before it got to the museum. We are very critical of what happened to it.

"Goodness knows how much evidence was destroyed by this rough treatment."

London Museum officials had to get permission from the Coroner to remove the coffin to the Museum in Kensington Palace.

There experts deciphered a Latin inscription on the side of the coffin, which revealed that the body inside belonged to Anne Mowbray.

Archaeologists were at first surprised at Anne being found in Stepney, for she had been buried originally in Westminster Abbey.

The coffin was probably moved about 1500 A.D., 20 years later, to make room for Henry VII's Chapel. It was moved to the Abbey of The Minoress, present day Clare Street, to join her mother's and grandmother's graves.

Born 1472

Anne Mowbray, born 1472, was the only child of John Mowbray, fourth Duke of Norfolk and Elizabeth, daughter of the Earl of Shrewsbury. When her father died in January, 1476, she inherited his vast estates and great wealth.

King Edward IV, eager to get hold of the Mowbray fortunes, offered the hand of his second son, Richard, to the young heiress.

Thus, after lengthy negotiations, five-year-old Anne and four-year-old Richard were married in St. Stephen's Chapel, Westminster, in January, 1478.

Anne died in 1481, Richard two or four years later, presumed murdered with his brother in the Tower.

East London Advertiser
1965

SING A SONG OF SIX-PENCE

and celebrate with **mothercare** where it now costs even less to have a baby!

Our prices are going down

NO MORE 'ODD ELEVENPENCES' AT MOTHERCARE
This means that 447 items are going to cost less in all Mothercare Shops.

GOING DOWN every item **over 5/-** to the nearest 6d. Examples: Mother-to-be dress at 29/11d. **NEW PRICE 29/6d.** And our 'Pied Piper' wears an appealing dark blue 'wrap-over' dress edged in red check, with an amusing matching check animal motif. In cotton, sizes 16″, 18″, and 20″. **NEW PRICE: 9/6d.**

GOING DOWN every item **under 5/-** to the nearest 9d, 6d or 3d. Examples: Baby vests and petticoats at 2/11d. **NEW PRICE 2/9d.**

REMEMBER: 447 items reduced under the new pricing system.

No wonder that more than ever it's a pleasure to shop at

mothercare

Marble Arch, London W.1. and shops throughout the country

Nova
1965

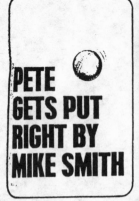

PETE GETS PUT RIGHT BY MIKE SMITH

WHAT'S UP, PETE? YOUR FIRST OVERS WERE SPLENDID. BUT NOW....

YES, THEY'RE BELTING EVERY BALL.

WHAT HAPPENED, PETE?

THIS IS MIKE SMITH, PETE.

I DON'T KNOW, MR. SMITH. I FELT ALL DONE IN.

I WONDER NOW... YOU DON'T SMOKE DO YOU, PETE?

WELL, YES, I DO. BUT WHAT...

SMOKING CIGARETTES WRECKS YOUR WIND AND STAMINA. I WOULDN'T TOUCH THEM FOR ANYTHING, PETE.

GOSH, MR. SMITH, I'LL TRY TO STOP.

DON'T JUST 'TRY', PETE. YOU CAN STOP IF YOU REALLY WANT TO.

TAKE A TIP FROM ME, THE BEST WAY TO STOP SMOKING IS NEVER TO START.

MIKE SMITH WARWICKSHIRE AND ENGLAND CRICKETER

Look and Learn
1964

Psychiatry challenges education

by ANDREW CROWCROFT

Listener
1965

Dr Crowcroft is a consultant child psychiatrist

WHEN THE MASS MEDIA cry out about the alleged antics of the young—seaside riots, delinquency, or what you will—some expert is supposed to be able to say what can be done about it. Which usually means 'what can be done to the young to stop them short?' Yet, when mutiny breaks out in the army, the most penetrating question is 'what's wrong with the officers?' Surely we, of the conspiracy of the adults against the young, surely we have questions to ask ourselves. And the most useful questions are questions about the past that created this present.

While psychiatry at work as psychotherapy cannot be prescriptive, I believe that as a technique and as a body of knowledge, psychiatry and its allied subjects have now reached a point where they can influence education. If we have the effrontery to impose education on the young, we should have the intelligence to let education be as much as it can be in the light of contemporary trends of knowledge—accepting that it will have to be reassessed again and again as the years pass. Fear of value judgments may lead us to no judgment at all. But value judgments themselves need not be so awful, if only we agree that we are making them. Educationists make them all the time.

We would probably agree that the mass media exaggerate, but nevertheless we do have crises in adolescence in our culture. We seem to accept them as inevitable, and we deal with them as they arise, piecemeal; but need we be so defeatist? I think not. In the past, psychiatry and education have worked together in certain limited situations—maladjusted schools, child guidance units, and so on. But I would argue that a more total approach can now be made to the whole school population.

Solitary play—first stage in the child's development

Henley Standard 1966

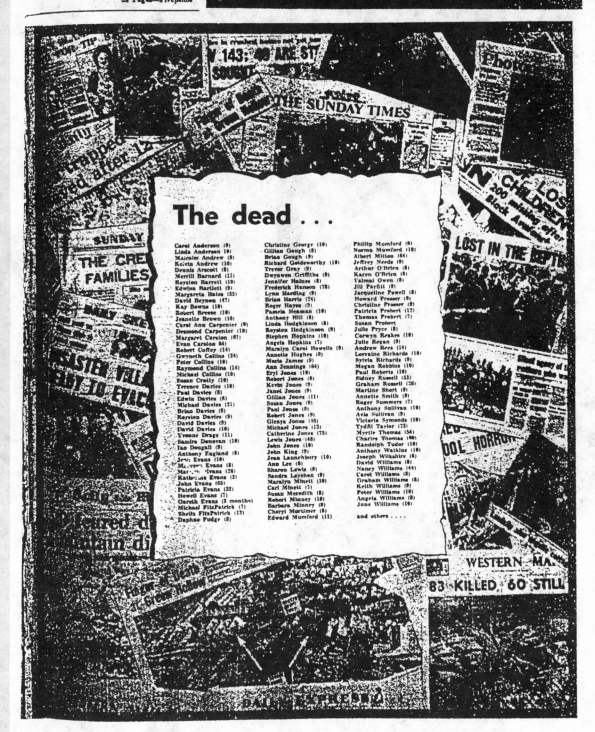

Rhymney Valley and Merthyr Express 1966

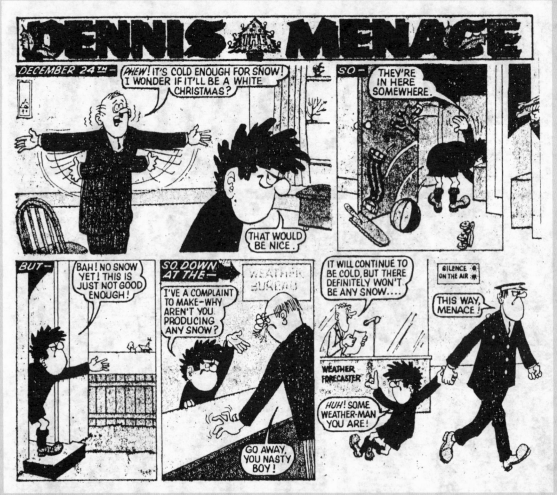

Beano 1965

All the thrills of the 'Monte' are emphasised in this 'Autocar' photo of a snowy night scene and right out of the picture onto your own track, come two gleaming Scalextric Minis!

Meccano Magazine 1965

Another boy for Lady Antonia

Lady Antonia Fraser, wife of former Tory Air Minister Hugh Fraser, gave birth to her sixth child, a son, yesterday. Mr. Fraser, who is M.P. for Stafford and Stone, and his wife now have three boys and three girls.

Daily Express 1967

target for the daleks

THE DALEKS — those tin canned monsters of the small screen—are on the paths of extermination once again, but this time on a much larger scale in an 84-minute film called "Daleks—Invasion Earth 2150 A.D." (Granada, Acton; Regal, Hammersmith).

Their object this time is earth and what a mess they leave us in.

They wipe out the whole world, except for a small group of resistance fighters in London who are helped in their battle against extermination —that word again — by the appearance of Dr. Who played by Peter Cushing, his niece Louise, played by Jill Curzon, his grand-daughter Susan, Roberta Tovey, and Tom, a policeman, who accidently stumbles upon the scene, played by Bernard Cribbens.

Shepherds Bush Gazette and Hammersmith Post 1966

Q. Jennifer (Hounslow). *I'm fifteen and all my friends are much more "with-it" than me. They're wearing these very short skirts right above the knees. My parents say it's indecent. There are continual rows over my clothes. I feel I'm a laughing stock in long skirts and I'm dreadfully unhappy.*

A. You're exaggerating, Jennifer. I understand your wish to be "with-it" in style, but it isn't of vital importance that you should show all that leg. I've actually heard people laughing at those who do! While you're dependent on your parents for dress money you'll have to do what you're told, but it won't be long now, will it, before you're earning, and can buy the clothes that you think desirable. Meanwhile, buy a few magazines which advertise teenage clothes and let your mother see them and realize these styles are for decent girls—not just Beatniks!

She 1966

The Monkees

WE would like to thank you for the fabulous, fantastic, gorgeous, wonderful, groovy picture of The Monkees in RADIO TIMES.

Also we want to thank you for settling our minds about the date of The Monkees' return visit (June). And thank you a million and one times for bringing them to our screens every Saturday night.

One complaint (there has to be one), in the last paragraph of your article you spelt Micky's name with an 'e.'

But we don't really mind and hope the BBC will continue with The Monkees programme until it no longer exists.—*Suzanne Craig, Teresa Fox, Prestwood.*

Radio Times 1967

4.40
JACKANORY
with
Wendy Craig
The Piemakers
by HELEN CRESSWELL
Today:
' The Biggest Pie-dish in the World '

Radio Times 1967

5.45

THE MAGIC ROUNDABOUT
Created by SERGE DANOT
English version
written and told by
ERIC THOMPSON

Radio Times 1967

TAXMAN TO TAKE A CUT FROM THE MINI-SKIRT

Mini-skirts and the "little girl look" will be taxed from November 1.

At present skirts shorter than 24in. are officially classed as children's wear and are not subject to purchase tax—and this is said to have been hitting the Exchequer.

Today the Customs and Excise announced that purchase tax exemption will apply only to skirts of 20in. or less and with a maximum 28-inch waistband.

Any garment described as intended for wear by other than young children are regarded as liable to purchase tax—irrespective of size or measurements.

A Customs and Excise officer in London, referring to the tendency for older people to wear the "little girl look," said: "Mini-skirts are included in this."

Bradford Telegraph and Argus 1968

Listen with Mother

AFTER listening to this programme with my four children in turn over the past eleven years (my eldest is thirteen and the youngest two), could we not please have a few changes in the nursery-rhyme collection which is so limited.

After all, there are hundreds of nursery rhymes to choose from, and surely it doesn't cost that much to make a new recording now and again when you consider the 'pop' rubbish we have to endure on Radio 1 (I am most grateful for Radio 4).

As I have three more ' listening ' years with my small son, please do something about it soon.

TV *Watch with Mother* has managed a few changes (most welcome) over the past two years.—(*Mrs.*) *Elizabeth A. Dinnage, Diss.*

Radio Times 1967

THE SOOTY SHOW

Sweep finds out that when things go wrong. Sooty is no help at all
AT 5.55

Radio Times 1967

★ **STAR LETTER** ★

I would like to tell you about a robbery I saw last year. One day I was doing some shopping for my mother, and I had to get a Postal Order from the post office. As I was passing the post office window to turn into the door, a tall man with black hair came bolting out of the post office. He had a sack in one hand and a shotgun in the other and a mask over his face.

I went in and I found that the manager had phoned the police and he was telling them that there had been a robbery. He gave the police the description of the robber. I told the post office manager that he went down the High Street and turned off at the first road junction. In a few days the police caught the robber and the money was found in his garden. I wonder if I was any help to them.

—*A Transistor Radio and a Postal Order to R. McCulloch, Lochgelly, Fife.*

Sparky 1967

SUPER SPORTS DINKY

by Chris Jelley

*Meccano
Magazine
1965*

IF you were given the opportunity to choose a sports car, what car would you pick? No doubt, many of you would choose the small jobs such as the Austin Healey Sprite or the MG Midget, while others would prefer the medium-range cars such as the Sunbeam Alpine and MGB. The 'big' sports, Austin Healey 3000 and TR4, also have a large following, but I think everybody must agree that the 'king' of them all is the Aston Martin DB5.

One very special version of the DB5 has won world-wide fame by its appearance in the James Bond film 'Goldfinger'. Unfortunately this fabulous car, with its ejector seat, twin machine guns, armour plating and similar 'extras', does not really interest us here, for it is the standard production version which Meccano have just released as a marvellous, new Dinky model under Sales No. 110.

The word 'marvellous' is not an exaggeration. Features include opening bonnet, covering a detailed engine, open-ing doors, windows, four-wheel suspension and Prestomatic steering, plus moulded headlamps, number plates, die-cast base and full interior fittings.

'Very good,' you may remark, 'but hardly unusual for Dinky Toys these days.' True, but this replica has another feature never before seen on a Dinky model—wire wheels! These have been die-cast from Mazak and a glance at the accompanying picture will show how realistic they look.

Latest release from Dinky Toys is the Aston Martin DB5, No 110, pictured here in a realistic setting

Holiday Wash-Out!

When we returned to school after our holidays last term, we were told to draw a picture of a place we had been to. I drew myself sitting by a pond, fishing, with trees and fields in the background. The teacher said it was good, and it was pinned up on our schoolroom wall.

This term when teacher asks us to draw a scene from somewhere we have been, I am going to draw myself sitting in the launderette with a bag of washing, as I was there more often than anywhere else during our last holidays!

—*A Postal Order to Joseph Colbeck, Liverpool.*

Sparky 1967

TROLL FAMILY

MY friends and I collect Trolls. I have five. I make all their clothes out of felt, but sometimes I use velvet for cloaks. I use shirring elastic for holding up trousers and skirts, and it's very useful. I converted a glass-fronted bookcase into a little two-roomed house for them.

Helen Probart, Wigan.

Penelope 1969

ADVICE TO SKIING PARENTS

Skiing for the Family - Erna Low
1967

A Few Important Hints

1. Even if you buy a set of train meals, it is advisable to take additional drink, biscuits, fruit and chocolate with you on the journey. Children are generally not patient travellers, and the occasional drink or snack keeps them occupied. Comics and games help to pass the time on the journey.
2. Each child should carry a little rucksack or bag with games and books to amuse him or her on the journey and at the resort, a bottle of orangeade and some sandwiches. Children appreciate a pocket dictionary and a little spending money for use on the journey and some currency for the country they are going to.
3. With small children it is advisable to fix a label on the child's coat and older children should be given written instructions on where to change and the name of the hotel and centre to which they are going, just in case they become temporarily separated on the journey.
4. All children must be warned about not opening train doors, not poking their heads out of train windows and about traffic on the Continent being on the right.
5. Let children travel in ski clothes, but take slippers for the train journey.
6. At the centre make sure that the children go to bed fairly early and do not overtire themselves.
7. If possible, discourage any over-exuberance in the hotel. If there are children's playrooms it is better for children and adults if children use them rather than playing in the hotel lounge.
8. Take any medicine or special food with you if your children are accustomed to it; although baby foods are available anywhere on the Continent, they may not suit your child. It is best to be on the safe side and give children boiled milk or mineral water rather than tap water.
9. Avoid over-exposure to the sun and make your child wear sun glasses.
10. Make sure that your child's ski boots fit well and that skis are well adjusted. Loose bindings are often responsible for accidents. Release bindings are advisable but they are by no means guaranteed accident preventers. The surest way to prevent an accident is to ski under the expert guidance of a fully qualified ski instructor.

"*We had Oscar Wilde today, sweetie.*"

Punch 1968

Let's bring Noddy back from exile!

by DIANA NORMAN

WHEN are British public libraries going to end their censorship of the writer who ranks alongside names like Stalin and Lenin in the world's best sellers? When, in fact, are they going to give a fair deal to Enid Blyton?

At this moment the English language sales of Enid Blyton are passing the one hundred million mark and her sixty-odd publishers are rushing out her books in nearly every language known to man.

Yet the success of this ageing conservative English lady, who has lived in seclusion since her husband died last year, has led to one of the biggest anomalies in modern publishing.

Censorship

For many, maybe most, of the public libraries in this country as well as Australia and New Zealand do not stock her books. Some have openly banned them. Others tacitly do not buy them. There is not a single Enid Blyton book stocked in any public library in Hertfordshire, for instance.

This doesn't worry her paperback publishers, mind you. Children who can afford to are rocketing their sales with their pocket money. One of them, Armada Books, for instance, sold one and a half million Enid Blytons last year at half a crown a time.

But shouldn't it worry us? For children who can't afford them the libraries' decision is a virtual censorship.

The Library Association says: 'The job of the public libraries is to educate and entertain. In the children's departments we put a heavier stress on education. It is thought that Miss Blyton does not present enough of a challenge to children.'

Individual librarians mutter charges of colour prejudice, limited vocabulary and middle-class bias. All of which are undoubtedly true and, coming from people who have immeasurably raised the standard of juvenile reading, have to be considered.

But in my mind they over-rate the susceptibility of children. No child is going to become a follower of Enoch Powell simply because Enid Blyton portrayed the golliwogs as baddies.

Her English is plain and simple—one of her great attractions for children.

Her Noddy Books have brought forth more vituperation from adults than Burgess and Maclean, yet he provides —as did the old folk tales—a healthy outlet for the original sins of envy, greed and name-calling which children are not allowed to indulge in in real life.

Enid Blyton is a phase which all children should be allowed to enter and then gently steered out of. The most highbrow of women can relapse into Georgette Heyer sometimes; the most intellectual of men indulge in thrillers. Then why not allow children to relax into the safety and comfort of a woman who knows better than anyone else how to please them?

Daily Mail 1968

ARE YOU UNTIDY?

Are you the despair of your Mum, who has to bribe you to clear up your bedroom? Do the contents of your cupboard fall on top of you when you open the door? Is your desk like a jungle? Well, that's the subject of this week's quiz. Try it, then see how you rate!

1 You hurry home from school, rush to your room and change into casual clothes to go swimming. Do you:

   a) Leave your school clothes in a heap on the floor?
   b) Throw them on to your chest of drawers?
   c) Hang them up in the wardrobe?

2 After a lesson do you:

   a) Put your books back in a special place in your desk?
   b) Toss them in anywhere?
   c) Leave them on top of your desk, to put back later?

3 Your Mum has persuaded you to tidy your room. Do you:

   a) Stack things up into neat heaps?
   b) Put things back in their proper places?
   c) Put a few things away, then say you must go out to your friend's?

4 You have a long hairstyle. For everyday wear, do you:

   a) Wear it hanging loose, because it's fashionable?
   b) Tie it back loosely with a pretty ribbon?
   c) Plait it very tightly, so it can't escape?

5 You want to find something quickly in your schoolbag. Can you:

   a) Find it immediately, because you know exactly where it is?
   b) Find it quickly if you empty some things out on to the floor?
   c) Find it after half-an-hour of rummaging?

6 Are you the type who:

   a) Hoards old comics, cuttings, pin-ups and things in stacks?
   b) Has special scrap books to keep things in?
   c) Throws them away and then wishes you'd kept them, later?

HOW TO SCORE

1. a) 3 b) 2 c) 1; 2. a) 1 b) 3 c) 2; 3. a) 2 b) 1 c) 3; 4. a) 3 b) 2 c) 1; 5. a) 1 b) 2 c) 3; 6. a) 3 b) 2 c) 1.

HOW YOU RATE

15-18: Well, you probably knew already, long before you tried this quiz, but seems you really are very untidy!

14-10: You're not too tidy, but you aren't that bad. And at least you're honest about it!

Under 10: You're too good to be true! Nobody could be that tidy, surely!

Penelope 1969

DAUGHTER IN THE HOUSE by GRAHAM

"Oh don't worry about them—they can go to a cinema or something!"

Punch 1968

Protest at 'pupil power'

By ROY NASH, Education Correspondent

EDUCATION Minister Mr Edward Short rejected a plea in the Commons yesterday that he should protect schools from the 'pupil-power' movement—the Sixth Form carbon copy of student rebellion.

He said : 'This problem can very well be left to the schools themselves to handle.'

Mr Patrick Wall, Tory MP for Haltemprice, Yorkshire, suggested that Mr Short should 'seek powers to prevent the spread of propaganda in secondary schools directed to the overthrow of pariamentary government.'

He told MPs: 'Trotskyist and anarchist forces who were behind some of the university unrest are now turning their attention to secondary schools.

'Organised attempts to undermine discipline and authority of teachers and parents can only disrupt our educational system.'

Strong

Mr Short replied : 'I do not consider this is really an appropriate matter on which to introduce legislation.

'It is not illegal to advocate the overthrow of our parliamentary institutions — and a good thing it is not, because this is one of the reasons why they are so strong.'

The pupil-power movement is demanding the abolition of corporal punishment and prefects, and a greater say for senior pupils in the running of schools. It is estimated to have around 15,000 teenage members.

Daily Mail 1969

Child 'called a heathen'

SIXTH - FORMERS at Worcester College for the Blind were threatened with expulsion if they "violated the tradition of compulsory chapel," according to a report on Religious Discrimination in Schools published yesterday.

But later the college denied the allegation. Mr L. Garner, the deputy headmaster, said: "There is compulsory religious assembly, but boys can be withdrawn by their parents." Some boys had, in fact, been withdrawn from assembly, he said.

The report, listing cases of alleged discrimination, says a child at a Primary school in Essex who wanted to "opt out" of scripture classes was called a "heathen" in front of the other children in her class.

In another case, a Surrey teacher who "opted out of worship" was told that he would not have been appointed if the headmaster had known in advance of his views.

The report, by the National Secular Society and the Humanist Teachers' Association, was published this weekend, according to Mr David Tribe, President of the National Secular Society, because the Secretary of State for Education and Science, Mr Edward Short, "is proceeding with a new Education Bill and has not yet announced a change of heart over religious clauses.

"We think it right to bring to his and the public's attention a few of the examples of what is happening under the present Education Act. The conscience clauses he makes so much of are plainly not working. If the examples in this report were occurring in a subject which was academically respectable, it would be bad enough. When the whole subject of religion is based on dubious philosophy and bogus history, the situation is deplorable."

Sunday Times 1969

Jackie 1969

AND HERE'S WOT MAKES YOU TICK...

THE best thing for a girl to fall in love with is a boy. You can love dogs, cats, toads, caterpillars or rice pudding but a recent survey has shown that the flavour of the month is boys.

There's a snag, though. You can't fall in love with just any boy. Love's a bit sneaky — it doesn't let you choose. You might see the most fantastic boy in the world and think 'WOWEE!' But 'WOWEE!' is not love.

Love's a small sledgehammer that flattens you when you least expect it. The most fantastic boy in the world probably has a weedy friend called Cyril and before you know it, you're looking at Cyril and the small sledgehammer goes 'Doinggg!!' on the back of your nut and that's it — you're in love!

SOMETIMES the feeling of love is mistaken for indigestion . . . except that stomach powders won't shift it.

Love is also very bad for your health—it brings you out in hot flushes, cold sweats and spots. Your heart does peculiar things. You go off your food, start daydreaming, get moody and depressed when the boy you love isn't around and light headed when he is.

But you're stuck with it and there ain't nuthin' you can do about it. You can't switch off.

But love has to be a two-way thing. It's no good you drifting around with stars in your eyes if your dreamy gaze is met by Cyril with a glassy stare. How are you going to make Cyril fall in love with you? Well, we all have our problems and that's yours.

Perhaps Cyril's glassy stare is the glazed look of love, but how are you going to know if he is too shy to tell you that he loves you? To answer this, it is necessary to do a bit of research . . .

Love is like measles. We all have to go through it. (Jerome K. Jerome.)

Love is blind. (William Shakespeare.)

My love is like a red, red rose. (Robert Burns.)

These quotations are valuable clues on what to look for. If Cyril is spotty, short sighted and plagued with greenfly you can be sure he is in love with you . . . or trying to frighten you off.

LOVE has a way of ending unexpectedly — it can just fizzle out or leave you with a broken heart. If you find your heart is broken, invest in a tube of strong glue and then hang around, waiting for the small sledgehammer to clunk you again.

If you're lucky, the next time you get clunked you'll stay clunked and live happily ever after, greenfly and all.

End of Teach In. More Next Week.

OBSERVATIONS
The Belgrade's bones

Last Thursday, 900 Coventry schoolchildren were packed into the city's Belgrade theatre for the first two performances of "Adventure." This is not a new children's play but a "total experience," devised by the Coventry "Theatre in Education" group. The producers have self-consciously set out to involve the children in every stage of the action by using the conventions which operate in children's games. The children in the audience are the adventurers, their involvement is not limited to taking sides with the hero; they are taking a trip to the centre of the earth (that much is decided for them). But they decide the equipment which will be taken and the route to be followed.

From their seats, they climb ropes, dig for precious minerals, and plunge down narrow rock chimneys. The plot, like the programme of a many branched teaching machine, goes where it is told; themes can be developed or omitted entirely. The director of the group, Stuart Bennett, doesn't like it if you call this children's theatre—"It doesn't aim to create the social habit of theatre—it is an imaginative experience in its own right, an extension of the games which children play in everyday life."

The Coventry "Theatre in Education" group is backed by the city council and the Arts Council and operates from headquarters in the Belgrade theatre itself. The office is an old costume store at the back of the circle. Originally, the group was set up as an "inspirational teaching service." Members, who tended to have both acting and teaching experience, went into local schools, took hold of events which were being discussed in history or English and tried to convince teachers that drama was something more than music and movement, that it could be used to brighten up traditional subject matter. They argued that drama could give children some appreciation of what terms like conquest, poverty, war and immigration meant, that learning should occur through empathising with historical individuals and groups. In recent years the acceptance of the group by teachers has allowed the members to move more towards initiating their own documentaries. Typically, they set up the bare bones of a situation and then bring in the audience to move the story along. The "Emergent Africa Game," for example, is started by a group of actors but the action is continually halted by the "game organiser" to allow children to make decisions about the allocation of finance, the possibilities of democracy, the necessity of socialism in a newly independent state.

The actor-teachers of Coventry don't talk much about "the theatre." They are embarrassed by suggestions that they are acting as public relations officers for the Belgrade. Stuart Bennett simply says that the group is trying "to hand back personal creativity and emotional experience to children who are increasingly becoming nothing more than passive recipients of information handed out by others."

New Society
1970

Woman's Own 1970